Global Governance and the Role of the EU

ISPI

ISTITUTO PER GLI STUDI DI POLITICA INTERNAZIONALE

Founded in 1934 upon the initiative of a group of companies and scholars from the Universities of Milan and Pavia, ISPI is one of the oldest and most prestigious research Institutes in Italy.

The vocation of the Institute is to promote the study of international affairs and strategic problems, train young men and women intending to work in international surroundings, as well as supply a forum for discussion and debate at a high level.

In particular ISPI's research area carries out studies in the fields of international politics and economics, strategic studies and history of international relations, whose aim is to further awareness and broaden understanding of international relations and foreign policy. Specific attention is devoted to the European Union and to its current challenges in the economic and political fields.

This volume – supported by the Compagnia di San Paolo – is realised in the framework of the European Economic Governance Monitor (EEGM) which is a network of leading European think-tanks. The EEGM partner institutes contributing to this volume are: European Policy Centre (EPC, Brussels); Istitut Français des Relations Internationales (IFRI, Paris); Stiftung und Wissenschaft Politik (SWP, Berlin); Istituto per gli Studi di Politica Internazionale (ISPI, Milan); Royal Institute of International Affairs (Chatham House, London).

Global Governance and the Role of the EU

Assessing the Future Balance of Power

Edited by

Carlo Secchi

Vice President, ISPI and Professor of European Economic Policy, Bocconi University, Milan, Italy

Antonio Villafranca

Senior Research Fellow, ISPI, Milan, Italy

In Association with

Edward Elgar
Cheltenham, UK • Northampton, MA, USA

Published by
Edward Elgar Publishing Limited
The Lypiatts
15 Lansdown Road
Cheltenham
Glos GL50 2JA
UK

Edward Elgar Publishing, Inc.
William Pratt House
9 Dewey Court
Northampton
Massachusetts 01060
USA

A catalogue record for this book
is available from the British Library

Library of Congress Control Number: 2011931010

ISBN 978 0 85793 304 1

Printed and bound by MPG Books Group, UK

Contents

Figures

Tables

Abbreviations

AWG-KP	Ad Hoc Working Group on Further Commitments for Annex I Parties under the Kyoto Protocol
BCAs	Border Carbon Adjustments
BCBS	Basel Committee on Banking Supervision
BIS	Bank of International Settlements
bmt	Billion metric tons
BRIC	Brasil, Russia, India and China
BTA	Bilateral Trade Agreement
BTAs	Border Tax Adjustments
CCP	Cities for Climate Protection
CCS	Carbon Capture and Storage
CDS	Credit Default Swap
CEPS	Centre for European Policy Studies
COP	Conference of the Parties
EC	European Commission
ECB	European Central Bank
ECOFIN	Economic and Financial Affairs Council
ECSC	European Coal and Steel Community
ECT	European Communities Treaty
EIA	Energy Information Administration
EIB	European Investment Bank
EIP	Excessive Imbalance Procedure
EFIGE	European Firms in a Global Economy
EMU	Economic and Monetary Union
ESAs	European Supervisory Authorities
ESCB	European System of Central Banks
ESM	European Stability Mechanism
ETS	Emission Trading Scheme
EU	European Union
EURATOM	European Atomic Energy Community
FASB	Financial Accounting Standards Board
FDI	Foreign Direct Investment
FED	Federal Reserve
FP7	Seventh Framework Programme

FSA	Financial Services Association
FSB	Financial Stability Board
FSF	Financial Stability Forum
GATT	General Agreement on Tariffs and Trade
GDP	Gross Domestic Product
GHG	Greenhouse Gas
IASB	International Accounting Standards Board
ICBC	Industrial and Commercial Bank of China
ICT	Information and Communication Technology
IFRI	Institut Français des Relations Internationales
IMF	International Monetary Fund
IPCC	Intergovernmental Panel on Climate Change
IPR	Intellectual Property Rights
LULUCF	Land Use, Land-Use Change and Forestry
MEA	Multilateral Environmental Agreement
MRV	Monitoring, Reporting and Verification
NATO	North Atlantic Treaty Organization
NGO	Non-Governmental Organization
OECD	Organisation for Economic Co-operation and Development
PBOC	People's Bank of China
PPP	Point-to-Point Protocol
QE II	Quantitative Easing (Second Round)
REDD+	Reducing Emissions from Deforestation and Forest Degradation
SCM	Subsidies Countervailing Measures
SDR	Special Drawing Rights
SDRM	Sovereign Debt Restructuring Mechanism
SGP	Stability and Growth Pact
SIFIs	Systematically Important Financial Institutions
SOEs	State-Owned Enterprises
TBTF	Too Big To Fail
TCC	Total Compliance Cost
TFP	Total Factor Productivity
UK	United Kingdom
UN	United Nations
UNFCCC	The United Nations Framework Convention on Climate Change
US	United States
WB	World Bank
WTO	World Trade Organization

Contributors

Carlo Altomonte is Associate Professor of Economics of European Integration at Bocconi University, Milan and Associate Senior Research Fellow at ISPI. He has held visiting programmes on Economics of European Integration, among others, at Panthéon-Sorbonne, NYU and Keio University (Tokyo). Involved in several research projects sponsored by the European institutions, he has published extensively in top journals in the field of international and industrial economics.

Franco Bruni is Professor of Economics at Bocconi University and Vice President of Milan's Istituto per gli Studi di Politica Internazionale (ISPI). He is past-President of the Société Universitaire Européenne de Recherches Financières (SUERF), member of the European Shadow Financial Regulatory Committee and of EuropEos, an ongoing forum for the discussion of European policy and institutional issues. He is author of many publications in monetary economics and financial regulation.

Jacques Mistral is a Professor of Economics, Head of Economic Research at the Institut Français des Relations Internationales (IFRI); he served as Financial Counselor to the Embassy of France in the United States of America from 2001 to 2006. He recently published two books on the American economy, a report on reforming financial accounting and numerous articles on recent global and financial issues.

Francesco Passarelli is Associate Professor of Economics at the University of Teramo and at Bocconi University, Milan. Recently, he has published several studies on voting, collective choice and political economics, with special reference to the EU.

Vanessa Rossi is Senior Research Fellow in International Economics at Chatham House, London. She has extensive experience in international macroeconomic analysis and financial markets based on a career in academia, government service, banking and consultancy, and contributes regularly to publications, conferences and media events. She has co-authored a book on

International Financial Markets and authored a chapter in the Chatham House publication *The Gulf Region*.

Daniela Schwarzer is Head of the EU integration division of the German Institute for International and Security Affairs (SWP). She is co-founder and co-editor of the *European Political Economy Review* and of www.eurozonewatch.eu. Previously, she worked for the *Financial Times Deutschland*.

Carlo Secchi is Professor of European Economic Policy at Bocconi University in Milan, where he is Director of ISLA (Institute for Latin American Studies and Transition Economies). He is Chairman of the Italian Group of the Trilateral Commission and Vice President of ISPI. He has been a consultant to the Italian Government, the European Union and various research institutions worldwide. He has published extensively articles and books on international trade, economic integration and European economic policy.

Antonio Villafranca is Senior Research Fellow and Head of the European Programme at ISPI. He is lecturer on International Relations at the Bocconi University in Milan. He has published several articles and edited volumes on the European governance and EU policies.

Xiaozu Wang is a Professor at the School of Management of Fudan University in China. He has served as a consultant for the World Bank. He has also published numerous academic papers in economics and finance.

Fabian Zuleeg is Chief Economist at the European Policy Centre (EPC). He is an economist by training and at the EPC he is responsible for the political economy programme, which covers topics such as Europe's economic future, EU health policy, Social Europe, the economic crisis and its long-term impacts, EMU, the EU budget and economic governance.

Foreword

The notion of living in a global village has been with us for a few decades now, but for economic policy-makers it has never been as close as in 2008. Virtually all over the world economies were shattered by an economic tsunami originating in the US's sub-prime mortgage market. The crisis spread globally and caused the first global recession on record.

A global crisis required global solutions. The world's leaders acted strongly and in a concerted way to prevent a financial meltdown and a replay of the 1930s. They gave a brand new look to the G20 process, which has become the main arena of policy coordination on a global scale. This was the moment which, I believe, defined the evolution of global governance for the next decade.

Europe has always been an active member of the international community. The EU's large and open economy is deeply embedded in the world's financial and trading system. The weight of the EU in the world economy also brings responsibilities at the global level. The EU is a committed member of the G20 and has played an important role in forging agreements among G20 members. The G20 agreement to shift country representation at the International Monetary Fund (IMF) towards large, dynamic emerging markets and developing countries would not have been possible without the EU's readiness to make compromises with the aim of building fair, balanced and representative world governance.

We practice what we preach. On the international scene, the EU is supporting the same values and principles that guide our internal economic policies and are enshrined in the Treaty. EU policy-makers firmly believe that open markets and free competition are the best way towards wealth and prosperity for all. The EU's attachment to unfettered international trade during the dramatic fall in world trade in 2008 and 2009 helped to avoid a spiral of protectionism of the kind we saw in the 1930s. At the same time the EU has been pushing hard to improve the regulation of the financial markets on a global basis so as to be effective in preventing financial instability and maintain an equal playing field for the financial institutions.

However, the international position of the EU will be as much influenced by the internal situation in the EU as by external developments. In other words, though it may sound trivial, only a strong EU can play a strong role globally. The global crisis put the EU and especially the euro area to test. Thanks to the bold action by EU policy-makers, the worst-case scenario was avoided, but the challenges before us are numerous: the prospect of low growth, fiscal consolidation, adjustment of macroeconomic imbalances, financial repair and an ageing population.

We are addressing these challenges head on. With the establishment of the European Systemic Risk Board and the European Supervisory Authorities, the EU has significantly strengthened its financial architecture. The EU2020 is a new EU reform strategy to deliver sustainable economic growth; the Annual Growth Survey published in January sets out the Commission's priorities in its implementation. In parallel, the EU is in the process of deeply reforming its rules for fiscal and economic governance in order to prevent effectively fiscal and macroeconomic excesses.

These reforms will strengthen the economy and the financial system, and prepare the EU to confront the global economic challenges of the future.

Olli Rehn
European Commissioner for
Economic and Monetary Affairs

Introduction

Carlo Secchi and Antonio Villafranca

The globalised world of the twenty-first century has experienced the most severe economic crisis since the Great Depression as a consequence of a dramatic lack of adequate economic governance and supervision at the international and national levels, with both sides of the Atlantic bearing high responsibilities for this. The effects of the crisis are still being felt painfully in many countries, but in less than two years economic growth has resurfaced across the world, thanks especially to a return to the pre-crisis growth rhythm in the leading emerging markets. Conversely, the mature economies are still confronting sluggish economic performance and are lagging behind (with the Eurozone, in particular, lagging well behind).

This volume addresses these topical issues and identifies two main challenges. The first deals with the economic and political conditions under which sustainable economic growth can be triggered in the future. Such growth needs to be built on solid ground if new global crises are to be avoided over the coming decades. In other words, global economic governance providing new international norms and rules – including in relation to the problem of increasing global macroeconomic imbalances – has to be put in motion. This new architecture should also mirror the post-crisis economic balance of power if it is to be credible. Besides, a sustainable and more balanced world economic growth can make a significant contribution to political stability around the world by lowering social tensions, which may be particularly intense in the post-crisis period (as demonstrated by the recent dramatic events taking place in the Mediterranean).

In this changing global context, the role and power of the European Union and its member states have been called into question. A new place in the future international arena needs to be carved out for the European Union, which is still struggling with the consequences of its sovereign debt crisis. This is the second challenge that the volume addresses, by suggesting the new route – in terms of changes in both internal dynamics and external representation – the EU has to take to escape the fate of a low growth area.

As far as the first challenge is concerned, Franco Bruni investigates the need for a new world economic framework in which monetary and financial stability are among the main pillars. In this regard, the author highlights the intimate relationship between financial stability and monetary policies. The former can be viewed as one of the objectives of the latter. The bankruptcy of Lehman Brothers demonstrated that overseeing the links between micro-risks of financial networks and systemic risks is key to avoid future crises. Provided that monetary policies can have a strong influence on (micro) financial risk-taking, such oversight of systemic risks cannot be located far from the monetary authority (as confirmed by the major financial supervision reforms introduced by the US and the EU in 2010). In addition, some forms of coordination of monetary policies are required to stabilize world-wide consumption prices and avoid new global bubbles in asset and raw material prices. More generally, a new global institutional setting should be put forward by scaling up coordination on a panoply of issues, including monetary and exchange rate strategies, adjustment of excessive current account imbalances, monitoring and regulation of a possible 'global supply of liquidity' (for example the creation of non-national currency instruments, such as the IMF Special Drawing Rights), budgetary rules, financial regulation and supervision, crisis management actions, and guidelines to manage unbalanced international capital flows. In a nutshell, a new Bretton Woods including, among other things, the re-definition of the mission and governance of the IMF and the G20, would be needed.

Jacques Mistral explores ways for the EU and the US to contribute to the governance of a multipolar and heterogeneous world. In particular, the author considers three major questions on the future of international cooperation: will the G20 continue to be a crisis management instrument or will it take a quantum leap toward effective policy coordination? Will bilateral interactions (especially in the form of the G2 comprising China and the US) overshadow multilateral efforts and, as a consequence, become a serious constraint to transatlantic relations? Should EU–US relations be revamped, and what should the goals of the new agenda be? Mistral points out that coordination of the two sides of the Atlantic can be expected to be satisfactory in the event of 'standard' financial turbulence in the future. But should the situation be more critical (due to another major banking crisis, a sovereign default threat or a mix of these) different views may emerge, and as a result issues should be better addressed at the G20 level. However, still in the G20 context, there is room for stricter cooperation between the US and the EU in some specific fields (including, for instance, development policies and aid to poor countries), where the two actors should attempt to take the lead or at least make a significant contribution within the framework of multilateral intervention.

But this can be done only if the needs and requests of the largest emerging countries – China in particular – are taken into due account. In his chapter, Xiaozu Wang explains the links between political leadership and economic growth in China and attempts to define the international role China is supposed to play in the coming decades. The author underlines that the impressive double-digit Chinese GDP growth has been significantly led by exports so far. But China learnt a lesson from the crisis and the growing international complaints about its huge trade surplus: it has to support national demand and improve the living standards of its citizens. This should eventually lower pressures on the appreciation of the renminbi and respond to international preoccupations with its trade surplus. In particular, the author points out that the convertibility of the Chinese currency can be predicted in the future, although it is not clear whether it will be in the 'near future'. In any case, a more balanced Chinese growth seems possible over the next decade, thus creating new opportunities for Europe and the US and making the growing international standing of China more acceptable.

The second part of the volume specifically tackles the challenge of the economic prospects of the EU, and the Eurozone in particular, for the next decade, and the need for a change in the internal functioning and external dimension of the EU. Vanessa Rossi depicts three key scenarios whose likelihood is strictly related to the ability of the EU to detect not only risks but also growth opportunities in the post-crisis global economic context. Such opportunities mainly stem from the robust growth foreseen for emerging countries (at a rate close to 5 per cent) but also from the possibility for the EU to correct internal imbalances and set up economic cooperation to an extent that was politically unfeasible in the pre-crisis period. In particular, the three key scenarios (and their respective foreseeable growth rates) are the following: (1) 'solidarity and discipline' in which the EU proves itself able to overcome the limits of its Stability and Growth Pact and engage in a stricter economic cooperation leading to moderate growth; (2) 'disorderly restructuring' in which cooperative efforts fall flat due to a bank crash (leading to a sovereign debt default) or to a large economy failing to control its public finances; (3) a 'new opportunity' in which a stronger EU growth scenario emerges by exploiting the potential offered by the new international context and succeeding in implementing catch-up processes in weak European countries (both inside the Eurozone and in Eastern Europe).

As mentioned above, the likelihood of the proposed scenarios depends on the decisions the EU will be willing (or politically able) to take over the next months and years. Daniela Schwarzer sheds light on the current reform of European economic governance which is emerging from the sovereign debt crisis. In particular, the author looks at the way the crisis has affected the EU and explains that the old East–West divide is fading while North–South divergence is increasing. Attention is given to the political and institutional impact of the crisis on the Eurozone reform proposals, and particularly to the sovereign debt resolution mechanisms. More generally, the author stresses the fact that the role and power of the EU in the evolving international context will ultimately depend on its ability to tackle internal matters (for instance by introducing a European liquidity fund, a debt restructuring procedure and joint EU bonds for a maximum of 60 per cent of GDP). But these measures may turn out to be insufficient if, at the same time, the problem of enhancing EU (and Eurozone) external representation in economic and financial matters is not properly addressed.

Shifting the attention from the current discussion on the changes in EU economic governance to a broader and long-term analysis, Altomonte, Passarelli and Secchi suggest some political economy decisions which may contribute to an economic growth consistent with the 'new opportunity scenario' (or at least the 'solidarity and discipline' scenario) presented by Vanessa Rossi. The authors point out that the emphasis of the current policy debate is mainly placed on the short-term aspects of the recovery (mainly focused on the financial stability of the euro area) but much more attention should be devoted to growth-enhancing 'structural' reforms. In order to solve the problem of the apparently inevitable trade-off between short-term and long-term objectives, viable options to complement policy actions needed in the short run with structural reforms of the economy (mainly involving labour and capital markets) are provided. The authors underline the risks of 'one-size-fits-all' recipes which may severely hamper economic potential in weak EU countries; rather they encourage policy responses which are tailored in such a way as to meet country-specific needs.

The long-term economic prospects of the EU and the problems it needs to face in the coming decade to meet the main target of the 'Europe 2020' strategy ('smart, sustainable economic growth') are further analysed by Fabian Zuleeg. The author identifies the following challenges for the EU as a whole and its member countries: globalization, scarcity of resources (be it energy, commodities or food), an ageing population (the elderly population will account for 20.1 per cent of the total population of EU-27 by 2020) and climate change. These challenges are aggravated by the fact that the pre-crisis potential growth rate was already low, mainly due to poor total factor productivity growth, especially in the Eurozone, with some significant exceptions (notably Germany). The author attempts to understand whether and to what extent the 'Europe 2020' strategy can help address the issues of long-term growth, by focusing on two specific areas for action: a newly-enhanced European level investment mechanism (including reforms of the EU budget and possible Eurobonds) and a further development of the Single Market.

The analysis of the pros and cons of the 'Europe 2020' strategy is completed by Antonio Villafranca who tackles the issue of fighting climate change. The latter is included among the seven flagship initiatives of 'Europe 2020', thus confirming the European willingness to be a front-runner in curbing CO_2 emissions and promoting the use of renewables and energy efficiency (the so-called '20,20,20 by 2020' targets). The failure of the Copenhagen Summit and the negligible results of the Cancún Summit (at least in terms of burden-sharing) are calling into question the current world governance model of fighting climate change, within which the EU targets had been set. In view of potentially unequal and unbalanced burden-sharing between the EU (the only region in the world with binding targets for the post-Kyoto period) and other major world emitters (including the US and China), requests for protection – for instance in the form of border tax adjustments – may emerge in Europe to re-level the international playing field. The compatibility of such measures with the current WTO rules needs to be carefully investigated. The author provides suggestions and comments which are not aimed at changing the overall 2020 strategy of the EU, but rather at adapting it to the emerging world economic governance of climate change, while avoiding possible conflicts in trade-related issues.

In summary, the volume provides analyses, insights and policy recommendations which attempt to match short-term interventions with long-term policies aiming at enhancing a sustainable and balanced growth. The quest for the latter must constantly rank high on the agenda of world political leaders over the next decade. As regards the EU in particular, the authors indicate tools and mechanisms which can enhance growth potentials in Europe, and in the Eurozone in particular. Their contributions help define the adequate place that the EU should take in the post-crisis international arena.

This volume has been realized within the framework of the EEGM (European Economic Governance Monitor), a network of leading European think-tanks: Istituto per gli Studi di Politica Internazionale (ISPI) in Milan, European Policy Centre (EPC) in Brussels, Istitut Français des Relations Internationales (IFRI) in Paris, Stiftung und Wissenschaft Politik (SWP) in Berlin, and Chatham House in London. Chapter 3 has been provided by Xiaozu Wang from the Fudan University in China.

The editors wish to thank Compagnia di San Paolo for its constant support of this volume and other EEGM initiatives. Special thanks are also extended to Mr Olli Rehn for his Foreword and for taking part in an EEGM

Conference to discuss the preliminary draft of this volume. Last but not least, the editors wish to wholeheartedly thank all the authors whose qualified contributions and constant support and suggestions have ultimately made this volume a reality.

PART I

Heading to 2020: a New World
Economic Governance?

1. Europe and the World's Economy Governance: the Monetary and Financial Perspective

Franco Bruni

1. INTRODUCTION: GLOBAL ECONOMIC GOVERNANCE AFTER THE FINANCIAL CRISIS

The international financial crisis that started in 2007 was much more than an accident caused by undisciplined financial innovations. It was a major failure of global economic governance. The globalization of finance and monetary systems has excessively prolonged the duration of unsustainable trends which a different form of governance could have resolved far earlier and far more painlessly. The term "subprime crisis" is as much an understatement as it would be to call World War I "the Archduke's War" (Padoa-Schioppa 2010, 2). The need to 'govern' the world economy with strong forms of international cooperation has now become much more evident.

In particular, the crisis has brought the objective of financial stability to the frontline of economic policies. Monetary stability, that is a stable and low rate of growth of price levels, was reached world-wide many years before the crisis, after a long and difficult struggle against the high, disordered inflation of the 1970s. The EU had become a champion of price stability by enshrining the latter as the overriding objective of its monetary policy strategy in its Treaty, into which the culture of the German Bundesbank was poured (Issing 2009). But financial stability is a different thing: one lesson of the crisis is that banks and governments can become seriously illiquid and insolvent even in an atmosphere of low inflation.[1]

The relationship between the European Central Bank (ECB) and financial stability has never been clear. While the bank often states that monetary stability is the central bank's contribution to obtaining stable financial markets, this idea is not included in the official ECB list of indirect benefits of stable prices.[2] The Treaty does not even explicitly mention the ECB's lending of last resort function, which is the standard textbook contribution of any central bank to financial stability policies. In fact the ECB has been given the instruments for lending of last resort[3] and is using them with great energy to manage the crisis, but the silence of its statute on this function seems like hypocrisy and is perhaps a consequence of the political preoccupation of leaving the powers of prudential financial policies to the national level.

Therefore, to the extent that redefining and relocating the responsibilities for financial stability policies is a major piece of the post-crisis change of global economic governance, Europe was not well placed to lead the reform process. After its very first stage, the financial turmoil originating in the US turned out to have many of its roots in the inefficient organization of financial supervision in Europe, where the consequences proved to be just as serious as on the other side of the Atlantic. With its supervisory architecture segmented along national lines and thus unable to control increasingly transnational financial markets, and with the ECB's unclear role in the provision of financial stability, Europe had little to teach a world in search of new governance schemes able to better prevent and manage financial crises.

But the weaknesses of the EU situation acted as a stimulus. A first step in reforming the prudential architecture was conceived and enacted in 2009–2010, with a conceptual scheme similar to that which guided the contemporaneous reform process in the US, consistent with the guidelines of the G20 and of the Financial Stability Board (FSB). The scheme innovates the relationship between monetary and financial stability. The relationship is still implicit though, and the monetary policy strategy of the ECB has not yet been reconsidered. In the meantime, both in the US and in the EU, the central bank has been deeply involved in providing large amounts of liquidity to help the banking system during the stress of the crisis. This task could weaken the central banks' ability to control the money supply, which would mean sacrificing monetary stability on the altar of (short-lived) financial stability.

It is increasingly difficult to implement the right governance of monetary policy, as the relationship between the supply of liquidity and inflation has weakened greatly in the last decade, all over the world. The transmission of monetary management to price level dynamics is complicated by two main factors: the increasing complexity of financial markets, where newly created money can remain and dangerously churn for long and variable periods without nourishing the aggregate demand for goods (Bruni 2010); and the gigantic positive supply shock originating from new cheap labor in the emerging economies of the globalized world.

Expansionary monetary policies can therefore go on for several years without producing decisive inflationary pressures. The following question arises: does it still make sense to define price stability as the overriding objective of a central bank's monetary policy? In the event that the answer is not a clear yes, a crucial characteristic of the European model of economic governance will be lost, at least partially, but some room will open up for adding pursuit of financial stability to central bank objectives.

It is even more complex to steer monetary policy after the lessons of the crisis in the US, where the Fed's mandate is already twofold: pursuing price stability and economic growth. If the latter is fine-tuned in the short run, the two objectives can be conflicting and the elusive trade-off between them can be considered one of the triggers of the excessive credit boom that led to the crisis. Before the crisis, Europeans could insist on the superiority of their single-objective monetary policy strategy. But if the third potential objective – financial stability – enters the discussion, transatlantic coordination of monetary policies will become even trickier.

The upshot of this discussion on the world's macro-monetary and financial governance can be summarized in at least three points of the reform agenda, attempting to answer three broad questions. First, how to re-state the optimal strategy and governance of monetary policies? The right way is probably to start from the current high-profile 'stability-oriented' European strategy[4] and better clarify the relationship between responsibilities for price level stability and stability of financial markets and intermediaries. Second, how to organize governance of the financial re-regulation that the crisis has proven to be indispensible and how to design the optimal architecture of prudential authorities that are in charge of financial regulation, supervision and stability? The best role of the central bank in this architecture is as important as it is difficult to decide. Third, how to coordinate at a global level the national or regional answers to the first two questions? Coordination should also allow monitoring of the degrees of implementation and success of the answers given to the questions, and take into account their interactions with the management and control of public finances and budgetary policies, another crucial section of macroeconomics. Coordination should also deliver the right degree of exchange rate stability: price and financial stability, besides economic growth, require changing today's 'currency wars' into something that can be defined as an international monetary system and that has disappeared since the 1970s and the end of Bretton Woods.

The following three sections are devoted to brief discussions of the possible answers to these questions. The last section concludes and emphasizes how the EU is entering the global perspective.

2. OBJECTIVES AND GOVERNANCE OF MONETARY POLICIES

The EU's 'monetary constitution' shaped by the Maastricht Treaty twenty years ago, at that time respected the world-wide consensus on the optimal governance of monetary policy. That consensus had been gradually reached, among both academics and policy-makers, starting from the late 1970s, in a period that saw the struggle against inflation, the crisis of naïve Keynesianism, the success of 'new classical' macroeconomic theory and the development of modern versions of 'monetarism'. The central characteristic of this consensus was that price stability had to be the primary goal of monetary policy. Formally, the US Fed did not adhere to this rule as its written objective function remained ambiguously targeted to reach the dual goal of price stability and real economic growth. But the substance of the Fed's actions and declarations had shifted towards the primacy of fighting inflation since 1979 when chairman Volcker started a strict control of the rate of increase in the money supply.

Volcker is a 'Deutschamerikaner',[5] however: the culture of price stability and the world-wide monetary orthodoxy that gradually prevailed in the 1980s–1990s were rooted in the German post-war economic culture and in Europe's monetary constitution. Taking the latter as the starting point for a post-crisis revision of the governance of monetary policies, it is important to note its other main characteristics. Price stability is measured by looking at consumption prices in the medium–long run, with no commitment to suddenly react to presumably short-lived changes in the inflation rate. To evaluate the prospects of price stability when deciding monetary policy changes, general macroeconomic analyses and forecasts are performed using all available statistical information and modeling; forecasts are then cross-checked, devoting special attention to the information derived from the growth rates of wide monetary and credit aggregates. The range of instruments used by the central bank is centered on open market operations where the counterparts are the banks and crucial decisions are taken on the target level of the short-term interest rate paid to the central bank to obtain liquidity. Central bank independence from political pressures is extremely important to secure central bank credibility and prevent the electoral cycle from causing monetary instability. Independence is favored by several institutional features of a central bank, including appropriate procedures to nominate its top officers, the length of their mandate, the impossibility for politicians to interfere in the maneuvering of monetary policy instruments, and the prohibition of direct central bank lending to the government. The independent central bank is accountable to political organs when delivering the results of its actions to be judged against its statutory price stability objective.

The experience of the international financial crisis suggests, first, to reinforce and spread worldwide the basic features of Europe's monetary constitution and, second, to supplement these features with new ingredients in order to benefit from the lessons of the crisis in improving the governance of money and finance.

In the first perspective, the central objective of price stability must be reaffirmed, together with the independence of central banks. The US Fed, in particular, must decrease its propensity to fine-tune the rhythm of real economic activity in the short run and must enhance its independence from government. In fact the crisis was preceded – and, to some extent, caused – by a global credit boom led by US monetary laxity aimed at over-stimulating the real cycle and supporting stock prices. This policy was dictated to please not only politicians but also banks and financial markets, which became oversized and enjoyed unsustainable profitability. It is therefore also essential to reinforce the independence of central banks from private market pressures. Special, demanding effort is required for defending central banks' independence, now that their involvement in the management of the crisis and in the special provision of liquidity to help troubled banks and stressed money markets has very much expanded their role and balance sheets.

Some other aspects of European-style monetary constitutions that deserve more serious consideration are the relevance of monetary aggregates and the medium–long-term orientation of the price stability objective. These aspects are connected: the crisis has shown that excessive growth of monetary and credit aggregates can also occur when prices remain stable in the short run. The governance of monetary policy must therefore be in a position to decide a more restrictive stance well before the credit boom results in the higher inflation which threatens the longer run. In fact the inflation potential of expanding money and credit can never materialize if the credit bubble bursts when consumption prices are still subdued.

The issues of credit booming and bursting and of the length of the policy horizon lie at the heart of the second perspective that needs to be adopted to improve monetary governance by adding new ingredients to the existing 'orthodoxy'. Steps in two directions are crucial: new attention regarding the countercyclical function of monetary stabilization and explicit attention to systemic risks in financial markets. Both steps are motivated by the fact that the crisis has highlighted the intimate relationship between monetary policy stance and financial intermediaries' and investors' attitudes to risk.

The dynamics of the credit supply are naturally pro-cyclical: when the economic cycle is in an upward phase, risks tend to be underestimated and credit is therefore over-abundantly supplied, thus nourishing an even more marked boom of the cycle, without attention to the fact that, precisely during that phase, risks are piling up that will become evident once the downward phase of the cycle moves in. When the cycle is negative, on the contrary, risks are overestimated and credit becomes too scarce, thus deepening the crisis. The credit supply mechanism is an intrinsic factor of instability. It must be an official task of monetary policy to counteract this phenomenon: monetary authorities must have the mandate to move in a restrictive direction, by increasing interest rates when the credit cycle starts to boom beyond a critical speed, while moving in the opposite direction when the negative wind intensifies the downward profile of the cycle.

Timely countercyclical action can be politically difficult when it implies an early interruption of the pleasant and profitable music of a boom party: it therefore increases the need to secure central bank authoritativeness and independence. On the other hand, the theoretical and empirical study of the current crisis is showing that monetary policy can be technically effective in stabilizing cyclical fluctuations in the propensity to take financial risks. Its effectiveness now appears greater than the macroeconomic paradigms implied before the crisis.

A crucial change is taking place in monetary thinking as the literature is highlighting a new channel of transmission of monetary policy to the real economy. Both theory and empirical research are forcefully arguing that there is a systematic and reliable inverse relationship between central bank-controlled risk-free rates and the risks taken by investors and financial markets.[6] When cheaper liquidity is provided by central banks, several reasons act as incentives to choose riskier investment strategies and riskier security and loan portfolios. The impact of accommodative interest rates on risk taking is somewhat intuitive, can be explained with sophisticated theoretical models[7] and cannot be disproved by rather robust and diverse analyses of data.[8] This impact also supports the idea that for several years before 2007, excessive and prolonged monetary expansion acted as a major cause of the crisis that followed.[9]

If, by controlling the risk-free rate on the money market, the central bank can influence the risk profile of banks and financial portfolios, then not only is monetary policy a powerful instrument to counteract the physiological pro-cyclicality of the supply of credit, but monetary authorities must themselves avoid being a cause of instability of financial markets and the whole economy.[10] The relationship between financial stability and monetary policy proves to be intimate, to the extent that the former must be considered among the objectives of the latter.

The inclusion of financial stability in the objectives of monetary policies is a non-trivial alteration of the orthodox model[11] of macroeconomic governance, in which the monetary authorities are asked to concentrate on price stability. The addition of financial stability appears even more complex and revolutionary when the monetary authorities' objectives already include real growth besides a stable price level, as in the US.

A further consideration can help the reader to understand the depth of this change. The current financial crisis is shedding light on a characteristic of financial risk that was not well understood previously. Financial markets consist of a very dense network of credit positions and flows, where certain sections of the markets and certain intermediaries are placed in critical locations analogous to crucial railway junctions. This network acts as a risk multiplier: when a financial operator becomes illiquid or insolvent, its troubles are disseminated all over the financial system as its creditors also suffer a loss of liquidity or solvency, and this dissemination accelerates when a 'crucial railway junction' is affected. Therefore, the size of the risk of the system as a whole is larger and more complex to calculate than a simple summing of the individual risk positions of the financial operators in the system. In other words there is a macro-dimension of financial risk that differs in nature from the micro-dimension characterizing each portfolio and each intermediary. This macro-dimension is called systemic risk. The best-known event that contributed to stress the importance of systemic financial risk was the bankruptcy of Lehman Brothers, a global financial services firm that proved to be highly systemic, and probably more so than the authorities thought when Lehman went under.

From the economic governance point of view the systemic nature of financial risk makes a great difference. Micro risks can be monitored and taken care of at the micro level: the single financial operator and its micro-prudential supervisor. But when the network of micro risks is considered as a powerful multiplier of individual troubles, then risks are viewed from a systemic perspective and systemic risk monitoring becomes a macro-prudential task,[12] to be entrusted to a macroeconomic authority. Consideration of systemic risk is thus an additional reason to involve monetary policy in targeting financial stability. Given the strong influence of monetary policy on financial risk-taking, discussed above, macro-prudential tasks must not be located far from the monetary authority.

Allocating responsibilities for different policies is an issue of economic governance which implies the search for optimal 'architecture' of authorities. As far as macro-prudential tasks are concerned, an additional problem arises considering that the origins of macro-systemic risk-taking are microeconomic anyway: they reside in individual financial operators' behaviors and balance sheet data. Macro-prudential analyses and actions are thus rooted in micro-prudential tasks. Does this mean that these micro tasks must also come under the responsibility of monetary authorities? The risk is to throw the governance of the economy off balance by concentrating excessive and inappropriate responsibilities in central banks.

But the opposite risk is to leave monetary policies without the information and instruments to optimize their contribution to financial stability. The next section discusses the possible solution of this 'architectural' problem of economic governance.

3. FINANCIAL RE-REGULATION AND THE ARCHITECTURE OF PRUDENTIAL AUTHORITIES

Inappropriate architecture of prudential authorities was among the major causes of the seriousness of the crisis[13] in the US, the EU and globally. Until 2010, the responsibilities of regulating and supervising financial activity in the US were dispersed over a legion of authorities, both at state and federal levels, thus implying many duplications and leaving large loopholes. The central bank also had a role but its prudential responsibilities were inadequately defined. In the EU, the most important defect of the prudential architecture was the decentralization of prudential powers, completely left to the member states. Inefficient European directives allowed national authorities to regulate and supervise in substantially different ways, and to refuse to share information on the health of financial markets and intermediaries operating under their jurisdictions. Nobody was in a position to monitor in a unified way the degree of liquidity and solvency of the European financial sector, which by contrast was becoming increasingly integrated partly as a consequence of the adoption of a common currency by a large number of EU member states. It is obviously impossible to obtain financial stability in a financially integrated region with decentralized and diversified regulatory, supervisory and crisis management policies. As regards the ECB, it had no responsibilities for financial regulation and supervision, and as noted above it even lacked a clear mandate in 'lending of last resort'. At the global level, the coordination of prudential policies was entrusted in an inorganic way to the International Monetary Fund and the Basel Committee on Banking Supervision (BCBS), with statistical and research work performed by the Bank of International Settlements and the OECD. In the wake of the 1997 Asian Financial Crisis, the G20 was established to increase cooperation between advanced and emerging market countries, and also to provide political direction to global financial stability policies using the Financial Stability Forum – a large 'technical' working group mainly composed of national supervisors and representatives of international institutions – as its technical arm. But the G20's prudential activities remained very soft and weak.

After the peak of the new crisis in 2008, G20 members were called upon to further strengthen international cooperation with summits held in Washington in 2008, London and Pittsburgh in 2009, and Toronto and Seoul in 2010. The Financial Stability Forum was widened, strengthened and renamed the FSB. The FSB quickly prepared a long and consistent global agenda to revise financial regulation and supervision methods, instruments and institutional organization. Along the lines of this agenda, with successive steps reported at the G20 meetings, detailed discussions and preparatory work for the required reforms were started in the US and many individual countries at the EU level, by national and international financial associations, lobbyists, standard setters, and working groups such as the BCBS.

A discussion of the FSB agenda items is outside the scope of a survey of the issues of governance, such as the present one. Going through the papers that the FSB prepared to summarize its work, take stock of progress in re-regulation and report to the G20, the list of items appears long, complex and organized in varying ways.[14] This list does, however, keep revolving around a group of crucial points including the following: the amount of own capital and liquidity that banks must keep to cope with the risks of their activities; methods of measuring financial risks; the accounting rules to be used in banking and finance; regulation of the markets for complex financial instruments, such as certain 'derivative' contracts; the role and the regulation of credit rating agencies; standards of financial supervision and the rules to enhance international cooperation between supervisors and between prudential authorities and central banks; enhancement of the effectiveness of crisis management, including ways to deal with the moral hazard generated by the expectation of bailouts – financed with central banks' or taxpayers' money – of 'systemically important financial institutions' that seem too large and important to be allowed to fail.

As far as the global governance of financial regulation is concerned, two problems emerge from the experience of recent years. One is the relationship between international technical-bureaucratic independent bodies, agencies, officers and politicians that are accountable to their electorates. Independent technical agencies are crucial to allow politicians to commit themselves to time-consistent supranational interactions and activities conducted to pursue the international collective interest. But supranational political agreements and institutions tend to result from complex, weak compromises, and international agencies' independence from political pressures from national political interests is often very limited, both de facto and de jure. Moreover, technical regulatory and supervisory bodies are liable to be 'captured' by regulated agents and industries, and have difficulties in keeping themselves independent from pressures from the private sector. These difficulties are more considerable when, as in financial matters, the technicalities of regulation are very complicated and must be faced in cooperation with regulated agents who have special competences and information that the regulators cannot master independently. Many of the delays and obstacles that the FSB-guided process is encountering in completing and, most importantly, implementing international financial re-regulation can be traced back to this issue of the relationship between independent supranational agencies and national politicians. The internal problems of governance of the EU provide a rich set of examples of this issue, which is perhaps the most important one to be tackled in the coming years in order to make substantial progress in governing the globalized economy.

A second problem inherent to global governance of financial regulation is that in reality 'not all financial regulation is global' (Rottier and Véron 2010). The geography of global finance is shifting from the dominant role of North Atlantic markets towards rapid growth of emerging economies' finance, with the center of gravity moving eastwards and also with some decrease in Western intellectual leadership in financial matters. These developments are generating a tendency towards financial multi-polarity. Moreover, in a period of crisis-induced re-regulation it is more difficult to harmonize rules than in an era of deregulation, when the tendency towards 'laissez-faire' naturally creates permissive common denominators. Balancing harmonization with national and regional specificities is a delicate task, even if paradoxically it calls for an even stronger commitment to a global agenda that contemplates solid global public institutions aimed at trying to achieve the right balance. Unjustified and distorting segmentations in international financial markets need to be avoided, by ensuring, for instance, that financial information be available in globally consistent ways and that the 'plumbing' of capital-market infrastructures (such as trading platforms and payment-settlement systems) be well integrated and homogeneous. Achieving a global level playing field, while preserving the right, unavoidable degree of local diversity, is a major challenge to the future governance of world finance.

National and regional supervisors will play a central role in this, and it is very important that the architectures of financial authorities be effectively shaped. As noted in the previous section, these architectures must give the right role to 'macro-prudential' supervision and central banking. In 2010 both the US and the EU decided on two major architectural reforms in financial supervision. In the US, the Dodd-Frank Act[15] has attempted to improve the allocation of supervisory responsibilities and decrease the loopholes that were a major cause of the financial crisis. In the EU, regulations[16] have been introduced to create three supranational supervisory authorities, for banks, markets and insurance and pensions respectively. On both sides of the Atlantic the reforms have substantially increased the powers of central banking and have established new bodies – the European Systemic Risk Board, and in the US the Financial Stability Oversight Council – to monitor the entire financial sector and support the implementation of system-wide macro-prudential controls. Macro-prudential policies have already been adopted by major emerging economies (Moreno 2011), such as China and Brazil, where combinations of monetary and regulatory measures have been enacted to defend financial stability by moderating bubbles in house prices and exchange rates. Macro-prudential strategies will require a complete, transnational and transparent flow of information from the micro to the macro supervisors and intimate cooperation between regulation-supervision and monetary policy. One important example of macro-prudential measures is the countercyclical capital buffer recently proposed by the BCBS: the amount of capital that each bank must hold should be increased or decreased when the macroeconomic ratio of credit to GDP increases faster or slower than its long-term trend.[17]

If defects in regulation and supervision were a cause of the financial turmoil that started in 2007, the crisis was then worsened by a lack of good procedures of 'crisis management' (Bruni 2009, section 4). Both in the US and in the EU, most decisions taken to manage the crisis were improvised, with a disproportionate role of central banks that grew enormously in size and endangered the credibility of their standard monetary policy actions by resorting to so-called 'unconventional policies'.[18] These improvisations were a cause of additional uncertainty for the markets, and of very great differences in the different countries' authorities' reactions to the crisis. Such differences distort international competition and are a source of very serious problems in dealing with multinational banks. Global re-regulation must therefore design more homogeneous rules that favor better-coordinated crisis management governance.

The rules, among other things, must avoid self-fulfilling expectations of bailouts of financial institutions that are considered too big to fail (TBTF) and, consistent with the governance of competition policies, address ways to avoid worsening the TBTF problem and dangerously weakening competition in the financial sector,[19] as a consequence of crisis-induced mergers and acquisitions of effectively or potentially troubled institutions – sometimes inspired and guided by the authorities themselves. Crisis management rules must also establish appropriate procedures to resolve bankrupt banks, minimizing contagion of the rest of the system; provide cross-border resolution mechanisms for multinational financial institutions; assign roles for dealing with (that is 'bailing-out') troubled financial institutions to central banks, government financing and for the involvement (that is the 'bail-in') of the institutions' creditors respectively. Within the EU, the crisis management problem is particularly pressing and includes the specific issue of managing sovereign debt crises. This issue is well-known world-wide – and much has been learned about dealing with it over the past decades – when troubled sovereigns were governments of less developed countries with debts denominated in foreign currencies. In the euro area sovereign debts have a peculiar profile as they are mainly denominated in the currency of the debtor country, that is in euros, but the currency supply is under the control of an independent supranational central bank and not the debtor government. The crisis that started with Greece in 2010 has acted as a powerful stimulus on the EU authorities[20] to reach agreements on how to deal with sovereign debt problems. The discussions involve the heart of the EU's economic governance, as they imply decisions on issues such as the degree of fiscal solidarity of member countries and of centralization of taxation, public expenditure and public debt.

4. AN INTERNATIONAL MONETARY AND FINANCIAL SYSTEM?

It is well-known that an 'inconsistent quartet' (Padoa-Schioppa 1985 and 1988, 372–375) results from trying to put together free trade, fixed exchange rates, freedom of capital movements and autonomy of national monetary policies. Different monetary policies cause differences in interest rates and capital movements, forcing the appreciation of the currency of the country where policy is more restrictive. Based on this concept, the EU decided to adopt a single currency, thus completely unifying monetary policy and giving up the last element of the quartet, in order to obtain stable exchange rates and preserve free trade – the original and most important achievement of post-war European integration – while increasing financial integration through complete freedom of capital movements.

At the global level, exchange rates have been free to fluctuate since the crisis of the Bretton Woods agreement in the 1970s. After a decade of major monetary disorder, Europe started to move back to fixed but adjustable exchange rates with the European Monetary System, from which the euro was later born. But problems with dollar instability remained, and the presence of an alternative reserve currency as important as the euro renders orderly conditions in foreign exchange markets both more difficult and more important to secure. If another currency, such as the Chinese renminbi, were to become a third widely-held international currency of denomination, means of payment and reserve instrument, the richness and fairness of the monetary system would increase but the dangers deriving from its potentially huge instability would imply very serious global costs for trade, finance and real growth. The demand for global governance of exchange rates is destined to increase. Speculative capital inflows in emerging economies, the various reactions of their authorities, and the highly controversial unilateral pegging of the Chinese currency have recently created conditions that deserve to be labeled 'currency wars' and no less. Will it be possible to gradually move in the opposite direction where there is a well-managed 'international monetary system'? According to the inconsistent quartet, with free trade and international financial integration, a substantial increase in exchange rate stability requires some coordination of monetary policies. After all, the demise of Bretton Woods was caused by the fact that the monetary policy of the central country, applied to the US dollar, was too expansionary and potentially inflationary to be acceptable to the other countries leading the world's economy and finance, in particular Germany and Japan. The exchange rate problem was really a monetary policy problem, which is precisely the idea that led to the adoption of the euro in Europe.

Coordination of monetary policies is also necessary in order to obtain stable world-wide consumption prices and avoid dangerous global bubbles in asset and raw material prices. With increasing international integration in real and financial markets, the effects of monetary policies of large-enough countries are felt everywhere and influence prices globally. Large countries are responsible for global inflation and financial stability, while small countries suffer the consequences of policies that they have not contributed to formulating. A lack of effort in coordinating monetary policies could lead to increasingly serious economic and financial 'wars', much worse than the current disputes on exchange rates. The world would then plunge into the only type of condition where policy coordination is not required, the opposite of globalization: trade and financial protectionism and economic nationalism, that slow down growth and impoverish the global economy.

Coordinated monetary policies need not be identical everywhere. Specific macro-shocks may require a certain degree of diversification in monetary policy stances, precisely to guarantee the right degree of stability of exchange rates and price levels. What markets require in order to act in a stabilizing way is a credible homogeneity of monetary policy 'strategies', that is in general rules that govern the reaction of the monetary authorities to a given change in macro-financial conditions, such as inflationary demand or a supply shock. The objectives, instruments and indicators of monetary policies must be well-coordinated and homogeneous, while the specific moves can differ when macroeconomic situations and expectations differ. These potential differences are also the reason for hesitating to plan for a single 'global currency', which would also require a powerful, independent global central bank that would lack a global political authority to which to be accountable for its policy results. However, such hesitations do not prevent the international monetary system from assigning a larger and stronger role, complementary to that of the major currencies, to a global reserve instrument like Special Drawing Rights (SDR), the basket of major currencies that is issued by the IMF.[21] The Chinese central bank has recently presented such a proposal (Xiaochuan 2009).

But coordination of monetary policies is insufficient for obtaining price and exchange rate stability and satisfactory macroeconomic governance of globalization. Once again, Europe is a crucial example. Credible monetary unification implies at least an additional factor of homogeneity: a reasonable degree of convergence of budgetary and fiscal policies and perhaps even a minimum degree of fiscal solidarity, allowing some stabilizing international fiscal transfers. Europe's decision to back the single currency with the Stability and Growth Pact, the evolution of the Pact, its failures and reforms, the complex and costly sovereign debt crisis that started with the Greek case in 2010 and the decisions that followed in order to provide those countries in difficulty with some centralized fiscal support, are a lesson on the relationship that must exist between monetary and fiscal integration. An 'international monetary system' cannot be sustainable without at least some centralized monitoring of budgetary policies.

The design of the macroeconomic governance of globalization must go beyond monetary and fiscal policies. As the previous sections of this chapter should have made clear, there are deep relationships between monetary policy, financial stability, financial regulation and supervision, and macro-prudential policies. In the economic literature the inconsistent quartet (exchange rate stability, international capital mobility, free international trade and autonomous national monetary policies) has a companion: the 'inconsistent trio' which comprises financial stability, international financial integration and autonomous national financial regulatory and prudential policies. When national prudential policies are too different and too-diverse measures are taken, international financial integration causes financial instability by allowing credit, securities, capital, banks and intermediation services to move across the borders of nations and financial jurisdictions in search of the most permissive stance of national authorities, that tend to compete in laxity and do not share prudential information on financial risks. Such instability cannot be fought with an inexistent central monitoring and supervisory authority.

The inconsistent trio is an important reason for the efforts made in the EU over the last three decades to harmonize and partially centralize financial regulation and supervision. These efforts were certainly initially targeted at creating a level playing field in the single European financial market, as 'financial stability' was not considered an important issue; at any rate, these efforts have been far from intense or successful, until very recently. The road towards a set of common financial rules and a centralized supervisory architecture is now being followed with more decision by Europeans. This development is partly a consequence of the crisis. But the crisis, as illustrated in the previous section of this chapter, is pushing the entire world to accelerate financial re-regulation in a coordinated way under the direction of the G20 and the FSB. Moreover, the crisis is bringing together prudential measures and traditional macroeconomic policies, to enact newly-conceived 'macro-prudential' policies for financial stability.

The European sovereign debt crisis has generated pessimistic views on the future of the euro and its role in the international monetary system. However, the euro can retain its natural, important place in the scenario of tomorrow's multicurrency world. The conditions for the sustainable global success of the European currency are complex and manifold. They should be clear from what has been noted above: European monetary policy must be consistently aimed at price and financial stability and be operated in close coordination with macro-prudential policies; fiscal discipline and EU-wide budgetary coordination must be at least as intense as the minimum required for the needs of a single currency area; sufficiently homogeneous and centralized financial regulation and supervision must secure a stable and efficient single market for credit, securities and financial intermediation, to be used by the entire world as a competitive place in which to borrow, invest and purchase up-to-date, sophisticated and reliable financial services; the governance of the world's monetary system must be such as to promote the right amount of stability of global currency markets, and to reward the currencies of those countries or regions with sounder and smarter monetary and financial policies with a more important role.

The global macro-financial governance scenario therefore comprises an integrated set of actions that require international coordination: monetary and exchange rate strategies, pressure on individual countries to adjust excessive current account imbalances for extended periods, monitoring and regulation of an appropriately defined 'global supply of liquidity' including the creation of non-national currency instruments such as SDRs, avoidance of excessive expansion of international reserves and monitoring of their currency composition and diversification, budgetary rules, financial regulation, supervision, international lending of last resort and other crisis management actions, and provision of guidelines to govern the temporary adoption of controls to limit disruptive international capital flows. The novelty here is the awareness that the actions needed on the different fronts must be consistent. The relatively new concept of global countercyclical macro-prudential policies is the best example of this requirement of consistency.

Finding a suitable global institutional setting in which to decide on and monitor the implementation of this integrated set of policies is one of the difficult tasks that should absorb the international community's energies in the coming years. A 'new Bretton Woods' is needed but it cannot be achieved in a single, short summit.

The IMF is obviously a candidate for playing a major role in the new setting. Since its Pittsburgh Summit of September 2009,[22] the G20 has assigned the IMF with the technical assistance for launching a 'Framework for Strong, Sustainable and Balanced Growth ... [guiding a] process of mutual assessment by developing a forward looking analysis of whether policies pursued by individual G20 countries are collectively consistent with more sustainable and balanced trajectories for the global economy'.[23] In order to be successful, a process centered on the combined work of the G20 and the IMF needs to find good solutions to the problem of the relationship between international technical bodies and politicians accountable to their electorates, which was mentioned in the previous section in regard to financial regulation, but which is also extremely important for the macroeconomic and monetary aspect of the cooperation needed in the comprehensive Framework launched in Pittsburgh. In this respect some pessimism can be grounded on the opinion that cooperation based on rules, and on sanctions for non-compliant countries, requires national politicians to give up the flexible discretion that comprises the favorite part of their sovereignty. As explained above, as macro-financial policies cover 'such a broad area, this would require countries to give up a tremendous amount of sovereignty to an international bureaucracy, an unlikely scenario' (Rajan 2010, 211). The risk is therefore coordination based on useless exhortations, with no clear rules and no mechanisms for the effective enforcement of supranational decisions.

One possibility could be to articulate the G20–IMF governance in two parts: a limited and strictly rule-based set of policies, and wider action using a different approach. The rule-based part should include, at least, certain characteristics of monetary policy and exchange rate strategies and a core subset of financial regulations as well as of codes for financial supervision and crisis management. In these matters the sacrifice of national sovereignty must be clear and explicit, even if subject to periodic checks and reconfirmations based on a transparent process of accountability of the delegated authorities. As for the wider action of coordination, a leading suggestion has been put forward by Raghuram Rajan, a brilliant academic with an intensive, though somewhat frustrating experience at the IMF. In his view,[24] 'global policy discussions have to be introduced into the political debate in every country and thereby make their way back into the closed-door meetings of global leaders'. International multilateral organizations should strive to influence by appealing more directly to a country's citizens. 'This should facilitate the government's task in building support for reforms'. International organizations should use 'soft power and persuasion... and see engagement in the public debate in member countries as one of their most important tools in encouraging domestic policies that foster the global good'. An international agreement is needed as regards 'how domestic policies can be influenced by multilateral agencies' with the specific task of stressing, measuring and explaining the 'global good' that can only result by recognizing the full extent of international external economies and diseconomies, interactions and spillovers, and by enacting cooperative policies. Countries must agree on the idea that international agencies such as the IMF can also enter the democratic mechanism, 'using sophisticated web-enabled networks, going directly to the public, including political parties, nongovernmental organizations, and influential personalities in each country to explain their positions', as representatives of global collective interests, in order to indirectly obtain national decisions compatible with consistent plans of global coordination.

The IMF must be deeply reformed in order to fix, manage and implement a limited but carefully policed set of rules and also pursue a wider, persuasion-based coordination action, being accountable via appropriate procedures to a 'political' G20-type group. Some reform has already started:[25] the Fund is now larger and more representative than a year ago, and some important changes have been made to its objectives and organization. European countries have given up a portion of their voting powers to make room for China and other emerging protagonists of the world economy. But the reform must go much deeper and involve a radical redefinition of the institution's mission and governance. The role of the IMF must no longer be confused with its being a helper of weak (or poorer or developing) countries: on the contrary, its main task must be to coordinate and discipline the policies of the most powerful protagonists of the world economy. This requires an enhancement of its independence and a substantial upgrading of its mandate. Studies and proposals for reforming the IMF have also been prepared inside the Fund in recent years, but they are still far from what is needed for hosting most of the macro-financial governance of the world economy. If a scheme in two parts comprising rules and persuasion, as described above, must come to characterize the IMF, then its Articles of Agreement must be deeply reconsidered and rewritten with a major global diplomatic effort.

Among the delicate issues is the Fund's role in financial regulation and global prudential policies, where its relationship with the FSB must be rendered neater. A global agency specialized in financial regulatory and supervisory matters can be useful,[26] but its work must be intimately nested in the macro-monetary functions of the IMF.

As monetary, fiscal and exchange rate developments have an impact on the international competitiveness of different national productions, the macro-management of the world economy must be consistent with the promotion and defense of free trade by the World Trade Organization (WTO), which must remain an important institutional player in global economic governance. In addition, a reform of the WTO is desirable,[27] to explicitly bring all possible types of direct and indirect causes of trade protectionism, dumping, subsidization and distortions under its authority, and develop the linkage of its investigations and rulings with competition policies, anti-trust authorities and IMF monitoring of exchange rate manipulations. But as an institution using a quasi-legal approach, with a well-functioning and flexible dispute-resolution process concentrating on a specific set of precise rules clearly signed and ratified by member governments after arduous negotiations, the WTO already has governance that should not require revolutionary reform as in the case of the IMF.

Policies against poverty, for development and aid comprise another pillar of global economic governance, obviously connected with macro-financial issues. The United Nations is probably the right institutional environment for coordinating these policies (alongside policies for education, human rights, the environment etc.) and reorganizing the World Bank, which now has a uselessly competitive and confusing relationship with the IMF.

5. CONCLUDING REMARKS

'In a world so deeply inter-connected, economic outcomes in each country depend significantly on developments and policy decisions made in others. In such a world, there is a strong case for rules and processes to be developed to help ensure that major economic and financial policy decisions made nationally are mutually consistent and contribute to global stability' (Palais-Royal Initiative 2011, 4). This chapter has argued that the monetary and financial perspective of global economic governance has a rich agenda that contemplates institutional reforms as well as changes in policy strategies. The complexity of the agenda is increased by the fact that, besides the coordination of national policies, the consistency of the different types of global policies must be ensured by instituting a closely related set of national and supranational agencies.

No doubt a long 'new Bretton Woods' Summit would be appropriate. The disaster of World War II was the incentive for the 1944 summit in the

Mount Washington Hotel; the sudden acceleration of globalization in the last two decades, and the financial crisis that exploded after 2007, are now serving as less dramatic stimuli for a global multilateral effort that has already started the achievement of more concrete and innovative results, but must accelerate this. The fundamental justification for the effort is the recent discovery of sizeable global public interests resulting from the formidable external economies and diseconomies that have sprung from the growing integration of the world economy. To be successful, the effort must overcome several categories of obstacles: the conceptual and technical difficulties of the items on the agenda; the strength of the special interests that are opposed to reforms and exert a powerful lobbying activity; the nationalistic and parochial attitudes of governments and citizens that are against – or simply do not understand – the idea of tackling the challenges of globalization with supranational governance arrangements; the arduous task of establishing the right balance between the functions and powers of supranational non-elected bureaucrats, the multilateral institutions that receive the mandate to coordinate, and national politicians accountable to their electors.

The EU is in a very special position in this global political and diplomatic effort. There are three main reasons for this. First, some important elements of the global economic governance to be achieved are deeply rooted in the postwar European culture, both from the point of view of the methods of achievement, for example multilateralism in search of feasible supranational arrangements, and as far as the aims of governance are concerned, for example the special focus of Germany–continental Europe on monetary and financial stability. Second, for many years the EU has been making a very similar effort to strengthen its internal macro-financial governance, even if Europe has a much more ambitious target of international integration than the global community, with the dynamics of its institutional setting at times resembling a slow movement towards a fully-fledged federal state. The EU can therefore contribute the valuable fruits of its past and current very intense experience to the global governance effort. Third, the EU is a very large economic and political region with a great potential influence on the shape of future world governance. This constitutes both a heavy responsibility and an attractive opportunity for Europeans, provided that they are able to deepen their internal integration and 'speak with a single voice'.

It is important to note that in recent decades, when globalization was proceeding quickly and without any major obstacles and crises, global integration trends often acted as challenges and drivers for EU internal integration. This is no longer happening in the bewildered global atmosphere of today, where initiatives for improving the functioning of the world must move bottom-up and be rooted in the explicit strategies of individual states and regions. We are currently in a phase where Europe must find from within both the energy to improve its own governance and deepen its own integration, and the strength to contribute to the building of a more integrated and better governed global economy.

NOTES

1. See, for instance, White (2006). The Bank of International Settlements had understood this lesson *before* the crisis and had unsuccessfully tried to influence monetary policies in time to avoid the disaster.
2. While the list (ECB, 2004, 42–43) includes the indirect contribution of price stability to reaching 'high levels of economic activity and employment', by 'improving the transparency of relative prices, reducing inflation risk premia in interest rates, avoiding unnecessary hedging activities, reducing distortions of tax systems and social security systems, increasing the benefits of holding cash and preventing the arbitrary redistribution of wealth and income'.
3. The so-called 'standing facilities'.
4. As proclaimed, for instance, in ECB (2004, Chart 3.2, 66).
5. In 2010 he was awarded the title of Distinguished German-American of the year.
6. A path-breaking contribution on the subject is in Rajan (2006).
7. From the literature, potential channels linking monetary policy stance and markets' risk propensities emerge in abundance, even if a clear taxonomy is still unavailable and models are still very diverse and specific. For example, the informational structure of credit markets is the basic hypothesis behind the formalization of the channel in Dell'Ariccia and Marquez (2006). Agency costs of high risk investments, that are preferred when the risk-free rate is low, are crucial in Matsuyama (2007). A simpler 'asset substitution channel', where lower yields on safer assets shift investors' demand towards riskier assets, can be found in De Nicolò *et al.* (2010). Rajan (2006), describes the channel connecting monetary policy and risk taking through a 'search for yield' mechanism and from managers' compensation schemes. Adrian and Shin, 2009, analyse a channel based on 'target leverage ratios' of financial intermediaries. See also Bruni (2009, par. 2.1), and Giavazzi and Giovannini (2010).
8. For example, three empirical contributions that, using very different sets of data, reach consistent results that are very far from disproving a net positive impact of low interest rates on the riskiness of banks' credit supply, are: Jiménez *et al.* (2007), Ioannidou *et al.* (2009), Altunbas *et al.* (2010).
9. An influential exposition of this thesis is in Taylor (2009).
10. 'Low interest rates: do the risks outweigh the rewards?' is the title of Chapter III in BIS (2010).
11. To appreciate this alteration in an historical perspective, see Goodhart (2010).
12. For a discussion of the definition of the expression 'macro-prudential', see, for instance, Borio (2009). The concept is also carefully explained in Chapter VII of BIS (2010).
13. See, for instance, the general introductory analysis conducted in the report by De Larosière (2009), which was the basis for the European architecture reforms.
14. The papers are on the website of the Board: www.financialstabilityboard.org. The evolution of the list starts with a document (FSF 2008) still authored by the Financial Stability 'Forum' in April 2008, five months before the disastrous bankruptcy of Lehman Brothers, detailing 67 recommendations organized in five groups.
15. US Government Printing Office (2010). *Dodd-Frank Wall Street Reform and Consumer Protection Act*, 5 January 2010, www.sec.gov/about/laws/wallstreetreform-cpa.pdf.

16. An overview and the texts of the European reform are in: http://ec.europa.eu/internal_market/finances/committees/index_en.htm.
17. Countercyclical capital buffers should be decided by national authorities on the basis of credit growth in individual countries. The buffers of internationally active banks should then result from the weighted average of the buffers in effect in the countries where they have credit exposure (see BCBS 2010).
18. 'The response of leading central banks to the current financial crisis has raised the magnitude of the financial and governance risks they face. … In engaging extensively in unorthodox policies – bearing similarities to fiscal policies – a number of central banks have risked… their monetary policy independence. In order to forestall these risks, … unconventional policies [should] be placed under a separate governance structure that would allow them to be brought under greater political control and accountability while preserving the operational independence of monetary policy' (Stella 2010, vii).
19. For a discussion of the behavior of competition authorities in the banking systems before and during the crisis, see Vickers (2010).
20. A comprehensive view of the package of proposals to cope with the crisis of the euro area and the specific issue of sovereign debts can be retrieved from: http://ec.europa.eu/economy_finance/articles/eu_economic_situation/2010-09-eu_economic_governance_proposals_en.htm.
21. On SDRs see the IMF website at: www.imf.org/external/np/exr/facts/sdr.HTM.
22. www.pittsburghsummit.gov/mediacenter/129639.htm.
23. Ibid., emphasis not in the original.
24. The citations that follow are from Rajan (2010, Chapter 10). The emphases are not in the original.
25. See the history, lines and documents of the reform process in www.imf.org/external/np/exr/key/quotav.htm.
26. Levine (2010) proposes a particular type of second-level institution specialized in financial regulation, that he labels the 'Sentinel', with the sole responsibility of continuously commenting and officially reporting to the legislative and executive powers, on regulatory policies decided at national and international levels.
27. For a critical summary of recent proposals for WTO reform, and a rich bibliography on the subject, see Hoekman (2011).

BIBLIOGRAPHY

Adrian, Tobias and Hyung Song Shin (2009), *Liquidity and Leverage*, Federal Reserve Bank of New York Staff Reports No. 328, January.

Altunbas, Yener, Leonardo Gambacorta and David Marquez-Ibanez (2010), *Does Monetary Policy Affect Bank Risk Taking?*, BIS Working Papers No. 298, March.

Bank for International Settlements (BIS) (2010), *80th Annual Report*, Basel, 28 June.

Basel Committee on Banking Supervision (BCBS) (2010), *Guidance for National Authorities Operating the Countercyclical Capital Buffer*, December, www.bis.org/publ/bcbs187.pdf.

Borio, Claudio (2009), *Implementing the Macroprudential Approach to Financial Regulation and Supervision*, Financial Stability Review, Bank of France, September.

Bruni, Franco (2009), *Do We Understand it? Forbidden Questions on the Financial Crisis*, in Carlo Secchi and Antonio Villafranca (eds), *Liberalism in Crisis?*

European Economic Governance in the Age of Turbulence, Cheltenham, UK and Northampton, MA, USA, Edward Elgar Publishing, 24–54.

Bruni, Franco (2010), *L'acqua e la spugna*. *Troppa moneta: i guasti di oggi, il controllo di domani*, seconda edizione, Milano: Università Bocconi Editore.

De Larosière, Jacques (2009), *Report of the High-Level Group on Financial Supervision in the EU*, Brussels, 25 February, http://ec.europa.eu/internal _market/finances/docs/de_larosiere_report_en.pdf.

Dell'Ariccia, Giovanni and Robert Marquez (2006), 'Lending Booms and Lending Standards', *Journal of Finance*, 61, 2511–2546.

De Nicolò, Gianni *et al.* (2010), *Monetary Policy and Bank Risk Taking*, IMF Staff Position Note, July 27.

European Central Bank (ECB) (2004), *The Monetary Policy of the ECB*, www.ecb.int/pub/pdf/other/monetarypolicy2004en.pdf.

Financial Stability Forum (FSF) (2008), *Enhancing Market and Institutional Resilience*, 7 April, www.financialstabilityboard.org/publications/r_0804.pdf.

Ioannidou, Vasso, Steven Ongena and José Luis Peydró-Alcaide (2009), *Monetary Policy, Risk Taking and Pricing: Evidence from a Quasi-Natural Experiment*, CentER Discussion Paper Series No. 2009-31S, Tilburg University, September.

Jiménez, Gabriel, Steven Ongena, José Luis Peydró-Alcaide and Jesus Saurina (2007), *Hazardous Times for Monetary Policy: What Do Twenty-Three Million Bank Loans Say About the Effects of Monetary Policy on Credit Risk?*, CEPR Discussion Paper No. 6514, October.

Giavazzi, Francesco and Alberto Giovannini (2010), *Central Banks and the Financial System*, CEPR Discussion Paper No. 7944, August.

Goodhart, Charles A.E. (2010), *The Hanging Role of Central Banks*, Bank of International Settlements, Working Paper No. 326, November.

Hoekman, Bernard (2011), *Proposals for WTO Reform: a Synthesis and Assessment*, Policy Research Working Paper 5525, The World Bank, January.

Issing, Otmar (2009), *In Search of Monetary Stability: the Evolution of Monetary Policy*, Bank of International Settlements, Working Paper No. 273, March.

Levine, Ross (2010), *The Governance of Financial Regulation: Reform Lessons from the Recent Crisis*, Bank of International Settlements, Working Paper No. 329, November.

Matsuyama, Kiminori (2007), 'Credit Traps and Credit Cycles', *American Economic Review*, 97, March, 503–513.

Moreno, Ramon (2011), *Policymaking from a 'Macroprudential' Perspective in Emerging Market Economies*, Bank of International Settlements, Working Paper No. 336, January.

Padoa-Schioppa, Tommaso (1985), 'Squaring the Circle, or the Conundrum of International Monetary Reform', *Catalyst, a Journal of Policy Debate*, 1 (1), Spring.

Padoa-Schioppa, Tommaso (1988), 'The European Monetary System. A Long-Term View', Chapter 12, in Francesco Giavazzi, Stefano Micossi and Marcus Miller (eds), *The European Monetary System*, Cambridge: Cambridge University Press.

Padoa-Schioppa, Tommaso (2010), *The Ghost of Bancor: The Economic Crisis and Global Monetary Disorder*, Louvain-la-Neuve, 25 February, www.notre-europe.eu/uploads/tx_publication/Speech-TPS-LouvainLaNeuve-25.02.2010.pdf.

Palais-Royal Initiative (2001), *Reform of the International Monetary System: A Cooperative Approach for the Twenty First Century*, January 18, www. elysee. fr/president/root/bank_objects/2011-007.Palais-Royal_Initiative-Final_version_of_ the_Report-Jan_18.pdf.

Rajan, Raghuram G. (2006), *Monetary Policy and Incentives*, Address at the Bank of Spain Conference on Central Banks in the 21st Century, 8 June, www.imf.org/external/np/speeches/2006/060806.htm.

Rajan, Raghuram G. (2010), *Fault Lines*, Princeton, NJ: Princeton University Press.

Rottier, Stéphane and Nicolas Véron (2010), *Not all Financial Regulation is Global*, Policy Brief PB 10–22, Peterson Institute for International Economics, September, www.piie.com/publications/pb/pb10-22.pdf.

Stella, Peter (2010), *Minimising Monetary Policy*, Bank of International Settlements, Working Paper No. 330, November.

Taylor, John B. (2009), *The Financial Crisis and the Policy Responses: An Empirical Analysis of What Went Wrong*, NBER Working Paper 14632, January.

US Government Printing Office (2010), *Public Law 111-203 – Dodd-Frank Wall Street Reform and Consumer Protection Act*, approved July 21, www.gpo.gov/fdsys/pkg/PLAW-111publ203/content-detail.html.

Vickers, John (2010), *Central Banks and Competition Authorities: Institutional Comparisons and New Concerns*, Bank of International Settlements, Working Paper No. 331, November.

White, William R. (2006), *Is Price Stability Enough?*, Bank of International Settlements, Working Paper No. 205, April.

Xiaochuan, Zhou (2009), *Reform the International Monetary System*, The People's Bank of China, 23 March.

2. Transatlantic Economic Policy Co-ordination at a Crossroad: Why it is Badly Needed and How it Would Improve the Work of the G20

Jacques Mistral

1. INTRODUCTION

Toronto, the fourth G20 Summit held in June 2010, not only delivered little tangible progress but was the first to show cracks in the spirit of international economic cooperation which prevailed after the eruption of the financial crisis. Just to recall the mood in Toronto: governments expressed vocal and public opposition regarding the need to pursue stimulus measures or to prepare exit strategies, to tax or not to tax their banks, to control or not to control bonuses in the financial industry; the whole process of negotiating bank regulations within the Basel committee was stagnating.

Thanks to a dedicated, meticulous and wise preparation by the Korean presidency, the Seoul Summit in November 2010 delivered more results but was also deeply clouded by the threat of a 'currency war' trumpeted by many officials in the run-up to the summit.

What a difference two years make! When initially meeting in Washington (November 2008) and London (April 2009), leaders clearly had to manage pressing and common challenges and they did that successfully. In response to a broad-based and bitter anger from the public, the leaders initially had no choice but to act bravely and co-operatively. Pushed by necessity, they quickly embarked on a spate of government activism based on huge macroeconomic policy measures and financial re-regulation.

Months of experience later, it appears very different to agree on broad principles and objectives at the peak of an unprecedented crisis and to adopt the design of macroeconomic or regulatory policies as the new norm. The uncomfortable truth is that – as frequently evidenced in the past – international economic co-operation is not straightforward.

In 2011, three major questions regarding the future of international economic cooperation have thus to be considered. First, as President Sarkozy observed in August 2010 in a speech devoted to the future French presidency, the G20 faces a bifurcation. Will the G20 continue as a crisis management instrument or will it make a significant step forward into effective policy coordination? Second, while the final communiqué in Toronto repeated previous commitments, the statement also recognized that 'countries should be free to examine a range of policy approaches'. Does this come-back to national solutions mean that the G20 is already *passé*? Third, the cohesion of the transatlantic world is under threat. Europe and the US are faced with different challenges and they are looking for different solutions: should transatlanticism be revived and, if yes, what should be the goal and the agenda?

This chapter builds upon a previous contribution on the same issue (Mistral 2009). This 2009 contribution argued that we were not facing a cyclical adjustment after which things would come back to 'business as usual' but that we had entered a period of severe crisis; globalization was said as to be under new threats and the paper, recognizing the merits of the newly created G20, called for a better international governance. These arguments have been vindicated: in January 2011, Asia is booming but the economic future of the West remains clouded by many economic, financial and social uncertainties – no one would pretend that the crisis is definitely over. Following the failure of Copenhagen (see Chapter 7) and the mixed results of the 2010 G20 summits, a better global governance appears more than ever crucial but shaky. In this context, the present chapter, in brief, focuses on the transatlantic relationship. This chapter emphasizes the need of a reinforced transatlantic cooperation in the fields of macroeconomic and financial regulatory policies; it also argues that this would be a positive and welcome contribution to a better functioning of the G20 summits. In the middle of a deep and prolonged economic crisis, facing the threat of clashing national interests, now is a moment of opportunity, to use or to lose.

2. ENCOMPASSING A MORE UNSTABLE AND UNPREDICTABLE WORLD

The state of the world at the beginning of the twenty-first century is framed by the continuing movement of globalization and by the unfolding consequences of the economic and financial crisis. We can discern a number of major trends now shaping the transformation of international economic relations.

Asia is now recognized as the driving force behind globalization, with China in the lead (see Chapter 3). China's conversion to an authoritarian sort of capitalism relying heavily on export successes has been the most powerful engine of world growth, putting China on the path to becoming the world's top importer and exporter within a matter of years. Meanwhile, India has become a world leader in technology and electronic services. By the year 2025, OECD (Organisation for Economic Co-operation and Development) countries will produce only 40 per cent of the world's wealth (as compared to 55 per cent in 2000), while Asia's share will increase from 24 to 38 per cent, practically on a par with the OECD zone. China, which has become *the* dominant regional power and the US's as well as the EU's leading trading partner, holds some of the keys to the future of the world economy as well as to its financial stability.

Decreased Western influence in global affairs is the inevitable corollary of globalization. While the Western model of economic liberalism has imposed itself above all others as the only viable option, the Western powers that embody and sustain it are gradually being moved out of their position of dominance, and the vulnerabilities of the Western model of economic liberalism are further exposed by the financial crisis and global warming. Not only is the West relatively weak, it is also the object of widespread mistrust. The very notion of liberal internationalism is under attack. Politically, Western leadership is on the wane. Americans and Europeans are no longer able to defuse international crises alone; no major issue, be it Iran, Iraq, North Korea or the Middle East conflict, and no global challenge such as climate change and health, can be dealt with without the help of Russia, China and other regional powers. As for the world financial crisis, the G20 has already supplanted the G7, establishing itself as the relevant forum for handling such matters.

Multipolarity is one of the main political effects of globalization. But it is overoptimistic to see multipolarity promising the fruits of a consensus-based multilateral system. At the other extreme, overpessimistic observers could see multipolarity carry the seeds of disorder, anarchy or conflict. In Copenhagen, it is true, we witnessed a sharp divide in the vision of globalization and its management. Yet, faced with the challenge of governing our multipolar world, most international institutions are in the throes of a crisis of legitimacy and effectiveness, in part because the status and relative weight of member states in these institutions reflect the situation that prevailed in 1949 and not the reality of 2011. New forms of international cooperation, such as the G20, have become necessary to deal with the economic crisis.

These forces contribute to make the world more unstable and unpredictable. The United States has not relinquished its ambition to be the world's leader, but the conditions of this leadership must be revised. A Sino-American duopoly, the 'G2', or some form of power-sharing arrangement remains possible. Others artificially divide the world along new bipolar lines into the 'West and the rest'. What we have learned since the crisis broke out is that, in principle, 'global problems call for global solutions'. But the problem of the global economy today is to manage relationships which more than before have to combine elements of cooperation and rivalry. This is why the issue of global governance and the effectiveness–legitimacy issue of the G20 are so indispensable to the pursuit of a successful globalization.

3. GOVERNING A MULTIPOLAR AND HETEROGENEOUS WORLD ECONOMY

The financial crisis has re-inaugurated a period of activist international economic co-operation. Experts, politicians, governments and international institutions have been successful in their first and decisive actions, but they are poorly equipped to effectively embrace this new roadmap. The dismantling of the state has been the word for more than two decades. Macroeconomic policies have been reduced to a minimalist sphere, financial markets have been left over to self-regulation. These trends have been backed by a very strong theoretical argument, efficient market theory. Huge efforts have been made to turn this abstract academic research into policy recommendations. Where did the idea of 'a soft regulation' of finance come from, where did the idea of 'transferring risks to those most able to bear them' come from, and where did the idea of relaxing capital standards because financial institutions were 'more able to gauge risks than before' come from if not from a powerful conceptual framework turned into an ideological and political force?

That government intervention is harmful, that fair value is the quantitative incarnation of reason and that securitization is the secret of risk evaporation are not a result of science, they are one side of economic realities which for a period of time had been carefully manufactured into sort of a religious belief. Now, we have to live with the legacy of this faith-based strategy. The trade-off between risks and rewards had been grossly tilted towards the minimization of risks and the overvaluation of rewards; it is time to choose another point on this trade-off, but which one? Market failures are well recognized but governments are ignorant about the long-term consequences of huge deficits and accommodative monetary policies, they are poorly equipped to back their efforts towards financial re-regulation. The efficient market theory that brilliantly inspired a homogeneous vision of global finance is now broken; without the equivalent theory for a time of re-regulation, the world we inherit is foggy and heterogeneous.

In such a situation it is better not to expect a sort of a pure and perfect international economic co-operation. All participants are not created equal in the global summits. History suggests that international co-operation in the field of economic and financial policies is a (relatively) simple task in only one geo-political context which is frequently referred to as the 'hegemonic' case: this is when one country plays a prominent role and when leading can effectively inspire and combine economic and financial policies designed – according to historical circumstances – either to extend or to curtail the role of the state.

After the war, the US enjoyed a global leadership based on a new understanding of the responsibilities of governments (the Musgrave typology) and on financial innovations like deposit insurance, supervision of financial markets and proper accounting standards as enacted by the Roosevelt administration and subsequently adopted in other countries. Reversing these trends, the US acted powerfully during the last three decades to extend the use of financial innovations, to broaden the horizon of global finance and to oppose foreign proposals to reduce its procyclicality. This period is over. In a world which is becoming multipolar, it is time to think more seriously about the difficulties of international economic policy cooperation.

The world is no longer the bipolar one of the Cold War nor the brief unipolar moment which followed the fall of the Berlin wall. 'Multipolarity' is not a concept backed by a rigorous analysis, it is rather a suggestive word which undeniably captures something important. The G20 has been celebrated precisely for bringing the global summits in line with the present geo-political realities. But others, as we already mentioned, are skeptical about its present results and about its future achievements. This is a very premature conclusion. Those who dismiss the summits have to consider how much of this would have occurred in their absence and it is always worthwhile at that point to remember the failure of the London conference in 1933. History reminds us that big shifts in global power such as what we are witnessing can derail the process of globalization and prompt turn to economic wars, competitive devaluations and protectionism. We need the sort of global economic governance that the G20, for the first time in history, encapsulates. But initial expectations have been excessive; now is a time to more coolly assess its workability. This question is frequently raised in terms of legitimacy and effectiveness of the summits. In this chapter, we explore another theme: what role could the US and the EU play to energize, or, if unsuccessful, to hamper the governance of this multipolar and heterogeneous world? How, more precisely, do their convergences and divergences affect their ability to frame the future of the G20 discussions on macroeconomic policies and financial re-regulation?

4. NAVIGATING BETWEEN MACROECONOMIC ACTIVISM AND FINANCIAL VIRTUE

Looking first at the origins of the crisis, there is a great deal of consensus. In one word, the generally accepted view is that the origin of the crisis is 'excessive leverage'. But besides that broad consensus, a difference of emphasis can easily be perceived between the two sides of the Atlantic:

- In Europe the dominant perspective is one of systemic failure: lax macroeconomic policies; insufficient oversight; policy adopted by the industry; the ideology of self-regulation. As evidenced by the Larosière report to the European heads of state and government, the policy conclusion is that a proper balance between markets and regulators has to be restored with a strong determination. The public remains deeply dissatisfied with 'bankers' and, in short, asks for more protection. The Greek sovereign debt crisis has created a widespread sense of financial fragility.
- America also recognizes the failure but rather sees a broad failure of judgement: the failure of supervision is not denied, but it is in human nature that banks skilfully learnt to play the system! Now, trying to eradicate failings of human nature could prove more damaging than useful: regulation exposes institutions to serious unintended consequences; risk-taking is the very source of economic progress and should not be discouraged. American voters are disgusted by Wall Street as well but their anger is directed mostly against 'big government' and what has been seen as the failure of the new administration's activist policies.

The combination of these attitudes creates an uneasy situation for debating the orientations and priorities of macroeconomic policies. Transatlantic public debates have on different occasions evidenced strongly diverging views about the desirability of stimulus versus exit strategies. A widely-shared perception in this regard is that the message of the US administration has been 'nothing is off-limits' while the attitude in Europe has been more cautious. Following the Lehman Brothers failure, there has been a moment of panic. European leaders, who initially saw the crisis as an American problem, have been badly caught out. Deflation has been quickly recognized as a serious threat in the US, not in Europe. It is certainly true that Germany, for one, took too long in late 2008 to take full measure of the crisis. It is always important to remember that automatic stabilizers are a major difference between the EU and the US in this regard; despite weaker discretionary measures, the European countries – France and Germany among others – recorded high deficits in 2009 and 2010 and actively played their part in the fight against the 'great recession'.

Regarding monetary policy, contrary to many biased assessments, the European Central Bank (ECB) clearly rose to the challenge. When the financial markets tensions first erupted in August 2007, the ECB immediately cast off its reputation as a sluggish, timid institution by swiftly announcing very large-scale injections of emergency liquidity; the Bank continuously acted with a similar determination, even massively intervening to stabilize the market of peripheral sovereign instruments. The ECB has taken aggressive steps to pump unlimited liquidity in the banking sector, yet there is a widespread impression that the Fed and the Bank of England showed a stronger determination to counter the recession. It is true that the ECB did not – for excellent reasons – change its monetary policy as much as the Federal Reserve which is now, under QE II (Quantitative Easing – Second Round), directly financing the US Treasury. Now, with the ultimate inflationary risk being the central bank financing of deficits, the question is whether the long-term inflationary impact of recent policies can be reversed in time. What is needed in such a context is a credible fiscal regime. If investors and the general public doubt the willingness of the authorities to restore fiscal sanity and deflate the huge expansion of central banks' balance sheets, inflationary expectations may very well gain a firm hold, driving interest rates up and exchange rates down.

All this suggests that policymakers in the US and in Europe have a slightly different view of inter-temporal constraints facing them. What are the implications in terms of international policy co-ordination? Surmounting a lot of scepticism, the sequence of G20 summits can cautiously been assessed as a success. To have expected anything more substantial would be to misunderstand the nature of the exercise and underestimate the difficulties. Every leader has its own historical reference and political constituency. Consider the pre-summit exchanges about the size of the stimulus package. The US and Germany both have in mind the dramatic consequences of the inter-war period, but the German Chancellor recalls the ruinous consequences of hyper-inflation under the Weimar Republic while the US President has in mind the misery of the Great Depression. The goal of such a summit cannot be to erase these differences but, more modestly to align as far as possible national and mutual interests.

The conclusion is straightforward. Until now, neither huge deficits nor massive liquidity expansion are unmanageable threats. For the future, the ability to navigate through the crisis using both fiscal and monetary measures will depend crucially on the credibility of governments' commitment to long-term monetary and fiscal stability. The European debt crisis of 2010 has come close to but still not reached its conclusion, in January 2011; the next big crisis could very well be triggered by what markets would see as excessive fiscal debt in countries with large current account deficits, notably the US.

5. THE DANGERS OF MISMANAGING MACROECONOMIC POLICY CO-ORDINATION

Macroeconomists are comfortable with the idea of uncoordinated, diverging economic policies between Europe and the US if their economies are proved to be in genuinely different situations: if growth potential, unemployment, balance sheets and/or other parameters are materially different, it is not only comprehensible but desirable for macroeconomic policies to differ across the Atlantic. This is also the basic argument explaining why, generally speaking, international economic policy coordination is difficult to achieve: it is thus a frequent argument that each government doing what it thinks is best for its own economy (the US fighting excessive unemployment and Europe cleaning its own problems) is the most appropriate contribution to the common good. In a deep crisis, things are more complex and economic policy coordination really matters.

The first reason is a very traditional macroeconomic argument. As in the 1930s, transatlantic interdependencies on the products and capital markets have proved strong and these interdependencies generate spillover effects likely to produce undesirable outcomes if improperly managed. Tightening governments, for example, expect to gain on net exports by relatively constraining costs, income, indebtedness and demand in comparison to their trading partners; Germany's performance in 2010 is a successful demonstration of this strategy. But the tightening country's efforts will drag on demand in the other countries, so that governments who see a need for significant additional stimulus will have to do more to get the same effect. Capital flows might well amplify the consequences of asymmetric policy moves. Capital usually flows from tightening countries to stimulating countries. In a context of widespread uncertainty dominated by concerns about sustainability of fiscal policies, lax tax policies risk aggravating those concerns and lead to a depreciation of the currency.

Initial depreciation benefits could be welcome but they also fuel inflationary pressures that could well swamp those benefits in the medium term, if not immediately. Monetary policy would be faced with an unwelcome trade-off, which is exactly the situation of the Bank of England in the winter of 2010–2011. Monetary divergence also has counterproductive consequences. In a situation (like in the autumn of 2010) where the central bank undertakes additional ease – in the form of large-scale asset purchases – while others would try to reduce monetary accommodation, capital is expected to flow from the stimulating to the tightening currency areas which works contrarily to the initial and desired impact of policies on each side. Even more seriously, such movements can overshoot and eventually have extremely damaging effects on the exchange rate, like those observed in the spring of 2007 when capital flows pushed the euro–dollar exchange rate to 1.6, its highest level ever.

A second argument is related to political economy considerations. Differences between the US and Europe exist but should not be exaggerated. As we have already recalled, the preparation of recent G20 summits has been characterized by transatlantic divergences regarding the urgency of immediate action to restore fiscal sanity or a higher level of activity. No one should underestimate the seriousness of this dilemma and this should be debated within an ongoing transatlantic conversation. But when the arguments turn into public disputes, this could quickly erode confidence and limit the effectiveness of both policies at stake, particularly in their impact on investment, with unpredictable consequences on capital flows and currency movements. The fear of the great recession turning into a great depression has hopefully been averted, but the risks facing the western economies are not eliminated. It is for sure an uncomfortable perspective but policymakers – not only academics – have the responsibility to make a judgment about the risks (like the ones of Japan's lost decade or, worse, of the Great Depression). Current policy discussions on both sides of the Atlantic probably underestimate the relevance of these parallels: in short, euro area policymakers could very well, under German inspiration and influence, exaggerate the benefits of immediate and general rigor; following decades of benign neglect regarding debt, American policymakers could very well underestimate the coming limits of global investors' willingness to finance US tax and monetary profligacy. It is reasonable to conclude that premature tightening as well as uncontrolled stimulus are symmetric threats so that the optimal macroeconomic policy probably lies somewhere between the stated positions on opposite sides of the Atlantic. We now turn to the micro-economic aspects of our post-crisis financial world.

6. THERE IS NO PURE AND PERFECT FINANCIAL RE-REGULATION

'Financial regulation' usually indicates a cluster of interrelated policies aimed at insuring a proper functioning of the financial system. Some of these regulations are, or should be, similar to those enacted in other industries regarding the protection of consumers, the safe design of products or the supply of appropriate information to the public. But finance is different in very important aspects. International financial regulation does not obey the same logic as the one, for example, embedded in international trade agreements and institutions. 'Free trade is good' and has been (within regulatory limits exemplified by food security concerns) pursued as such; but what about finance? Capital flows are good as well, but finance regularly triggers crises; more than trade, finance needs rules. There is an underlying tension beneath financial liberalization. Free trade means going forward on a linear axis; free capital movements immediately expose a trade-off between risks and rewards. The trade-off between risks and rewards had been grossly tilted towards the minimization of risks and the overvaluation of rewards; it is time to choose another point on this trade-off, but which one?

Market failures are well recognized but governments are poorly equipped to back their efforts towards financial re-regulation. Getting a financial international agreement is much more demanding than liberalizing trade. The efficient market theory brilliantly inspired a homogeneous vision of global finance that is now broken; the world we inherit is heterogeneous. We must not be satisfied with purely pragmatic answers backing the process of international re-regulation only due to the pressure of domestic politics. Regulatory competition is destabilizing. This is why the US and the EU need to work together to design a new balance between market efficiency and supervisory security: we need to back-up regulatory efforts by sharing a view adapted to a time of re-regulation.

First, the center of gravity of the global economy is moving eastward. The share of emerging countries among the top 100 listed banks has surged from practically nothing to one third of the world total, a significant part of it reflecting the rise of Chinese institutions. A similar picture emerges when looking at global financial centers among which Hong Kong, Singapore, Tokyo (and Shanghai tomorrow) rank at the top of the league. The combination of deleveraging in the West and wealth accumulation in Asia will certainly reinforce this trend. This still does not translate into Asian countries playing a major role in the global financial policy debate. Emerging economies are considering the financial crisis as a Western mess, they are not re-regulating in the Western style but rather withholding their cards, and that does not contribute to make the world of global finance flat.

Second, continental Europe is looking for emancipation. Its financial culture and its financial structures are different from those of the City or of Wall Street. A distinguished observer of European financial realities recently characterized Europe as the combination of a port – the city of London – oriented towards the ocean, and a vast hinterland – continental Europe – both being strongly inter-connected. In many aspects, continental Europe only reluctantly adopted the mantra of self-regulated efficient markets; one should remember the harsh words of German officials going so far as to qualify American bankers as 'locusts'. More importantly, Europe appeared disarmed when facing the financial crisis. A more unified financial single market had been recognized for years as a desirable goal but, despite the creation of the euro, action remained timid and delayed due to conflicting national interests. After the crisis, because of public anger, inaction was no more an option.

According to many observers, the global crisis is relentlessly demonstrating the EU's flaws and limitations, particularly regarding the organization and supervision of the financial markets. After months of delay, due to the political bickering following the installation of a new Parliament, a new Commission and new European institutions, lawmakers and governments finally agreed in September 2010 to a radical overhaul of the patchy system of financial oversight. Besides the creation of a Systemic Risk Council (described in the following section), the new regime will rely on three new European Supervisory Authorities (ESAs) (see also Chapter 1) for banks (located in London), markets (in Paris) and insurance (in Frankfurt). This decision is a new example of a European tradition to use every crisis as an opportunity: the creation of such agencies was considered as necessary to really organize European-wide financial activities but opposed by national governments. Their creation out of three pre-existing pan-European committees is a logical consequence of the crisis. On paper, the supervisory structure is a wise balance of national and EU-wide responsibilities.

The main task of the new European agencies will be to set standards and rules, day-to-day supervision remaining with national authorities. The new ESAs are formal European institutions made up of the heads of the 27 national supervisors; they will make their decisions by simple or qualified majority voting even if they certainly extend the tradition of the previous committees to work mainly by consensus so as to bring everyone on board. The ESAs will have binding powers in certain circumstances, in particular in case of 'emergency situations', but they cannot enforce decisions that have budgetary implications: if facing a financial crisis, the market-authority could temporarily ban certain products but the banking authority could not order a bail-out. The size of the agencies will be modest (say 100 people for each as compared with 3000 for the British FSA – Financial Services Association) and they willingly will depend on significant member states' inputs. All this is a sensible, harmonized rule-making process which is an important aspect definitely needed for a better functioning of the European financial industry and markets; it is also a subtle shift of power to Brussels.

Multipolarity eventually changes the behavior of the main actors. A multipolar world is one which simultaneously faces asymmetry between the West and the rest and between the US and the EU. In its previous phase, for example, EU institutions were instinctively working on the basis of free-market and internationalist considerations because these were the drivers of intra-European harmonization. The dynamics are changing as more political objectives are now, as everywhere in the world, fed into the debates; this in particular reflects the increased role of the European Parliament. This European reaction is a striking demonstration of what we have to expect when entering a heterogeneous and multipolar world. The G20 is not the expression of a global political constituency; beyond the summits, decisions are made in Washington, Beijing, Brussels and other capitals where, as we know, 'all politics is local'. Re-regulation lies in the hands of domestic constituencies; this inspires a widespread reluctance to delegate formal powers to a supra-national level. Differences in the financial industry structures also make uniform rules meaningless and unreachable. There is nothing like an ideal harmonization of legislation: the G20 has to engineer a 'workable convergence' and what could prove workable, and due to the reality of the G20 there is no better place to initiate this conversation (or to block its momentum) than in transatlantic dialogue.

7. SYSTEMIC RISK AND BANK REGULATION ON THE RIGHT TRACK

The crisis has demonstrated the importance of strengthening the resilience of the banking industry by implementing tougher rules on capital and liquidity. The package prepared by the Basel Committee has been delivered in time after detailed consultations. It is very comprehensive and addresses these issues by improving the level and quality of capital for credit institutions as well as developing a framework for liquidity risk. The main elements of the proposal are: first, to improve the quality of capital constituted especially under tier 1 and to introduce capital buffers to increase the loss-absorption capacity of banks; second, to rely on a non-risk-based leverage ratio as a supplementary measure to the Basel II risk control framework in order to curb excessive balance sheet growth; and third, to introduce a range of measures like forward-looking provisioning intended to mitigate the inherent pro-cyclicality of the financial system. Does all this rise to the challenge?

The Basel Committee has, in short, concluded a complex agreement in a short period of time; good news for its future work. The compromise, with the above mentioned limits, offers the chances of a level playing field even if several countries, among them the US or Switzerland, could find it not demanding enough. This would be a sort of a reverse controversy seeing the US willing more stringent regulations than continental Europe! Some will conclude that, in the current context, harmonization efforts might only lead to weak global standards: this is an unnecessarily cynical argument. Anyway, the Congress will always follow its own way – and the adoption of any Basel agreement in Washington remains an open question. With many others, I would finally consider the Basel proposals as an example of a workable convergence.

The financial crisis has demonstrated that safe banks were a necessary but not sufficient condition of a safe financial system. Deep and complex interconnections between financial intermediaries are the source of risks of systemic nature. The key to preventing financial crises is the establishment of a process to identify and monitor these vulnerabilities that threaten financial stability. It is easy to remember in the past decades a lot of situations – Mexican and many other debt crises, savings and loans, dotcom or housing bubbles – where such a process would have been more than desirable. Briefly said, the historical record is not encouraging in this regard. Could it be different this time? Should we prove irremediably naïve, we are tempted to think that the short answer is yes. The true question relates to political will but the task is not unmanageable; the idea of weaknesses accumulating before the crisis being, at least for now, widely shared. These imbalances and risks have first to be recognized, rather than denied, as we have too frequently witnessed during the last decade; they have thus to be calibrated in terms of their potential adverse effect on the economy which is both more important and more difficult. This process is a continuous one of information gathering, technical analysis and synthetic assessment. It should be systematic in nature, comprehensive and monitoring both the macro and micro aspects. We have witnessed a political will to meet these challenges. Are EU and US reforms appropriately designed? Will they prove up to the task?

At the moment credit should be given to the reforms adopted on both sides of the Atlantic. Prominent among other policy bodies, new institutions are created to face the unique nature of systemic risk. In Europe, the new actor is called a Systemic Risk Board in the US, a Systemic Risk Council. Both will comprise policy officials, central bankers, members from regulatory and supervisory bodies; the chair is held by the Central Bank in Europe, and by the Treasury in the US. There is a debate about the effectiveness of both arrangements. In both cases, participants represent different interests and are subject to different public and private influences; this is the nature of the game and consensus will not be easy to achieve. It can be argued that the US solution relies exclusively on federal officials, and when consensus is reached, each agency has the authority to implement decisions. Effective enough 'if' consensus can be reached; the experience of the past decade invites a cautious assessment in this regard. The EU Board is sometimes wrongly qualified as a 'reputational body' – it has real even if less direct power than its American counterpart, but more importantly it is chaired by the independent and powerful ECB. The ECB has already proved to be an important player in the middle of diverging views among member states.

In short, the distinctions between the American and European solutions to cope with systematic risk are of second order, and the Board and the Council are reliable frameworks to track and prevent financial excesses. Experience suggests that coordination between the two will be satisfactory in case of 'standard' financial turbulence. Things would be tenser if facing a more severe situation (another major banking crisis, a sovereign default threat, a mix of both, a divergence regarding the pursuit of quantitative easing, and so on). In such a case, issues could be elevated to the G20 level. The final answer would depend on the degree of consensus regarding the risk–reward balance of the financial outlook and on the political will to act accordingly and cooperatively. There is no known solution, as we already witnessed in particular about the size of the stimulus package, to oblige convergence and overcome diverging political priorities regarding the use of budgetary and monetary rescue instruments.

8. SEEKING THE PROPER BALANCE BETWEEN FINANCIAL RISK AND REWARDS

Another major systemic vulnerability of the system is the question of 'too big to fail'. In the US, several big financial firms, now called 'Systematically Important Financial Institutions' or SIFIs, faced insolvency. As the Lehman's failure demonstrated, this was posing a threat to the whole system. Government intervention was needed, as had been the case in previous financial crises, but the government did not have the tools to do the job. US authorities had to provide bridge loans to sponsor mergers, to extend Federal Reserve funding and to recapitalize these institutions with an unprecedented amount of taxpayers' money. Europe too faced similar risks in the UK and Ireland. On the continent, individual banks suffered, sometimes severely, without endangering the system. The question raised by SIFIs is at the heart of modern finance; these institutions have grown in a way that put them outside the very logic of capitalism which is to reward success by profits and to punish failure by bankruptcy. There cannot be a proper functioning of the whole system if such an important part of the economy is able to withdraw itself from market discipline. Solutions have been debated and a report is to be submitted later to the G20 by the FSB (Financial Stability Board). If capital requirements alone are not up to the task, what other solutions can be implemented?

Markets can also have a systemic impact if they are insufficiently transparent thereby leading to mispricing of risk and laying the basis for destabilizing adjustments; this was the case in the CDS (Credit Default Swap) market. Efforts to reform the CDS market are focused on making the market more transparent and reducing counterparty exposures. Consensus has emerged that over-the-counter markets need to be moved to central counterparties or be subject to additional requirements. Where such central clearing mechanisms existed before the crisis, payments flowed smoothly and defaults were handled well. Looking forward nonetheless, it is important to act carefully so that the benefits of multilateral counterparty netting are not offset by the concentration of operational risk inherent to such big institutions.

The future extent of securitization will crucially depend on how regulation is formulated. New regulations have already constrained some of the more complex products but securitization benefits for economic growth should be secured by creating a secure environment for long-term investors (insurers, pension funds and so on) which need to be convinced that abuses which occurred in the run-up to the crisis are definitely under control. Incentives should be designed in a way which promotes a stricter view of credit supply which implies originators keeping a significant share of these credits on their books. On the other side, should regulations be too strictly designed and applied, originators may well find it un-economical to originate loans unnecessarily restricting the usefulness of securitization. Facing this trade-off, and with the benefits of the previous financial boom and bust, policymakers should preferably err on the side of caution.

Second, capital markets need consistent financial information; this is a clearly desirable goal but this could also fuel a serious transatlantic rift. First, a lot of issues deserve to be taken into consideration by the G20 and its regulatory network and could be other examples of a workable convergence. Current risk-disclosure practices could certainly be improved; lessons could, for example, be drawn from the stress tests conducted both in the US and the EU, and these exercises integrated into a more coherent framework. The public supervision of rating agencies remains very much unconvincing; that calls for new initiatives which should be as converging as possible. Surprisingly, audit firms have remained out of the radar screen despite the fact that the Sarbanes-Oxley Act produced a transatlantic uproar after granting extraterritorial competence to US authorities; designing a stronger international body should be part of the agenda. This said, everyone knows that a more painful hurdle lies on the way towards a 'better' financial information, fair market value at any price. There is no issue where the theme of pro-cyclicality is more provocative. Prematurely recognizing unrealized capital gains, it can be said, is the mother of all financial excesses. There is no issue where the intellectual candor of a financial body has been more deeply and systematically captured by the industry. Raising the lessons of the crisis, the London Summit took the initiative to ask the International Accounting Standards Board (IASB) and the Financial Accounting Standards Board (FASB) to deliver convergence of their standards in June 2011; this hope has been (indefinitely?) postponed by the FASB. There are few reasons to believe that Europeans would accept convergence at a price which would be a return to what is considered as a key ingredient of the crisis; convergence of accounting standards is a worthy objective as long as the content and quality of the standards are designed to increase convergence, not volatility.

9. THE FUTURE OF THE TRANSATLANTIC PARTNERSHIP

The transatlantic partnership is strong – it is not necessary to underline its strength and endurance: 6 June 1944 is in everyone's mind on both sides of the Atlantic. It comes as no surprise that such a close relationship has gone through ups and downs. The Bush presidency for sure counted among the latter, but only a few observers thought that the divorce could be as deep and durable as rhetoric at that time suggested. Today, the relationship has turned to a new normal but remains under pressure – a pressure of a different sort, apparently more benign but which could prove in reality more damaging. This malaise originates in the discordance between the goals and tools of the alliance. The world that created 'transatlanticism' is fading fast. Europe and the United States should urgently recast their relationship as a more effective and a more strategic partnership focused on economic policy co-ordination. Two arguments, finally, suggest the need to reassess the relationship: one relates to the economic pressures of the time, the second to the geo-political dimensions of globalization today.

On the economic side, the West is in trouble, which is not good news for the world economy. The two-speed recovery continues. In advanced economies, activity has strongly recovered and growth remains subdued, unemployment is still high, imbalances are not correcting and renewed stresses in the euro area periphery are contributing to downside risks. In many emerging economies, activity remains buoyant, inflation pressures are emerging, and there are now some signs of overheating, driven in part by strong capital inflows. Upside risks are visible but downside risks are not absent. The most urgent requirements for robust recovery are comprehensive and rapid actions to overcome sovereign and financial troubles in the euro area and policies to redress fiscal imbalances and to repair and reform financial systems in advanced economies more generally. These need to be complemented with policies that keep overheating pressures in check and facilitate external rebalancing. The world is faced with daunting policy challenges; nothing equivalent has been witnessed since the 1930s.

On the geo-political side, we have to take into account three essential realities. First, the West – even if Europe and the US work together – is diminishing in terms of demography, power and influence. By 2050, the US and Europe combined may no longer account for more than 7 per cent of world population. A similar relative diminution is to be expected in terms of economic heft. With this will go the erosion of the 'West's' ability to determine the terms and organization of global governance. Second, following the biggest financial crisis since 1929, governments are faced with pressing socio-economic demands: public opinions have been patient but history shows that long-term mass-unemployment is dangerous for democracy. The pressure is growing on both sides of the Atlantic to focus more on the domestic economy than on international relations. Finally, the time has come to recognize that the Cold War is over. The twentieth century was shaped by major political clashes that led countries into war or took the form of nuclear stand-off. Most conflicts burdening the transatlantic couple are no longer NATO issues. Be it Iraq or energy policy, the Middle East or climate protection, Iran or development in Africa, NATO is no longer the most appropriate institution to carry transatlantic relations. And for all that they produce, institutions related to transatlantic economic cooperation (the Summits and Dialogues) have until now had very small traction. This is what dramatically needs to be energized to manage transatlantic economic divergences and organized as a tool to help to work of the G20 successfully.

All this makes a better world governance both necessary and difficult to achieve. Three years after its creation, the G20 perfectly reflects today's world in its two dimensions: the need to go beyond the old Western-style G7 steering committee and the frigidity of a broad but heterogeneous summitry. In fact, integrating new powers as responsible stakeholders will be far trickier than currently expected for many reasons. First, the world remains more driven by national interest than frequently asserted in a wave of excessive 'globalization enthusiasm'. Renewed strategic competition and serious clashes of interest complicate efforts to enlist emerging powers in managing common global challenges. Second, rising powers are more inclined to enjoy the privileges than shoulder the obligations of power. Their status as developing countries reinforces an instinct to free ride on the contributions of established nations, including the United States, Europe and Japan. Third, most emerging powers do not share Western views on global order – at least not entirely. They have already demonstrated that they will test the West and try to renegotiate existing rules and norms, rather than celebrating their adoption as a proof of their 'successful modernization'.

In brief, the inertia of existing structures, the vested interests of existing power-wielders, and the inevitable trade-offs between efficiency, legitimacy and like-mindedness will make it hard to adapt old institutions to new players – and ensure the transition of the old international liberal order to a new phase. From the previous to the present stages, the American preeminence certainly remains' but things are now evolving into a much more complex canvas. This is why the transatlantic partnership remains so important. The common body of principles, norms, rules and procedures we have built and accumulated is sort of an *Acquis Atlantique*. But the actual functioning of the partnership does not match these challenges and makes this *acquis* less robust than frequently supposed. The ties that bind the global economy are a product of the Western, liberal economic order. The more integrated, united and dynamic those bonds are, the greater the likelihood that rising powers will rise within this rules-based order. The weaker or the looser those bonds, the greater the likelihood that rising powers will successfully challenge that order.

BIBLIOGRAPHY

Aglietta, Michel (2008), *Macroéconomie Financière*, La Découverte.
Bank for International Settlements (BIS) (2009), *79th Annual Report 2008–2009*, 29 June.
Bank for International Settlements (BIS) (2009), *80th Annual Report 2009–2010*, June.
Bradford, Colin I., Linn, Johannes F. and Paul Martin (2008), *Global Governance Breakthrough: The G20 Summit and the Future Agenda*, Brookings Policy Brief, No. 168, Brookings Institution Press, December.
Brender, Anton and Florence Pisani (2007), *Les Déséquilibres Financiers Internationaux*, La Découverte.
Brookings Global Economy and Development (2008), *The G-20 Financial Summit: Seven Issues at Stake*.
De Larosière, Jacques (2009), *Report of the High-Level Group on Financial Supervision in the EU*, Brussels, 25 February, http://ec.europa.eu/internal _market/finances/docs/de_larosiere_report_en.pdf.
Dervis, Kemal and Ceren Ozer (2005), *A Better Globalization: Legitimacy, Governance, and Reform*, Center for Global Development, April.
Frieden Jeff (2006), *Global Capitalism*, Norton: New York.

Friedman, Thomas L. (2005), *The World is Flat: A Brief History of the Twenty-first Century*, New York: Farrar, Straus & Giroux.

Fukuyama, Francis (1992), *The End of History and the Last Man*, New York: Free Press.

Grieco, Joseph M. and G. John Ikenberry (2003), *State Power and World Markets*, New York: Norton.

Institute of International Finance (2009), *Capital Flows to Emerging Markets Economies*, 27 January.

James, Harold (2001), *The End of Globalization*, Cambridge, MA: Harvard University Press.

Kahler, Miles and David A. Lake (eds) (2003), *Governance in a Global Economy*, Princeton, NJ: Princeton University Press.

Keohane, Robert (1984), *After Hegemony, Cooperation and Discord in the World Political Economy*, Princeton, NJ: Princeton University Press.

Kindleberger, Charles (1973), *The World in Depression*, University of California Press: Berkeley, CA.

Kindleberger, Charles and Robert Aliber (1978), *Manias, Panics and Crashes: A History of Financial Crises*, Wiley Investment Classics.

Lewis, W. Arthur (1978), *The Evolution of the International Economic Order*, Princeton, NJ: Princeton University Press.

Mistral, Jacques (2007), 'Comment réformer la gouvernance mondiale', in Le Cercle des économistes, *Un monde de ressources rares*, Librairie Académique Perrin: Paris.

Mistral, Jacques (2009), 'Shaping a New World Economic Governance: A Challenge for America and Europe', in Carlo Secchi, and Antonio Villafranca, (eds), *Liberalism in Crisis?*, Cheltenham, UK and Northampton, MA, USA, Edward Elgar Publishing Ltd.

National Intelligence Council (NIC) (2008), *Global Trends 2025, a Transformed World*, US Government Printing Office.

Pisani-Ferry, Jean (2005), *The Accidental Player, the EU and the Global Economy*, www.Bruegel.org.

Sapir, André (ed.) (2007), *Fragmented Power, Europe and the Global Economy*, Brussels: Bruegel Book.

Reinhart, Carmen and K. Rogoff (2008), *The Aftermath of Financial Crises*, www.economics.harvard.edu./rogoff.

Ruggie, John (1983), 'International Regimes, Transactions, and Change: Embedded Liberalism in the Postwar Economic Order', in St. Krasner (ed.), *International Regimes*, Ithaca, NY: Cornell University Press.

Slaughter, Anne-Marie (2004), *A New World Order*, Princeton, NJ: Princeton University Press.

Truman, Edwin (ed.) (2006), *Reforming the IMF in the 21st Century*, Washington D.C., Peterson Institute for International Affairs.

Wolf, Martin (2004), *Why Globalization Works?*, London: Yale University Press.

3. Understanding China's Role in the Post-financial Crisis World

Xiaozu Wang

1. INTRODUCTION

In 2010, China's GDP reached yuan 39,798bn, or $6,009bn at the end-of-year 2010 exchange rate. Surpassing Japan, China has become the second largest economy in the world, with GDP about 41 per cent of that of the US, $14,660bn in 2010 GDP.

China's economic achievements have foremost benefited Chinese people. In 2010, the urban household per capita income reached 19,109 yuan, an increase of 11.5 per cent over the previous year and almost 10 times as much as that in 1978 in real terms. In 2009, only 35.79 million people lived under the national poverty line of annual income of 1,196 yuan per capita, a reduction of more than 85 per cent from that in 1978 (Ministry of Foreign Affairs 2010). In 2009, China overtook the US as the world's biggest car market, and in 2010 13.8 million passenger cars were sold in China, 33 per cent higher than in 2009.

Although China's large population will continue to make it one of the poor countries in the world in terms of per capita income, China's overall economic power will also make it one important player in the multipolar world. With its size of the economy, momentum of growth, increasing level of technological sophistication, sound financial position and importance in global trade, China will play an important role in the global economy. China's growth presents an opportunity to the world by providing the world with a larger and more mature market in goods and services. It also challenges the rest of the world to realign their interests and competitiveness in the world.

In this chapter, I discuss some key elements to understanding the rising role of China. The chapter is organized as follows. I first outline the political and institutional features of China in order to set up the context of our discussion. I then examine China's domestic agenda and its implications for the global economy. Next consider how China will respond to its international challenges and particularly renminbi exchange rate and China's foreign exchange reserve. I conclude with some forward-looking remarks.

2. THE GOVERNMENT'S ROLE IN PROMOTING ECONOMIC GROWTH AND MAINTAINING SOCIAL AND POLITICAL STABILITY

China achieved its great economic success under a quite different political system than that in the Western countries. The Chinese Communist Party has been the dominating political power since 1949, and the political leaders have been chosen by the Party. This political system is often criticized as lacking popular representation and is treated with much suspicion in the West with regard to both its legitimacy and stability. But such critique focuses too much on the form rather than the substance of the system.

Historically, the Communist Party came to power in 1949 after the civil war and years of popular revolt against the Nationalist Party, which retreated to Taiwan after its defeat in mainland China. China attempted to get rid of decades of colonial influence of the West, of the corrupt political system, and to achieve economic prosperity and equality. The Communist Party provided an answer to these demands, and that gained it political legitimacy. In the next 30 years, China made economic progress (Lin 2009) but lagged further behind relative to developed economies (Deng 1978) due to the mismanagement that was driven by communist ideology. The central planning economic system became a barrier of economic development.

In 1978, seizing the opportunity of economic crisis, Deng Xiaoping led the Party to refocus its attention to improving China's economy and made it clear the Party must gain its legitimacy by improving the economic welfare of Chinese people. This has ever since become the guiding principle of the Communist Party. Deng also made clear that political and social stability is a necessary condition for economic development. There is an implicit social contract between the Communist Party and Chinese people that the Party will provide the stable economic and social environment for Chinese people to pursue their economic interests, and the political legitimacy of the Party is grounded on the steady economic improvement of Chinese people.

Given its political mandate and power, the Communist Party has the duality of acting swiftly and gradually. Under most circumstances when the political stability is not under threat, the government chooses to play safe and implement changes slowly. But in case of economic or political crisis, the Party can switch gear and change course with urgency. When at odds, political stability trumps economic efficiency. Such seemingly self-contradiction or inconsistency is founded on the same Party doctrine: political and social stability is of paramount importance and stability promotes economic growth. After enjoying more than 30 years of social stability and economic prosperity (Figure 3.1), Chinese people are ready to submit themselves to building a 'harmonious society'.

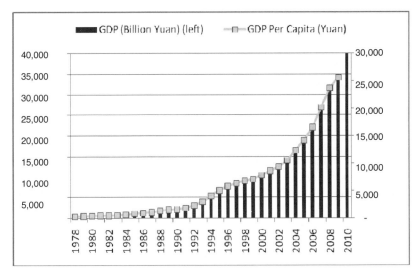

Source: Ma (2011), National Bureau of Statistics of China (2011)

Figure 3.1 China's GDP and per capita GDP (1978–2009)

One key feature of Chinese economic reform since 1978 is gradualism (Qian 2002). The economic development since 1978 took a number of stages, which usually starts with a local small-scale trial-and-error experiment and goes on to larger-scale implementation of the successful policy (Lin 2009). For example, when China started to reform state owned enterprises (SOEs), it started in selected cities. Later on, when nationwide reform started the government allowed different modes, from outright sale of the SOEs to private entrepreneurs, joint-venture with foreign investors, public listing in stock exchanges and enhanced management under state ownership. In 30 years, the economy has been transformed from almost 100 per cent of industrial output produced by state-owned enterprises to two-thirds by private enterprises.

Gradualism allows time for bargaining and adjustment of all parties involved, and ensures the economic benefits are shared or redistributed. Making reform inventive-compatible for major parties is a key to the success of China's economic reform and development, and the government should be expected to adhere to the principle.

The majority of businesses in China are privately-owned. The central government directly controls only 121 companies, through state-owned assets supervision and administration. But those controlled by central government are mostly very large and of strategic importance, such as energy, telecommunication and aerospace industries. The five largest companies listed in the Chinese stock market are controlled by the government, and they account for close to a quarter of the total market capitalization of all listed companies in China. Local governments also control a small number of companies.

A central role played by the Chinese government is to set the country's agenda of economic reform and industrial policies. For example, when China set out to build its high-speed train system, it was the government-controlled companies that spearheaded the efforts in acquiring foreign technologies and developing their own. In fact, the role Chinese government is playing in directing the country's economic priority is not much different from other Asian countries, such as Japan and South Korea, particularly during their earlier states of development. This system is proved to be effective when the country is attempting to catch up with developed economies, where the goals can be clearly set. But once the country reaches the technology frontier, when further growth must come from new technologies invented and market demand cultivated, which will require individualistic efforts and many times of trial and error through market competition, such a government-led approach may become less effective.

To foster economic growth, the government can direct public resources to the SOEs either by tax subsidies or by granting monopoly power. It can also sacrifice the interests of these SOEs if it deems it necessary for the greater and longer-term social and political good. When facing high inflation pressure in 2007 because of the global high price of energy, the Chinese government directed its oil companies to keep down the price and help keep inflation down. It was quite effective in the short run (the most imporant reason why China escaped the high inflation of 2007 was the global financial crisis, as this made China's imports of energy and raw materials much cheaper).

The Chinese government is in a strong position to direct the Chinese economy. First of all, the economic success since 1978 has earned the government credits. Secondly, the government is in a strong financial position to support its economic agenda. The central and local government fiscal revenue kept growing at an average annual rate of 17.9 per cent from 1978 to 2010, with only small deficits. In 2010, the central government ran a fiscal deficit of yuan 585.3bn, which is 13.8 per cent of the fiscal revenue. Thirdly, the government controls the banking system. The central bank of China, People's Bank of China (PBOC), is under the direction of the State Council and not independent (Xinhua News Agency 2003). The monetary policy is set as part of the government's economic policies. The five largest state-controlled banks account for 50 per cent of the banking assets in China.

The strong position allows the Chinese government to mobilize large amounts of financial resources quickly. After the collapse of Lehman Brothers in September 2008, in response to the threat of economic recession, the Chinese government quickly introduced a yuan 4,000bn stimulus package in November 2008, consisting largely of government-sponsored investment in infrastructure, housing subsidies for low-income families, and subsidies for environment and technology upgrades. It would not have been possible without the strong political power of the Communist Party. The central government committed roughly one quarter of the funds, with the balance contributed by local governments and companies that carry out these projects. In 2009, the commercial banks also provided large amount of loans to government-sponsored investment projects. At least partly due to the government's concerted efforts, China was able to avoid the severe economic recession experienced by most of the world, and kept its GDP growth above 9 per cent, reaching 10.3 per cent in 2010 (see Figure 3.2).

However, such government power and heavy-handed interventions do not always come without a price. After banks made massive loans in 2008 (Figure 3.3) as part of the government's efforts to avoid economic recession, the government became very concerned about the quality of those loans and the capital adequacy of the banks. Most of the banks recapitalized in 2009 and 2010 by issuing stocks and bonds. Many economists believe the massive loans increased the money supply and was partly responsible for high inflation in 2010. In order to calm the middle–lower income population, the government also introduced direct price controls in 2010, and central government issued orders to local governments to limit food prices. The local governments then used their financial resources to subsidize food producers or make rent concessions to food vendors who rent stores from the government property. These measures alleviated the inflation pressure in the shortrun through redistribution of wealth without tackling the deeper causes. Because of its central economic role, the Chinese government may take the undeserved credit or unaccountable blame.

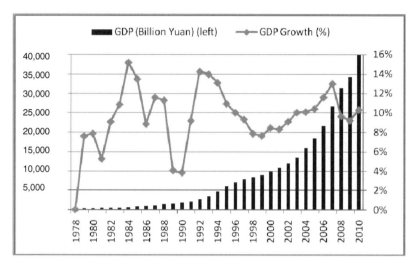

Note: GDP is in current yuan and growth rate based on constant yuan. 2010 figures are preliminary, based on the Commissioner's Report of National Statistical Bureau of China. In China, GDP figures are released three times during approximately a two-year period: preliminary, preliminarily-verified and finally-verified. The figures can be subject to further revision when the national survey is conducted.

Source: Ma (2011), National Bureau of Statistics of China (2011).

Figure 3.2 China's GDP growth rate (1979–2009)

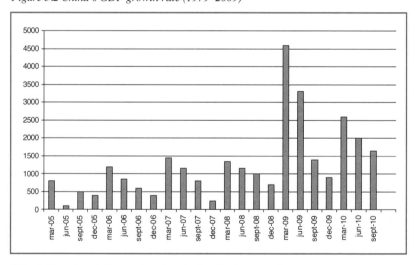

Note: Net loan issue is the new loan issued minus the loans repaid.

Figure 3.3 Quarterly net loan issues (billion yuan)

3. THE DOMESTIC AGENDA

China enters its 12th Five-Year Plan in 2011. In its 'advice' for devising the 12th Five-Year Plan, The Communist Party set the guidelines that follow the concept of 'scientific development', as advocated by President Hu Jintao, which emphasizes social development over simple GDP growth (Xinhua News Agency 2010).

China has planned to cut energy consumption and make economic growth more environmentally friendly. It has paid a very heavy price in the past development in environment and resources and it is now trying to undo some of the damages. It encourages both foreign and domestic investment in environment-friendly and energy-efficient technology by providing tax incentives, has made some progress in solar energy and wind energy, and become an important production base for new energy equipment.

In the past three decades, China had a very high savings rate, ranging from 34 to 53 per cent of China's GDP (Yang *et al*. 2011). Total Chinese household savings reached yuan 26tn. It enabled the massive investments China made during the period possible. But it also has the negative implication of depressing consumption. One commonly cited reason for the high savings rate is that consumers need savings for 'rainy days': medical care, education and retirement. In the 12th Five-Year Plan, the government plans to improve the social safety net dramatically, in both cities and rural areas in order to boost consumption.

Another item high on the 12th Five-Year Plan is to develop middle and western China. In 2010, the investment in eastern, central and western regions grew by 22.8 per cent, 26.9 per cent and 26.2 per cent respectively. This trend should be expected to continue. This will not only bridge the economic gap between the east and the rest of the country, it will become the next important catalyst of China's economic growth.

One characteristic of China's economic growth in the past three decades is that the eastern coastal region developed faster and contributed much more to the nation's economic growth. But three decades of development has also made the eastern China land scarcer, environmental requirements more stringent, and the overall costs higher. In the meantime, the infrastructure in middle and western China is so much developed that more and more companies choose to locate or relocate there. Migrant workers who used to leave home and work in the eastern region now can find jobs near home and choose not to go to the east. This increases the labor costs further in the east and makes middle and western China more attractive.

Since businesses are guided by their desire to seek lower costs and serve untapped markets, the economic growth in China will expand inland. This economic dynamics will be strengthened by the government's desire to level the regional differences. The development of middle and western China will enhance productivity in China, and the government's investment in infrastructure, which made private investments in middle and western China possible, will eventually pay off. China has benefited from its size in many ways and will continue to do so in western region development. Once the virtuous cycle of investment, economic growth, higher income and larger domestic market ensues in middle and western China, just as it did in the eastern coastal region in the past, we can expect China to enjoy high growth for another decade or two.

Another reason to be optimistic about China's growth is the development of middle and western China as it will offer a buffer in China's competition with other emerging economies in labor-intensive industries. Businesses that would otherwise seek low costs in other countries may view middle and western China as a viable alternative. Of course, China's competitive advantage in international trade is not merely low costs. Many countries around the world offer lower costs than China. The reason for China to attract investment, maintain high growth and become the world's factory must include social and political stability, organizational and human capital, the size and maturity of the domestic market, which are not easily provided by other emerging economies (Wang *et al.* 2009).

Inflation is one evil the Chinese government is determined to fight. In 2010, the consumer price index was 3.3 per cent up year-on-year, with the December 2010 rising at faster pace of 4.6 per cent. Given China's GDP growth of 10.3 per cent in 2010 such inflation should be quite tolerable. In fact, in the past three decades, China's higher GDP growth was often followed by higher inflation (Figure 3.4). But the food price was up by 7.7 per cent, which disproportionately affected lower income households. Housing prices were stubbornly moving upward, which made the younger population particularly unhappy. For fear of inflation causing social instability, the Chinese government did not take any chances and made a great effort to control inflation, including setting limits on food prices and providing subsidies to vendors. The local governments also introduced severe measures to control real estate prices, including limiting the number of apartments one family can buy.

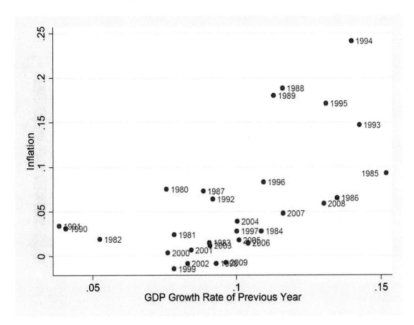

Note: Annual GDP growth and inflation, in decimals.

Source: Ma (2011), National Bureau of Statistics of China (2011).

Figure 3.4 Inflation and economic growth

China has emerged from the global financial crisis with its financial sector virtually unscathed. The Chinese banks had very limited exposure to 'toxic assets'. When Lehman Bothers collapsed, the largest bank in China, the Industrial and Commercial Bank of China (ICBC), had only subprime-related assets of $3.7bn on its book, or about 0.27 per cent of its total assets.

China pulled itself out of the global financial crisis by making massive investment. Although the efficiency of those investments can be dubious, its role in setting China back on the path of growth and keeping unemployment low is undeniable. In 2009, the contribution of net exports to GDP growth was negative (40 per cent). That negative impact had to be made up by the contribution of investment to GDP of close to 100 per cent, while consumption remained stable (Figure 3.5).

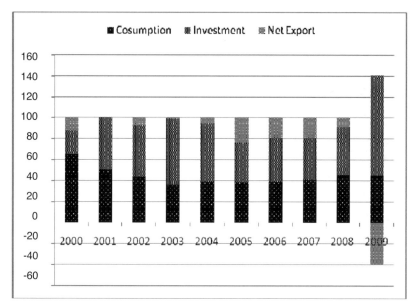

Source: Ma (2011), National Bureau of Statistica of China (2011).

Figure 3.5 Contributions to GDP growth (%)

4. INTERNATIONAL CHALLENGES

Since China joined the World Trade Organization in 2000, its international trade grew more than sixfold, from $474bn in 2000 to $2,973bn in 2010 (Figure 3.6). China is often criticized for being mercantilist, running a large trade surplus, which stood at $183bn in 2010. A less well-known fact is that although China runs a large trade surplus overall, it runs large deficits against mineral-rich countries, such as Russia, Australia and Brazil. China also runs large deficits with Germany, South Korea and Japan, which have set up extensive production facilities in China that require imports of parts and provide equipment for China to expand its production capacity.

Another less well-known but important development in China's international trade is that trade surplus decreases quite dramatically in recent years. After reaching a peak of $298bn in 2008, China's trade surplus dropped to $196bn in 2009 and further to $183bn in 2010. While the 2009 figure was partly a result of the collapse of global trade after the financial crisis, the 2010 figure may signify a more profound change. One may be quick to point to this as being a result of increasing pressure from trading partners. But it is also likely to be caused by changes in China's economic structure. As Bhidé and Phelps (2007) pointed out, China's 'trade surplus in the early years is central for an optimal growth trajectory'. This is because initially China needed to maintain the trade surplus and use accumulated reserves to buy advanced technology from the US and other developed countries. As Chinese economy develops and income rises, Chinese consumers will be buying more from the developed countries and the trade surplus will decline. As China develops, the technological gap between China and the US will narrow and trading opportunities will improve. This should give reason to be optimistic about the 'global imbalance' without any consideration of renminbi exchange rate.

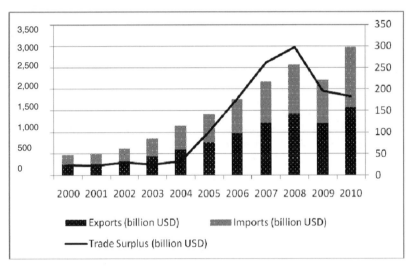

Source: Ma (2011), National Bureau of Statistics of China (2011).

Figure 3.6 International trade since China joined WTO

It should also be pointed out that China has played and will continue to play a very positive role in the global economic recovery by offering the rest of the world, the US and other developed economies in particular, a large and growing market. According to a recent study (Hsieh and Ossa 2011), from 1992 to 2007, China's improvement in productivity was responsible for 2.2 per cent of the wealth gains of the rest of the world. From 2008 to 2010, China imported $3,532bn products. Moving forward, as China further improves its productivity, exporting products such as solar panels and wind turbines at lower costs, the rest of the world will benefit even further.

The global financial crisis also made China rethink that strategy. The crisis made China's export markets, Europe and the US in particular, stagnant, and that made China realize the limits of the export-driven growth strategy. For many years, exports contributed a significant portion to China's GDP growth (Figure 3.5) and export sectors employed large number of workers. In 2005, net exports contributed 24 per cent of China's overall 10.4 per cent GDP growth, and the contribution dropped to 9.2 per cent in 2008. In 2009, with a lower trade surplus than in the previous two years, net exports contributed negatively to China's GDP growth. The negative impact of net exports on GDP growth had to be offset by a dramatic increase in investment growth. With its increasing size of the economy, it had become apparently unrealistic for China to continue to count on exports as a significant engine for growth.

Despite their large volume, exports often have a low value added. Many of China's exports are assembled using imported parts with most of their value created and received by other countries. For example, apparel accounted for 6 per cent of China's total exports in 2009 and phones accounted for another 6 per cent, most of which carry foreign brands. Made-in-China iPhones exported to the US, for example, superficially gave rise to the US $1.9bn trade deficit. But China actually contributed only 3.8 per cent of the total; the rest was simply a transfer from Japan, Korea, and Taipei, China (Xing and Detert 2010).

Realizing the limit of exports on economic growth, the Chinese government has redirected its growth strategy to domestic structural change and consumption. In its 12th Five-Year Plan, China has specifically set up the agenda to start transforming its economic structure from being low-value-added and highly-polluting to higher-value-added and more environmentally friendly.

China maintains a closed capital account and foreign capital cannot freely enter or leave China. Renminbi is not freely convertible in international currency markets. The exchange rate of renminbi is managed against the US dollar by the People's Bank of China. When companies bring foreign capital to invest in China, they must get approval from the government. When companies remit to China the foreign exchange that they receive from exporting, they can convert the foreign exchange at banks in China with proper documents showing the source of the funds. The commercial banks can then choose to keep the foreign exchange or send it to the central bank in exchange for renminbi. The central bank of China, PBOC, becomes the last holder of the foreign exchange that flows into China because of trade or investment. This is the foreign exchange reserve. Over the years, China has accumulated large amounts of foreign exchange reserve, which stood at $2,847bn in December 2010 (Figure 3.7).

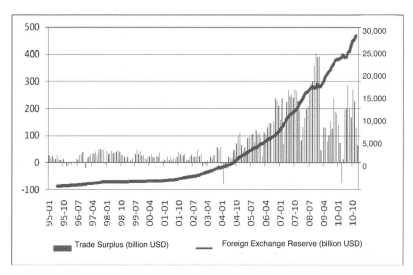

Trade Surplus (billion USD)   Foreign Exchange Reserve (billion USD)

Note: By December 2010, China's foreign exchange reserve reached $2,847bn.

Source: State Administration of Foreign Exchange of China (2009).

*Figure 3.7 China's monthly trade surplus and foreign exchange reserve, 1995–
    2010 ($ billion)*

Foreign exchange reserve has important implications for money supply in
China. Since PBOC must issue renminbi to buy foreign exchange, foreign
exchange reserve increases the money supply. To sterilize the extra amount of
money supply, PBOC has to issue central bank bills to commercial banks. The
system requires it stands ready for any approved inflow of foreign exchange, so
PBOC loses autonomy over monetary policy. As China accumulates more and
more foreign exchange reserve, PBOC's operation of central bank bills
becomes more cumbersome and costly. More importantly, foreign exchange
reserve builds up inflation pressure.

So when Chinese Premier Wen Jiabao told his European audience
during his 2010 trip to Europe that China is not pursuing trade surplus he
most likely meant it. For much of the time since 1978, it was China's
official policy to increase exports and foreign exchange reserve. But too
much of a good thing has become increasingly a domestic pain.

China is already on its way to alleviate the pain by adopting a more
flexible and market-oriented foreign exchange system. The 12th Five-Year
Plan has set the goal of 'eventual convertibility of renminbi'. In the past
few years, PBOC has made a number of small-scale and localized
experiments in China's foreign exchange system, and they may have
significant implications for the global financial system.

One such development is that China, through both the government-controlled companies and private enterprises, has dramatically increased its investment overseas (Figure 3.8). In 2009, China made outbound direct investment (over $55bn), with Asia being the number one destination by far, followed by Latin America and Europe. One recent high-profile case is Geely (a privately-owned Chinese car maker), that bought Volvo in 2010. This should be a welcoming development not just for companies that are cash-strapped in Europe and the US. Those companies in Europe and the US which join a partnership with Chinese investors enjoy Chinese production capacity and markets; in return, they provide technological know-how, distribution channel and branding. It should be a win–win situation for many companies around the world. But some foreign countries remain suspicious of Chinese companies' intention and make Chinese investment rather difficult.

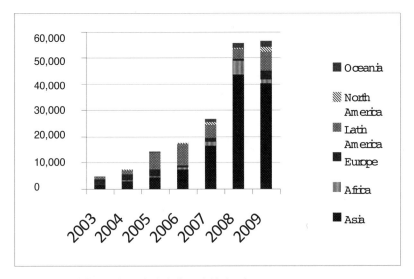

Note: 2003–2006 figures do not include financial industries.
Source: Ministry of Commerce of China (2010).

Figure 3.8 China's outbound FDI ($ million)

In 2005, China started allowing renminbi to appreciate against the US dollar and, after a two-year pause from mid 2007 on, the process has accelerated since mid 2010. The accumulated appreciation since 2005 is more than 20 per cent (Figure 3.9). It is worth noting that China's trade surplus increased quite significantly since 2005, not decreased. With the

US running the largest trade deficits against China, it suggests the renminbi exchange rate may not be the main cause of the US trade deficit. The higher productivity of China's export sector may be.

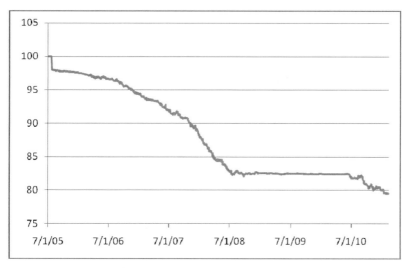

Source: China State Administration of Foreign Exchange of China (2009).

Figure 3.9 The renmimbi exchange rate with the US dollar (indexed at 100 on July 1, 2005)

More recently, China has allowed more off-shore renminbi products in Hong Kong. Caterpillar and McDonald offered renminbi bonds in Hong Kong to fund their businesses in China. Hong Kong Stock Exchange will also allow renminbi products. China is making more renminbi available offshore by allowing Chinese banks to accept renminbi deposits. PBOC signed currency swaps with a number of central banks around the world to facilitate renminbi trade payments.

When these small steps are examined through China's gradualism prism, they point to the eventual convertibility of renminbi and inevitable arrival of renminbi as one of the world currencies. Although we cannot be certain how fast it is going to happen, the direction should not be mistaken.

5. CONCLUSION

China will continue to enjoy high economic growth despite global uncertainties. To improve the living standard of its people and maintain social stability by providing more and better jobs, the Chinese government will try to maintain high GDP growth. But China will focus more on quality than quantity. The government will continue to implement its economic growth strategy that emphasizes domestic demand over exports and consumption over investment, and to upgrade its technological infrastructure to be more energy-efficient and environmentally friendly.

Along the way, China will contribute to the world's economic growth and become one stabilizing force. China will become an even more important power for the world to both reckon with and benefit from. China will be more integrated with the global economy. For its self-interests, China will be more sensitive to the interests and demands of other countries and make adjustments accordingly. But the pace of China's adjustment will be gradual and ultimately be determined by its domestic agenda, both economic and political, and not by outside pressure or coercion.

BIBLIOGRAPHY

Bhidé, Amar V. and Edmund S. Phelps (2007), 'A Dynamic Theory of China–U.S. Trade: Making Sense of the Imbalances', *World Economics*, **8** (3), July–September.

Deng, Xiaoping (1978), 'Open Up and Learn from the Advanced Science and Technology Around the World', in *Collected Works of Deng Xiaoping*, People's Press, 1989, 132–33.

Hsieh, Chang-Tai and Ralph Ossa (2011), *A Global View of Productivity Growth in China*, NBER Working Paper Series, w16778, available at SSRN: http://ssrn.com/abstract=1759850.

Lin, Justin Yifu (2009), *Economic Development and Transition: Thought, Strategy, and Viability*, Cambridge: Cambridge University Press.

Ma, Jiantang (2011), *National Economy Showed Good Momentum of Development in 2010*, National Bureau of Statistics of China Commissioner's Report, available at http://www.stats.gov.cn/english/newsandcomingevents/t20110120_402699463.htm.

Ministry of Commerce of China (2010), *2009 Statistical Bulletin of China's Outbound Foreign Direct Investment* (in Chinese).

Ministry of Foreign Affairs of the People's Republic of China, and United Nations System in China (2010), *China's Progress Towards the Millennium Development Goals 2010*, Report.

National Bureau of Statistics of China (2011), *China Statistical Yearbook 2010*, China Statistics Press, Beijing (in Chinese).

People's Bank of China (2010), *China Financial Stability Report 2010*, http://www.pbc.gov.cn/publish/english/959/2010/20100917102952632398099/20100917102952632398099_.html.

People's Bank of China (2010), *China Monetary Policy Executive*, Report 2010, 3rd Quarter.

Qian, Yingyi (2002), *How Reform Worked in China*, William Davidson Institute Working Paper no. 473, available at SSRN: http://ssrn.com/abstract= 317460.

State Administration of Foreign Exchange of China (2009), *China Foreign Exchange Management Yearbook*.

Wang, Xiaozu, Lixin Colin Xu and Tian Zhu (2009), *Foreign Direct Investment Without the Rule of Law: Explaining Cross-Regional Variations in FDI in China*, Working Paper, The World Bank.

Xing, Yuqing and Neal Detert (2010), *How the iPhone Widens the United States Trade Deficit with the People's Republic of China*, Asian Development Bank Institute, Working Paper no. 257.

Xinhua News Agency (2003), *The People's Republic of China Law of People's Bank of China*, 26 May.

Xinhua News Agency (2010), *The Chinese Communist Party's Advice for Devising the 12th Five-Year Plan for National Economy and Social Development*.

Yang, Dennis Tao, Zhang Junsen and Zhou Shaojie (2011), *Why are Saving Rates so High in China?*, NBER Working Paper Series, w16771, available at SSRN: http://ssrn.com/abstra.

PART II

Carving out a Place for the EU

4. The EU Economy to 2020: Coping with Divergence and Debt

Vanessa Rossi

1. THE SHORT-TERM CHALLENGE: A CRITICAL PERIOD AHEAD

The parameters that will determine the shape of the EU economy over the next decade critically depend on what happens over the next couple of years – this looks set to be a watershed period for the Western economies in general and for the EU and the euro in particular. Even if talk of the possible disintegration of the European Union can be dismissed as alarmist,[1] the events of 2010 have provided real grounds for concern about potential debt defaults and stability within the monetary union. Prospects for the EU economy are clearly clouded by the continuing crisis of confidence in debt management, uncertainty over euro membership and even an unusual divergence in economic growth across member states.

Such uncertainty is in itself bad for investment, growth and financial stability but sentiment will not fully recover until the debt crisis – the question mark hanging over not just the periphery of the euro area but also the major European countries and the banking sector – has a clear and credible solution. To be fully convincing, all EU states – not just a few such as Sweden, Germany and the UK – must demonstrate their capability for both controlling debt (including liabilities for national banking systems) and sustaining adequate economic growth and employment. Yet this requirement may take several years to address, especially in view of the forthcoming electoral cycle in the major economies with elections in key regions of Germany through 2011, the race for the 2012 Presidential election in France just starting and the possibility of a change in leadership in Italy and Spain as well.

The creation of the European Stability Mechanism (ESM) in mid-2010 was intended as a short-term expedient to reassure markets about the scope of assistance for Greece and any other small countries facing debt crises, indeed

Ireland was to become the second recipient of aid in November 2010. However, even the IMF's own analysis for Greece, pointing to further increases in its debt burden to around 150 per cent of GDP over the next three years (IMF 2010b), illustrates that the 2010 bail-out can only have postponed the question of some form of debt restructuring. In addition, it would be impossible to prevent the failure of a large economy, such as Spain or Italy, as bail-outs are ultimately limited by the ability of the major economies to provide assistance without endangering their own stability. These are questions not just of liquidity but also solvency – they have not gone away and will become more pressing as most countries' sovereign debt continues to rise over the next few years to levels generally considered risky for both stability and growth.[2]

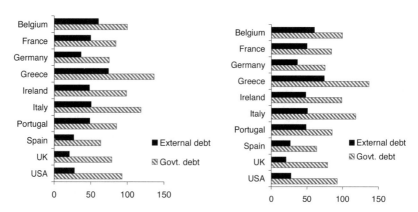

Source: EC (2010b), IMF (2010c, 2010d).

Figure 4.1 Comparison of budget deficits, external balances and debt show the widespread vulnerability of the advanced economies (2010 estimates, % of GDP)

However, although overshadowed by concern over debt and the euro's future, some more optimistic trends have also emerged in 2010, most obviously the export stimulus provided by booming China and other emerging markets. Some large economies countries have benefited significantly and may be able to sustain robust rates of growth, helping the EU to perform well and to more quickly exit its debt crisis.

In this chapter, we examine the EU's economic outlook to 2020 as it works to overcome its internal tensions:

• The impacts of the 2008–2009 recession, followed by the 2010 debt crisis and now fiscal austerity point to a difficult period of policy clashes and sluggish domestic demand growth across many European countries but especially in the most indebted economies.

• Further divergence in economic performance across member states is likely: the most indebted, cash constrained economies are continuing to suffer from prolonged recession while the richest focus on restoring public finances and improving their own growth prospects. For example, thanks to a new surge in exports to China and other emerging markets, Germany has seen a far stronger than expected recovery in 2010, even creating new jobs, while Greece has collapsed into deeper recession.

• 2011 will see the income inequality gap widen in the EU. While all growth should be welcomed, the implications of divergence are challenging for the EU given the political capital expended on the concept of economic and social convergence.

• However, European solidarity and mutual interest in maintaining the stability of the euro area have provided financial aid for Greece and Ireland in 2010, even if the guarantees given and the scope for extending aid remain uncertain.

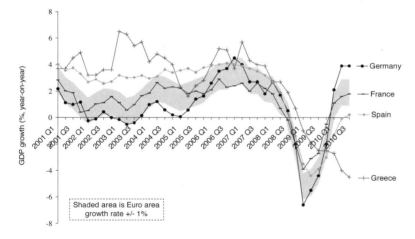

Source: Eurostat (2010a).

Figure 4.2 GDP growth across the EU shows unusual divergence in 2010 with Germany doing well and Greece now the worst performer (%, year-on-year)

How will these tensions be resolved? Can the EU leverage external growth opportunities and accept a multi-speed Europe? We examine the implications of alternative assumptions regarding risks and policy choices for the economic outlook to 2020, focusing on the following key scenarios:

- 'Solidarity and Discipline'. To uphold a cooperative approach, keep the euro area intact and avoid a dangerous spiral in debt for all member states, the focus must be on tough policing of the Maastricht rules for public sector finances and improving macro prudential oversight. The previous regime – a cosy club based on congenial neglect of the limited set of Maastricht rules – has been exposed as not so benign after all. Monetary union cannot be built on ignoring poor economic fundamentals and the build up of unsustainable debt. There must be a new reality injected not just into government budgets but also into expectations for growth and convergence.
- 'Disorderly Restructuring'. If the cooperative approach fails – perhaps provoked by a bank crash leading to a sovereign debt default or by a large euro economy failing to control its public finances – a disorderly scramble for alternative solutions will ensue. Persistently weak European growth and austerity fatigue may also lead to voter rebellions and an outbreak of 'can't pay, wont pay' debt restructuring. Whether or not it is rational, such a scenario cannot be ruled out, with unpleasant consequences for economic and financial stability in the EU. This could even open up the question of euro membership although we would expect the euro itself to survive.
- 'New Opportunity'. A stronger EU growth scenario could emerge if the impacts of global trends and trickle-down throughout the EU economy provide more favourable, more powerful stimulants, than presently expected. Arguably, the squeezed periphery may also start to look towards new alliances and growth opportunities. The developing world is capable of sustaining high growth rates in the 6–7 per cent range yet the outlook for emerging Europe seems far less bright unless it can tap into this alternative dynamic. If emerging Europe succeeds in finding a new growth model, this will alleviate concerns about debt repayment and long-term prospects – nevertheless, attention must be paid to maintaining sound public finances to avoid incurring new debt problems in the future.

The international background and general economic outlook are discussed in the next section, followed by further analysis of the alternative scenarios presented above.

2. GLOBAL CONDITIONS. RELYING ON EMERGING MARKETS AS THE KEY DRIVERS OF GROWTH

The financial crisis of September 2008 brought to an end the developed world's 'great moderation' and the convenient assumptions that were broadly encompassed in that comfortable concept, especially regarding the stability of economic growth, the benefits of free flowing capital and the virtue of easy access to cheap credit. Although the epicentre of the financial crash was the US, the recession was particularly harsh in Europe, making it the worst performing region in the world during 2009. Nevertheless, the so-called 'North Atlantic' crisis only brought world growth to a temporary halt thanks to the resilience of the emerging market economies in general and the vigorous response of China in particular.

Fortunately for the world economy – and the recovery in the developed countries – the performance of the developing world has become stronger and steadier, increasing both its weight in world GDP and its internal trade. The major emerging market economies have become the main determinants of global growth over the last decade and they are also becoming less dependent on exports to the advanced countries. By about 2015, half their trade will be with each other compared with around 40 per cent today and only 25 per cent a decade ago (as illustrated for China in Figure 4.3).

The factors supporting strong growth in the developing world are well rehearsed: a relatively robust financial background and stable governance in the major emerging markets, buoyant trade, rising cross-country investments and rapidly growing domestic demand as more households reach the level of income at which consumption starts to take off on the so-called 'S curve'. Asia, the leading growth region, provides a large, cost-effective global manufacturing base, while commodity producers are benefiting from expanding demand, higher world prices and new investment into their key sectors.

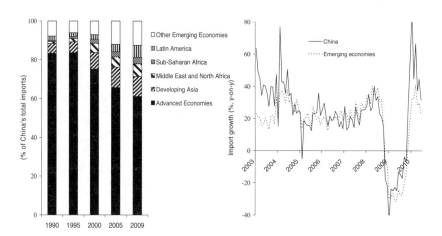

Source: IMF (2010a).

Figure 4.3 China's imports by origin (lhs, %, share of total) and growth rates (rhs) – developing economies' share is growing rapidly

Concerns tend to focus on the impact of rising food and energy prices, symptomatic of pressure on the resources sector. Such inflation has been seen as a factor behind political turbulence in north Africa in early 2011. However, although these events have raised investor awareness of risk, confidence generally remains high. This is illustrated by buoyant consumer and business sentiment and the steady, low-risk premia for most developing countries in global capital markets, in spite of the increases seen in emerging Europe and north Africa.

Excluding 2009, the year of the global recession (when emerging markets, chiefly China and India, accounted for 100 per cent of global growth), the share of emerging markets in global GDP growth has steadily risen from around 50 per cent twenty years ago to 65–70 per cent over the past decade, and this is seen edging up to about 75 per cent over the next five years (Figure 4.4).

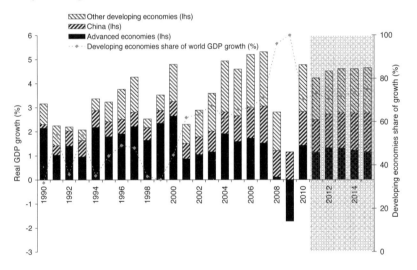

Source: IMF (2010d).

Figure 4.4 Developing countries contribute most to global growth (%, measured in PPP terms)

Effectively, the world economy is now being driven by two-and-a-half engines – China and the rest of the developing world are the two strong performers pulling each other along while, lagging some way behind, the advanced economies are only firing at half strength. Consensus forecasts point to growth in the developed world averaging 2–2.5 per cent over the decade to 2020, similar to the average over the last decade. However, to illustrate how robust world economic prospects are, even if the advanced countries average only 1 per cent growth (in line with Japan during its 'lost decade' after the collapse of the bubble economy in the early 1990s), global growth will probably remain in the 3.5–4 per cent range thanks to the developing half of the world economy continuing to expand at a rapid rate of 6–7 per cent (Figure 4.5).

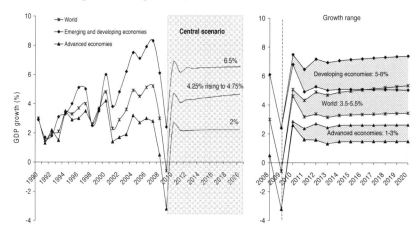

Source: IMF (2010d) and own estimates. The central scenario and growth ranges are own estimates based broadly on consensus forecasts. The reason for world growth trending upwards in the long run is due to the rising weight of the emerging markets

Figure 4.5 Long-run projections based on a return to trend growth (GDP growth, %)

In fact, in the absence of a massive shock generating dislocation effects similar to the late 2008 financial crisis – or a serious and prolonged setback in the Chinese economy – world growth should remain steady in the 4–5 per cent range.

The varying pattern of forecasts for emerging markets, the US and the EU are similar to the stylised scenarios A, B and C depicted in (Figure 4.6). From mid-2009, the emerging market economies have forged ahead and pulled the world economy along: they have already recouped the short-lived losses caused by the global crash in late 2008 and early 2009 and are now set to return to trend growth. Effectively, they have succeeded in achieving a strong V-shaped recovery that looks like scenario A, just as Asia did following the 1997–1998 crisis (IMF 2010e).

However, for the EU economies, estimates for long-run trend growth have been scaled back for some countries due to predicted long-tailed impacts of the global recession and debt crisis on investment and productive potential – this is particularly the case for the troubled periphery of the euro area.[3] Consensus forecasts suggest average growth rates close to 2 per cent for the EU, slightly weaker than the historic trend, and a lower rate for the euro area. This is commensurate with a scenario between B and C. While US growth could remain weaker for longer, for the same reasons as the EU, US analysts tend to be optimistic about the economy recovering to growth rates commensurate with its pre-crisis performance, that is, around 2.5 per cent per annum, as illustrated by scenario B.

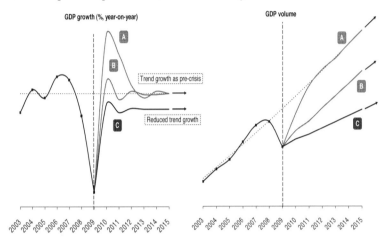

Note: IMF (2010d) historic data to 2008 based on estimates for the Eurozone.

Figure 4.6 The ABC of recovery scenarios – A (just a cyclical blip), B (one-off loss in output, growth recovers) and C (permanent loss in output and growth)

Might this pessimistic prognosis for Europe be wrong? In spite of the debt crisis and continued recession in some countries, results for the EU economy in 2010 have actually been better than expected, thanks to the rebound in world trade (Figure 4.7) driven by the massive rise in demand in emerging markets. Could the EU recover to scenario B or better, boosted by its strongest performers such as heavyweight Germany?

Most of the EU gains are due to Germany enjoying a better-than-forecast recovery while, amongst the mid-sized economies, Sweden has performed particularly well (Figure 4.8). Germany's GDP rose by about 3.5 per cent in 2010 but the rest of the euro area's recovery has been quite feeble, with growth just over 1 per cent compared to the euro area average of about 2 per cent including Germany. Moreover, many interpret Germany's 2010 surge as simply a one-off rebound in exports after the global recession in 2009 (similar to the temporary bump shown in scenarios A and B in).

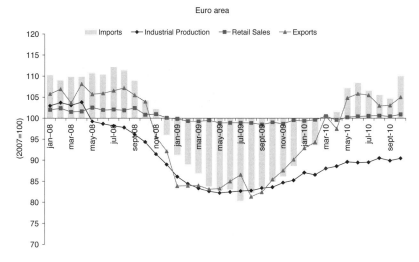

Source: ECB (2010b).

Figure 4.7 Euro area indicators illustrate the strong rebound in exports in 2010 but weaker recovery in industrial production and retail sales

If Germany's (and Sweden's) export-led growth does drop back sharply in 2011, then this would be a blow to hopes of sustaining the EU's performance. But perhaps the most cogent reason for concern about a drop in EU growth over the coming 6–12 months is the risk of a renewed slowdown in still fragile European demand (Figure 4.7), driven chiefly by the negative impacts of fiscal austerity and the on-going threat of instability in financial markets and the banking sector.

Most of the developed world will be embarking on so-called 'exit strategies' to reverse fiscal policy and halt the deterioration in public sector finances before this becomes unmanageable. For example, Germany, Spain and the UK have already agreed tough budgets to bring down deficits and curb the rise in debt by 2014–2015, while France and Italy are also proposing tighter policies. In addition, tougher regulations are being imposed on the banks, leading to capital raising to meet higher prudential requirements – this may crimp economic growth as credit expansion is likely to stay subdued, especially if confidence in the sector remains weak.

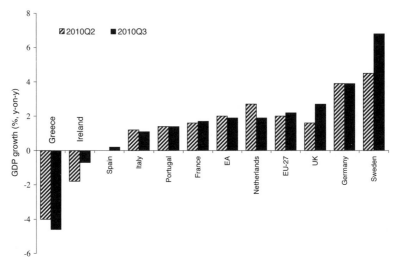

Source: Eurostat (2010a).

Figure 4.8 GDP growth in selected European economies in mid-2010 (%, year-on-year) – unexpectedly strong growth in some countries but also wide divergence

The impact of policy tightening will be particularly negative if this process is badly managed. While the need for policy reversal is widely understood and policymakers have prepared the way for fiscal austerity, if economic growth and jobs are to be maintained then private sector confidence is essential. If the private sector does not take up the running as the government cuts back, there will be a relapse into a situation of little or no economic growth and a deteriorating jobs market. And governments would have few resources available to do anything to counter this – indeed fiscal deficits could even deteriorate due to falling tax revenues and higher social expenditure, a risk which is already worrying Greece and Ireland. Maintaining positive consumer and investor sentiment is therefore a crucial part of sustaining the recovery at the same time as improving public finances.

Effectively, policy is balanced on a knife edge at this moment – there must be sufficient adjustment in fiscal balances to eliminate suspicions of a looming sovereign debt crisis but not so much that it kills the economic recovery. The greatest threat is probably over the coming 6–12 months: judging the initial timing and scale of policy adjustment is critical. Once the process of adjustment is smoothly underway in the major economies, risks should ease. But if the process of fiscal consolidation is destabilizing to the EU economy, then further market turbulence will ensue, and with less ability to reassure investors than in 2010.

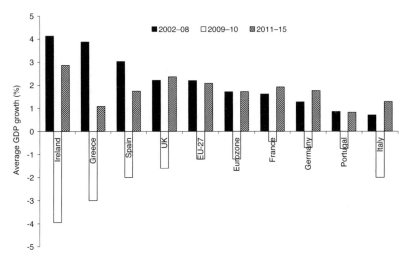

Average GDP growth (%)

■2002–08 □2009–10 ▨2011–15

Ireland Greece Spain UK EU-27 Eurozone France Germany Portugal Italy

Source: IMF (2010d).

Figure 4.9 Average GDP growth pre-crisis and during the crisis versus IMF forecasts for 2011–2015 (ranked according to pre-crisis growth)

Forecasts for 2011 therefore remain cautious. However, estimates for trend growth over 2011–2015 (Figure 4.9, based on IMF forecasts) are very familiar as they are close to historic averages, with only a small drop in the EU average growth rate and a slightly lower euro area figure. Given the scale of debt burdens and concerns over how to regenerate growth in a number of countries, consensus forecasts look remarkably bland or even overly optimistic (for example, Italy in Figure 4.9). However, the pattern of growth has shifted plausibly: Greece and Spain are now seen as lower growth economies (Ireland will probably be revised down) while Germany is expected to improve its performance, reversing the rankings seen pre-crisis. Poland and Sweden are also expected to perform well. Arguably, forecasts should be bolder in showing greater divergence but there has been clear reluctance to adopt such projections.

3. 'SOLIDARITY AND DISCIPLINE': AN ORDERLY EXIT FROM THE DEBT CRISIS

Although a sovereign default or break up of the euro area is no longer considered unthinkable as a risk scenario, consensus forecasts such as those presented above continue to assume that there will be no defaults and that the euro area's structure will essentially remain stable. In effect, the debt crisis will be orderly and manageable thanks to discipline being maintained under current funding arrangements.

While consensus forecasts essentially reflect the 'Solidarity' scenario, if this tough but cooperative solution is to prevail, what more does it require? What are the basic assumptions regarding the scale of any debt crises and the policies available to address these?

Firstly, it means that there can be no failures too large for a country to plausibly tackle either itself or in conjunction with the aid offered by the Stabilisation Fund. For example, any threat that might emerge from the banking sector must be small enough for the home country to absorb – or there would have to be some form of collective bank bail-out solution, a de facto acceptance of a European rather than national banking system.[4] Indeed, the financial aid offered to Ireland in late 2010 came close to such a position although this was accounted for as an EU bail-out not of the banks but the government, which then bailed-out the banks: the test would come if the Irish banks were to require a further bail-out, which could not plausibly be incorporated into government debt.

Table 4.1 The countries most at risk from excessive debt (all figures as % GDP, 2010 estimates)

	Government deficit	Government debt	External debt	Short-term external debt	Current account balance
Belgium	-4.8	99.6	60.3	11.8	0.5
France	-8.0	84.2	49.8	9.9	-1.8
Germany	-4.5	75.2	36.3	2.9	6.1
Greece	-7.9	136.6	74.0	0.9	-10.8
Ireland	-32.0	98.7	48.1	4.2	-2.7
Italy	-5.1	118.6	50.5	4.4	-2.9
Portugal	-7.3	85.1	48.4	7.7	-10.0
Spain	-9.3	63.6	26.4	3.7	-5.2
UK	-10.1	78.8	20.5	2.1	-2.2
USA	-11.1	92.7	27.5	5.0	-3.2

Source: EC (2010b), IMF (2010c; 2010d).

While Europe has been quick to criticise credit rating agencies,[5] risk analysts do take into account a wide range of indicators in assessing the health of economies and debt – unlike the Maastricht rules, which focus on an extremely limited range of variables, essentially inflation (the ECB target), budget deficits and public sector debt. Although it is well known that financial and economic crises can rapidly explode government debt, this risk seems to have been ignored until 2009. The connections between the scale of banking sectors, external debt and national debt were not examined until it was too late, even though there was ample evidence of such risks, for example from the Asian crisis of 1997–1998.

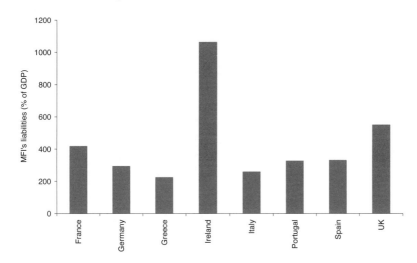

Source: ECB (2010a), IMF (2010d).

Figure 4.10 Monetary and financial institutions' liabilities (excluding Eurosystem and National Central Banks, % of GDP)

Secondly, the total amount of money committed to bail-outs, as indicated in mid-2010 when the ESM was first announced, may be insufficient. The proposed figure (including IMF funds) was around € 700bn: this can assist Greece and Ireland, probably Portugal and possibly Belgium if needed, but it would be inadequate to aid a large country such as Spain or Italy. The fund could be extended but ultimately the limit would be dictated by the burden imposed on the remaining countries, primarily Germany and France (which must remain solvent themselves), and the risk of contagion in the senior European bond markets. Breaching such thresholds would lead to a disastrous outcome. Therefore, the 'Solidarity' scenario has to assume that none of the major economies fail – they must survive and recover by controlling their own debt.

In addition, the EU's flawed economic model and macroprudential supervision must be addressed. For example, the reasons for the crises in Ireland and Spain being so important are not just their scale but their origin: unlike Greece, and a number of other Eurozone members, Ireland

and Spain were not Maastricht offenders but exemplary member states with solid public sector finances – until their overblown property sectors collapsed and dragged down employment and the banks as well. The EU actually fell into recession in early 2008, with Spain already showing worrying signs of a collapse in its property sector before 2008. And Europe was the worst performing region in the world during the global crisis of 2009 – this poor performance was not simply caused by the faults of the US property market and Wall Street but by fundamental flaws within Europe itself.

While these faults have now been recognised, there has to be further progress on addressing weaknesses:

- Tougher debt management is essential. Most EU states will have to impose a prolonged programme of fiscal austerity in order to curb the crisis-driven increase in public sector debt: the average level of debt for euro member states will soon reach almost 90 per cent of GDP[6] compared with a pre-crisis level close to the Maastricht limit of 60 per cent. For the euro area to survive, policing of rules and bail-outs must get tougher in spite of voters' reluctant appetite for fiscal austerity.

- Export success must be encouraged, not held back. Sales outside of the region, especially to fast moving emerging markets that are now the drivers of global demand, will be a key determinant of the EU's economic prospects. Most of the export gains seen so far have accrued to just a few countries, notably to Germany. Indeed, in the first three quarters of 2010, BMW's profits alone reached almost 70 per cent of the value of Greece's total exports over the same period,[7] highlighting the gulf in the scale of exports across Europe. Looking ahead, China is likely to become Germany's major trade partner within the next couple of years, displacing France. But such success has to be encouraged if the EU is to retain its presence in the world economy and if the major economies are to continue growing robustly, providing a locomotive for the weaker EU states.

- Greater divergence may have to be accepted as a feature of the EU economies. Divergence in economic growth across EU member states and the lack of trickle-down effects to the less successful countries are a source of friction. Some countries find it difficult to compete in international markets – and would do so even if they left the euro. Currency rates and cost competitiveness are not the only determinants of export growth and differences in external performance will have to be accepted, although more efforts could be made at a micro level to boost feasible areas of trade for poorer performers.

- 'Trickle down' must be improved. A key target for policymakers should be improving trickle down within the EU, as it would reduce resentment about differential success in external markets. However, this may require large regional variations in wages and local service prices to be sustained in order to attract business, boost economic growth and maintain sound public finances.

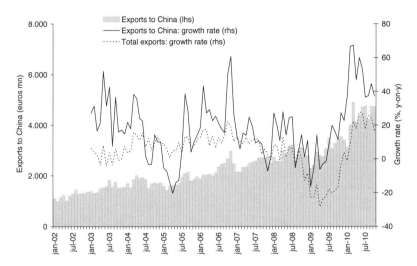

Source: Germany Federal Statistical Office (2010).

Figure 4.11 Germany's exports boosted by Chinese demand growth (exports to China, euros bn on lhs, export growth, % y-on-y on rhs)

Germany is the most obvious beneficiary of the boom in Chinese imports and inward investment into the EU but it is not the only country to gain from increased economic ties with China – significant deals have been signed with the UK and France, for example, and more is being promised in Spain. Given rapidly growing import demand in China and few signs that Chinese growth will taper off quickly, such trade can provide a significant stimulus to European economies with large, advanced manufacturing bases. Whether this translates into gains for the precarious peripheral European economies – that tend to be less competitive in advanced manufacturing – is doubtful. Arguably, products could be more carefully tailored to match demand in growth markets, including sectors such as food products as well as luxury goods that rely more on small-scale output and highly skilled labour. However, the smaller countries also stand to gain from capital provided for key infrastructure projects and for financial investments in their debt markets, where China may play an important stabilising role. This suggests that the channels as well as the rates of economic growth will be different across the regions of Europe.

The policy implications of economic divergence are challenging for a continent that has expended so much political and economic capital on the concept of economic and social convergence, including monetary union. But if the euro area is to hold together, the focus will have to be on tougher policing of Maastricht rules and bail-out conditions, on policies to curb fiscal excesses, not on increased social transfers. For most EU member states, it will be a struggle to cut budget deficits and halt rising debt by the target date of 2014–2015,[8] however, many more years of balanced budgets will have to follow to reduce debt to the Maastricht limit of 60 per cent (Figure 4.12). Only a handful of countries are likely to manage this by 2020.

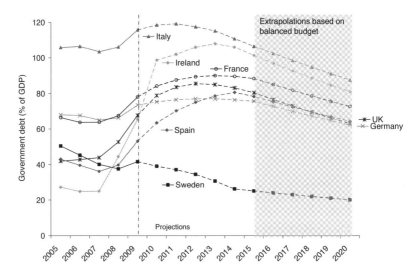

Source: Germany Federal Ministry of Finance (2010), Government Offices of Sweden (2010), HM Treasury (2010) Budget 2010, Ireland Department of Finance (2010), Italy Department of Treasury (2010), Spain Ministry of Economy and Finance (2010), and own extrapolations.

Figure 4.12 Public sector debt projections to 2020 have been badly damaged by the impacts of the recession and bank bail-outs (debt as % of GDP)

Tougher policing may also extend to other spheres, such as the scale of external debt, of the banking sector and even of property markets as these were all critical factors in bringing down the Irish and Spanish economies in spite of their governments running prudent policies in the pre-crisis boom years. Surveillance and supervision of member states' economies could become far more intrusive in order to prevent bailout risks recurring (see Chapter 1). Are member states and voters prepared for this?

While mainstream economic forecasts appear to be in line with the 'Solidarity' scenario, assuming the euro area stays together and debts can be worked off, all the conditions required for this scenario to be plausible are not necessarily made clear. Certainly there is heavy reliance on a benign policy stance with no further nasty surprises regarding the growth outlook and the Euro debt crisis.

4. 'DISORDERLY RESTRUCTURING' AND THE RISK OF INSTABILITY

Unlike the relatively friendly, consensual muddle that has pervaded the arrangements for the euro area over the last decade, the coming decade will see the infant moving on from the play-as-you-please kindergarten to disciplined schooling. But, if it does not make the grade, parts of Europe could be relegated to the debtors club alongside countries such as Argentina.

Against a weak European background, some of the most vulnerable economies such as Greece, Ireland, Portugal and Spain could remain in recessionary conditions, making it even harder to reduce budget deficits, cope with excessive debt burdens and, in the case of Ireland and Spain, recover from the collapse in the property sector and local banks. In late 2010, Greece already announced an upwardly revised figure for its total debt for 2009, bringing this to 130 per cent of GDP. Tax revenues have also proved weaker than expected.

Table 4.2 Government debt figures highlight extent of revisions over 2010 (% of GDP)

	2008[a]	2009		2010	
		Spring 2010 estimate[b]	Autumn 2010 estimate[a]	Spring 2010 projection[c]	Autumn 2010 projection[d]
Portugal	65.3	76.8	76.1	85.8	85.1
Ireland	44.3	64.0	65.5	77.3	98.7
Greece	110.3	115.1	126.8	124.9	136.6

Notes: (a) Eurostat November 2010 estimate, (b) EC spring estimate, (c) EC spring 2010 projection, (d) EC spring 2010 projection with Eurostat November 2010 estimates for 2009 debt and cost of Irish bank bailout included.

Source: EC (2010a), Eurostat (2010b).

Threatening further bouts of turbulence, financial markets remain uncertain about which way to turn. Although support for the dollar as the world's leading reserve currency has been called into question over the last couple of years, there is still little enthusiasm for what is presently the only significant alternative, the euro. Indeed, the euro area continues to be under the spotlight as analysts are not convinced about either the health of the European banking system or the ability of some of the most indebted countries to repay their heavy debts and bailouts. In 2011, there is even a risk of reduced liquidity as Basel III is leading some major European banks to make an early start on plans for capital raising, making it even harder for troubled banks – and countries – to attract funds in the market. Ireland's government is struggling to cope with an already high bail-out cost and cannot afford to offer further support to its banks if market funding fails to revive. Further restructuring may be necessary.

Although there appears to be progress in terms of backing for the EFSF and its success in raising funds, a full and convincing solution is still not in place for the euro area's solvency and liquidity problems. Until it is, financial markets and many global investors will be reluctant to strongly back the weaker euro area markets and will remain sceptical about the euro itself.

If there is a fully credible proposal to solve the EU debt crisis through feasible collective bail-out guarantees, then, to avoid market jitters, this will have to be backed up by the promise of greater discipline for the future. There has to be a strong and enforceable agreement over what parameters are acceptable for a club of countries that effectively agrees to bail each other out – such a guarantee cannot remain ill defined or poorly monitored.

On the other hand, if bailout attempts fail or simply become practically impossible to extend, then we cannot be sure what happens next apart from some form of immediate debt restructuring. Short-term concerns would focus on containing the damage and providing liquidity – as many fear, this could be similar to the disorderly Lehman disaster if there is no plan ready to ensure a speedy handling of any bank failures or country defaults. And what would follow on from this? It seems inconceivable as well as impracticable that the euro area could break up – this would risk adding monetary chaos to debt meltdown – yet one or two small countries might position themselves for exit over the next couple of years in order to open up the choice of breaking away. Spain is not going to do this, but it may not be impossible for Greece or Ireland if austerity drags on.

It is important to reflect on the scale of the debt problems that must be resolved and the potential for uncongenial outcomes. Although the attempt to forge a cooperative solution through a mix of ECB support and IMF tutelage continues, most observers believe that ultimately there will have to be some form of debt and bank restructuring within the next few years, the precise nature of which is yet to emerge. For example, as much as €150bn of debt may need to be cancelled, most probably gradually amortised (as Brady bonds were in the Latin American crisis), in order to bring Greek debt back to a level that might feasibly be repaid – that is, to make Greece solvent. A similar figure may be required for Ireland (possibly considerably more if banking problems persist in 2011).

These sums may seem a modest price to pay for preserving the reputation of the euro area, however, if restructuring were to prove disorderly, then more countries would require bail-outs and debt restructuring. Small countries' debts alone could double the estimated losses while Spain and Italy might add as much as €2–3tn to the cost. In total, the 'hair cut' could reach as much as €3–4tn to bring EU debt down to a more supportable 70–80 per cent of GDP.

In this case, contagion would be rife (also affecting the US) and there would almost certainly be a sharp drop back into recession for the EU economy in the midst of a sovereign debt crisis. Like Japan in the post-bubble era, the EU could suffer a 'lost decade', with growth averaging as little as 1 per cent or worse.

5. 'NEW OPPORTUNITIES': MAKING THE MOST OF GLOBAL GROWTH

While the risks ahead are uppermost in most analysis of the global outlook – and especially so for the euro area – there is also the chance of improved opportunities for growth. What might this mean for the EU? Which factors could offer a more optimistic outlook?

Firstly, the EU must recognise that the divergences in member states' economic performance that appear so worrying are small in comparison with the major global trends that will overtake the global economy over the next decade – for example the rise of China and India followed by other leading emerging market economies. Internal divergence in economic growth may also be necessary to maintain the competitive position of the EU in external markets.

Secondly, key exporters must be encouraged through maintaining openness to trade and reducing barriers – for both the exchange of goods and, more controversially, for cross-border investments. Europe cannot be hostile to such trends either internally or abroad. Germany and other countries such as Sweden are world leaders in manufactures exports, in fact Italy also performs quite well, And the UK excels in services. They must be encouraged to pursue and grow these business interests along with other exporters. Even for weaker economies unable to achieve such gains in trade, some trickle down is better than none.

Thirdly, the position of some of the smaller economies in terms of their cross-country business and scale of domestic demand means that they find it hard to compete in large-scale manufacturing industries – their economic futures cannot be based on idealistic hopes for industry relocation and growth. To help exporters target new growth markets and boost related labour market skills, EU aid could play a role provided it is carefully focused. Infrastructure is also critical, although Europe is generally well provisioned for this.

Finally, even more efforts to boost trickle down need to be made – whether through improved goods and services, better transport links, availability of leisure time or encouraging labour mobility. This should be part of a new growth bargain between member states.

If the major economies can succeed in sustaining their international competitiveness, higher growth in exports and gains in employment, with GDP rising at rates of 2.5–3 per cent over the next decade, then the potential to boost consumer demand will be significantly improved. In turn, this may mean that growth could rebound to rates of 2–3 per cent or more in the periphery countries, helping to alleviate the pressure of their high debts. Arguably, this may make it more likely that the EU would offer easier terms for debt repayment and even partial debt forgiveness over the longer run. However, this will only be acceptable if there are clear commitments to meeting the guidelines for public sector finances and avoiding destabilising economic trends in the future. Capital flows and credit conditions, mortgage and property markets and banking sectors will all need more careful monitoring than was the case over the last decade of debt-financed excesses: the understanding of macroprudential oversight, as well as its implementation, still has to be improved even if growth recovers to healthier rates.

6. CONCLUSIONS: THE EU'S PERFORMANCE OVER THE NEXT DECADE COULD BE BETTER THAN EXPECTED

There are some very positive trends in the global economy and Europe needs to focus on these and improve its ability to leverage the business opportunities offered. Surprising though it may seem after a shocking global recession, world growth has recovered well, reflecting the reality that the crisis in finance was largely a North Atlantic affair rather than a truly global phenomenon.

Although recent events, especially the debt crisis in Europe, have continued to focus attention on the risks to recovery, in fact the evident robustness of the global economy is boosting business confidence and the real investment outlook. And it is the next round of new investment – getting this right – that should be the new focus of attention.

There are five key points that emerge from our analysis of economic prospects, indicating risks but also growth opportunities:

- In contrast to fears of a prolonged period of weak growth, emerging markets are driving global growth at a rate close to 5 per cent – indeed, this could even reach a new peak of 5–5.5 per cent if all regions fire up simultaneously. The impact of emerging market demand on EU growth has been firmly registered in 2010.

- Even under fiscal tightening, export opportunities offer scope for continued robust GDP growth in the EU – there is easily potential for GDP to expand by around 2–2.5 per cent per annum over the next decade, provided no errors are made over the management of the debt crisis. Strongly performing exporters could raise their GDP growth while weaker, indebted countries might take several years to regain growth.

- Should disorderly debt restructuring be provoked, say by a major banking failure, then this may push the EU, possibly also the US, back into recession. This would probably imply that average growth would drop back to only 1 per cent over the next decade. This scenario would also incorporate significant variations in GDP performance, depending on the countries involved in debt restructuring.

- At the other end of the spectrum, if the major economies are successful in promoting export successes externally, and EU policies achieve both greater trickle down from the fast growing economies and improved export potential in the periphery, then there is scope for faster EU growth, possibly taking the average closer to 3 per cent.

- The euro will survive – indeed, even without taking into consideration the monetary chaos that would ensue from any break up of the euro area, the international community as well as the EU would be the poorer without the euro. The world needs a second major currency to take the strain off the dollar – in fact, it would benefit from acquiring another leg to this platform, which will probably come from the rise of China's renminbi over the coming decade.

The three key scenarios for the EU economy are depicted in Figure 4.13. The average rate of EU growth may vary from 1 to 3 per cent, which means that, by 2020, the EU economy could be worth some €4tn more under the more favourable 'New Opportunities' scenario than under 'Disorderly

Restructuring'. In effect, European citizens could be 20 per cent better off
by 2020 if their leaders manage the recovery well rather than badly.

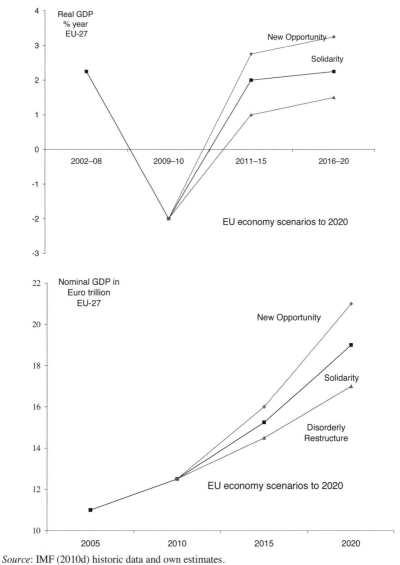

Source: IMF (2010d) historic data and own estimates.

Figure 4.13 EU economy scenarios to 2020

The EU needs to take a decisive stance on the management of its rising sovereign debt and on the bail-out issue. But it also needs to encourage the growth coming through in the major economies and to look realistically at a more microeconomic level at the possible ways in which depressed economies can be helped to create jobs and growth. Arguments about exchange rates and wage competitiveness will not resolve the problems of reviving and sustaining growth in the weakest economies – and neither will more borrowing. If China has shown other emerging markets how to grow successfully without becoming debt addicts, then Europe can learn the same lessons.

NOTES

1. For examples of discussions of the risk of a break up of the Eurozone, see Roubini (2011) and Krugman (2011).
2. According to assessments made by Reinhart and Rogoff (2010), who suggest that debt over 90 per cent of GDP is a critical threshold for markedly negative impacts on GDP growth.
3. See, for example, EC (2009).
4. An EU-wide bank special resolution regime is being discussed in some quarters – see, for example, Buiter (2011).
5. For example, EC (2010c).
6. For example, estimates provided in the IMF's Fiscal Monitor (2011).
7. Data from BMW Group (2010) and WTO (2010).
8. A target that Germany and the UK persuaded the G20 to adopt at the Toronto Summit in June 2010. See G20 (2010).

BIBLIOGRAPHY

BMW Group (2010), *Quarterly Report: To 30 September 2010*.
Buiter, Willem (2011), 'The Debt of Nations', *Citi Global Economics View*, 7 January.
European Commission (EC) (2009), *European Economy: Impact of the Current Economic and Financial Crisis on Potential Output*, Occasional Papers No. 49, June.
European Commission (EC) (2010a), *General Government Data: Table by Series*, Spring.
European Commission (EC) (2010b), *General Government Data: Table by Series*, Autumn.
European Commission (EC) (2010c), *Financial Services: The European Commission Consults on Further Policy in the Field of Credit Rating Agencies*, 5 November.
European Central Bank (ECB) (2010a), *National Aggregated Balance Sheets*, October.

European Central Bank (ECB) (2010b), *Statistical Data Warehouse*.

Eurostat (2010a) *National Accounts (Including GDP) Database*.

Eurostat (2010b) *Provision of Deficit and Debt Data for 2009: Second Notification*, 15 November 2010.

France Ministry of the Economy, Industry and Employment (2010), 'Projet de Loi de Finances 2011'.

G20 (2010), 'Toronto Summit Declaration', 27 June.

Germany Federal Statistical Office (2010), GENESIS–Online Database.

Germany Federal Ministry of Finance (2010), *Government Draft of the 2011 Budget and Financial Plan to 2014*, 7 July.

Government Offices of Sweden (2010), *2011 Budget Bill*, October.

HM Treasury (2010), *Budget 2010*, June 2010.

International Monetary Fund (IMF) (2010a), *Direction of Trade Statistics*.

International Monetary Fund (IMF) (2010b), *Greece: Staff Report on Request for Stand-By Arrangement*, May.

International Monetary Fund (IMF) (2010c), *Joint External Debt Hub*.

International Monetary Fund (IMF) (2010d), *World Economic Outlook Database*, October.

International Monetary Fund (IMF) (2010e), *World Economic Outlook: Rebalancing Growth*, April.

International Monetary Fund (IMF) (2011) *Fiscal Monitor*, 27 January.

Ireland Department of Finance (2010), *Budget 2011*, December.

Italy Department of Treasury (2010), *2011–13 Public Finance Decision*.

Krugman, Paul (2011), 'Can Europe be Saved?', *The New York Times*, 12 January.

Reinhart, Carmen M. and Kenneth S. Rogoff (2010), 'Growth in a Time of Debt', *The American Economic Review Papers and Proceedings*, January.

Roubini, Nouriel (2011), 'Saving the euro', *Financial Times*, 28 January.

Spain Ministry of Economy and Finance (2010), *General State Budgets 2011*, December.

World Trade Organization (WTO) (2010), *Monthly Series*.

5. The EU in Search of its New Shape: Economic Challenges and Governance Reforms in the Sovereign Debt Crisis

Daniela Schwarzer

In 2010, the Eurozone entered the third phase of the economic and financial crisis: a severe sovereign debt crisis which has raised serious doubts whether the single currency could survive. By the end of the year, two member states, Greece and Ireland, had to ask for financial support provided by their European partners and the International Monetary Fund (IMF). For a period of about three years, neither of the two countries has to refinance itself on the financial markets. At the beginning of 2011, it is possible that further governments of Eurozone member states will have to ask for credit and guarantees, as the mainly market-driven crisis may spread to Portugal, and in a worst case scenario also to Spain, Italy and Belgium.

In parallel to reacting to the sovereign debt crisis, the governments of the European Union's (EU) member states in spring 2010 committed themselves to reforming the economic governance mechanisms of the EU. There is a triple objective: improving budgetary policy surveillance and coordination, establishing a closer co-ordination of economic policies and installing a permanent resolution mechanism for debt crises. The latter is particularly important as the measures decided upon in spring 2010 will expire in 2013.

The years 2010 and 2011 are hence politically particularly complex: the sovereign debt crisis and the reform of economic governance need to be managed simultaneously. As recent experience has shown, ill-formulated reform proposals and disputes between member states stir market reactions and can aggravate sovereign debt crises. Meanwhile, an ambitious reform of the governance mechanisms of the Eurozone is now seen as an important condition for the eventual resolution of the current sovereign debt crisis. An institutional shake-up of the Economy and Monetary Union (EMU) – in parallel with national reform and austerity programmes and credible measures to reduce economic divergences – are key to regaining market confidence, to ending contagion and to improving the EU's competitiveness in global comparison.

This chapter first looks at the way the current crisis affects the European Union economically. It argues that divergence in North–South comparison has strongly increased and runs straight through the Eurozone. Although Slovakia and Estonia are the only two Central and Eastern European countries to have made their way into the monetary union six years after entering the EU, the old East–West divide among the 27 members of the EU is fading.

Second, this chapter turns to the political and institutional impact the crisis has had on the Eurozone. It sheds light on the broad reform process that has been launched in 2010 and that will at least partly be completed in 2011, discusses a probable scenario and evaluates current reform proposals, in particular on the sovereign debt resolution mechanism, against the background of the theories on self-fulfilling financial market crises.

The third section discusses the crucial issues ahead, not only with regard to internal matters, but also implications for the EU's fragmented and evolving external representation in economic and financial matters. As fairly good growth rates in 2010–2011 do not prevent Europe from losing economic weight with regard to other world regions, progress towards a formally more unified external representation should be sought. But so far, diverging national interests prevent the relative loss of economic and political weight of the EU in international comparison from being compensated by a leap forward in integration.

1. ECONOMIC PERFORMANCE IN THE CRISIS: A NEW LANDSCAPE EMERGING?

In 2009, hit severely by the economic and financial crisis, the Eurozone slipped into a recession for the first time since its creation ten years earlier. The economic downturn resulted in a massive increase in unemployment and strong pressure on public finances. Later in the year, the sovereign debt crisis started to unfold with several member states reaching very high deficits which pushed up public debt to unsustainable levels.

Like the previous economic downturn in the years 2002–2003, the real economic crisis did not hit all members of the Eurozone equally strongly. Divergence in competitiveness and fiscal performance has increased tremendously between member states. This has provoked economic imbalances, severe market reactions, political power shifts and strongly diverging interests between member states.

Not only the governments', but also the European Central Bank's (ECB) crisis management capacities have been put to a very tough test. Since the euro was launched in 1999, the ECB has been under close scrutiny. Initial fears that could become an inflation community have proved to date to be unfounded. With an average of around 2 per cent (1999–2009), inflation in the Eurozone was low, both in international and historical comparison (US inflation was 2.7 per cent in the same period). As the ECB quickly gained credibility in the markets and inflation expectations were revised downwards, interest rates in the money and capital markets sank. Only the year 2008 was an exception with an estimated price increase of 3.4 per cent mainly due to rising prices in the energy and food sector, as well as rising wages. Since 2010, the ECB has taken an active part in managing the sovereign debt crisis. It started to buy sovereign bonds of the mostly indebted countries as part of the overall stabilization strategy to save them from bankruptcy. This is resulting in new concerns about inflationary pressure that may build up.

Also the growth performance of the Eurozone had caused concern well before the current crisis. Even before the outbreak of the financial crisis, from 1999 to 2008, the GDP of the EMU countries only grew by 2.2 per cent (in the same period, the US GDP grew by 2.8 per cent, the overall EU GDP by 2.5 per cent). The years 2002 (0.9 GDP growth in the Eurozone) and 2003 (0.8 per cent GDP growth) had been particularly weak. The unemployment rate stabilized around 7 per cent on EMU average during the first decade of the euro's existence. Since the EU slipped into a recession in 2009–2010, unemployment has reached a level of around 10 per cent in the Eurozone. While this performance in terms of growth and employment is provoking a debate on the EU's ability to improve growth prospects, it is widely acknowledged that the disappearance of exchange rates among the EMU countries has prevented an even worse performance in the crisis. The 17 member states benefit from the fact that the serious downturn is not aggravated by additional costs due to currency movements among the participating member countries, just like in the sharp slump following the end of the New Economy boom.

Since the beginning of 2010, the European economy on average has recovered modestly. This happened in spite of the severe turbulences in sovereign debt markets. One of the drivers of economic activity is export-driven demand in Germany (GDP growth of 3.3 per cent in 2010). There are also some smaller member states whose growth rates have recovered, for example Finland, Slovakia and Slovenia.

The recovery of average growth cannot hide the fact that there are pronounced differences in the developments across member countries. Even before the outbreak of the crisis, economic divergence emerged as a problem in the Eurozone (Dullien and Schwarzer 2009). Now, they are all the more visible, as current account balances show. For instance, Germany and the Netherlands record net surpluses vis-à-vis their EU partners. After recording a deficit from 1999 to 2007, Germany jumped to a strong surplus of 6.7 per cent of GDP in 2008 which is increasing since. Countries like Spain, Portugal or Italy meanwhile have rather high current account deficits, indicating a loss of competitiveness. As these deficits go along with external debt, they can cause longer-term problems: paying back the debt can inhibit the development of domestic demand.

The evolution of unit labour costs as a result of repeated exaggerated wage increase is the major reason for the loss of competitiveness. Since the introduction of the euro, unit labour costs increased by roughly 20 per cent in Italy and Spain (Dullien and Fritsche 2007). In Germany, unit labour costs remained stable due to moderate wage agreements and successes in restructuring and reforming the economy. The wage restraint has led to low inflation rates and hence a real devaluation. Germany's economic activity has strongly rebounded in 2010 thanks to robust manufacturing exports but also to an improvement in both private consumption and investment. But given its strong export orientation, its growth prospects depend largely on demand developments in other world regions (mostly the US and China). Given Germany's size (27 per cent of Eurozone GDP), its substantial trade relationships and links through production, it has the potential to boost demand in the Eurozone. For the time being, for instance in France, the Eurozone's second largest economy which competes less well internationally, growth is picking up more slowly as private consumption is weakened by high unemployment and budgetary austerity. In Italy, both exports and investment have picked up in the first half of 2010. But persistent competitiveness problems limit the scope for export growth and planned fiscal consolidation is likely to weaken private demand.

The situation of those European states facing serious sovereign debt problems is worse. The economies of Greece, Ireland, Portugal and Spain have grown very modestly or even shrunk. These countries find themselves in a negative spiral of tight austerity measures, increasing deficits and low or negative growth rates and low competitiveness. It is today not clear how sustainable the political reform process is, both in terms of structural reforms in order to improve competitiveness and with regard to budgetary consolidation. There is a risk that the countries will not be able to break the vicious circle and regain growth unless there is a huge effort by the other member states to support this adaptation process, and this beyond the EU and IMF packages that have been granted to Greece and Ireland in return for ambitious reform programmes. The alternative would have been a partial default on their sovereign debt, which remains an option if it shows that the countries will not be able to reduce their public debt level and the envisaged pace.

Meanwhile, the Central and Eastern European member states which joined the EU on 1 May 2004 are no longer the rather homogeneous group they used to be. Two country clusters can be distinguished: on the one hand, there are countries which have major difficulties in recovering, for instance Bulgaria and Latvia which had previously suffered unsustainable booms; and Hungary, Latvia and Romania which had or have severe problems with public debt levels and had to request balance-of-payment loans from the EU and the IMF.

On the other hand there are member states like Poland and the Czech Republic with relatively strong private and public sector balances, which were able to create a competitive export base during the pre-crisis period. Thanks to their recovery, and in some countries budgetary austerity, they are converging economically and politically with the Eurozone's north (Germany, Netherlands, Austria, Finland). Estonia even met the convergence criteria for entering the Economic and Monetary Union and hence became the EMU's 17th member on 1 January 2011.

Despite their reasonably good growth prospects, these Central and Eastern European countries remain vulnerable to the growth performance of the EU and in particular the Eurozone. In most of these countries domestic demand is not robust, and lower growth in the euro area will put further stress on the banking sector and reduce capital flows to Central and Eastern Europe. This could delay the revival of credit growth and domestic demand, or fuel a depreciation of some currencies.

Interestingly, with these ongoing developments, the economic map of the European Union changes. Until the economic crisis, there was a rather clear East–West divide with most Western European countries recording rather stable growth rates, avoiding excessive public deficits and belonging to the European Monetary Union. In particular this latter fact promised them a comparable degree of stability in the first two years of the crisis. In 2010–2011, there are at least four Eurozone members with severe public finance problems and low degrees of competitiveness. In addition to Greece and Ireland which do not need to issue bonds because their financing needs are fully covered by IMF- and EU-backed credits and guarantees, Portugal or even Spain may request similar financial support. At the beginning of the year, Belgium and Italy are not hit by the sovereign debt crisis, but financial market reactions may extend the self-fulfilling financial crisis to these countries. Italy and Belgium are being closely scrutinized by investors, in the latter case mostly for political reasons as the general elections in 2010 have left the country in a situation in which no government can be formed and pressures for a disintegration of the state gain ground. In particular if large Eurozone member states run into trouble, the current €750bn rescue fund may have to be increased considerably.

One of the most important risks to economic recovery, facing even those member states which are not hit by the sovereign debt crisis, is that the financial sector gets under further stress. This could cause a credit crunch as banks are less and less willing to provide credit to the corporate sector. Demand could break down, also as an effect of fiscal austerity which weighs heavily on domestic consumption in some member states (International Monetary Fund 2010). An overarching challenge is the re-establishment of trust by financial market actors who have become prudent in their decisions to invest in public debt issued in the European Union. Interestingly, investors are no longer primarily interested in real economic performance, but also considerably in the political ability of the member states to handle the crisis and to re-shape governance mechanisms in the Eurozone.

2. REFORMING INTERNAL ECONOMIC GOVERNANCE UNDER THE PRESSURE OF THE CRISIS

In spring 2010, reforms have been launched which are supposed to ensure that a crisis similar to the current one will never happen again. In order to tackle its root causes, reforms concern three areas: European surveillance and coordination of 'national budgetary policies', European surveillance and co-ordination of 'national economic policies' and the creation of a 'mechanism to solve and prevent sovereign debt crises'. As the European Council has decided in December 2010, this reform should include a revision of the EU Treaty, which Germany in particular sees as a necessity in order to create a permanent crisis resolution mechanism which includes a rescue fund compatible with primary law.

In spring 2010, the Heads of State and Government installed the so-called Van Rompuy Task Force. This was a reaction to the creation of the € 750bn rescue fund which was installed to provide credit to Eurozone member states facing a liquidity crisis. Some member states, in particular Germany, insisted that the emergency aid should be accompanied by reforms which, in the future, would prevent similar crises in Eurozone member states. The working group chaired by the new Council President Herman Van Rompuy tabled its reform proposals in October 2010. A few weeks ahead of the Van Rompuy Report, the European Commission published first drafts of six related legislative acts, after having sketched its own proposals in several Communications published since spring 2010. The details of the reforms are the subject of heated negotiations between the member states and the European Parliament which co-decides on four of six proposed regulations. But the major elements of the renewed economics governance rules in the Eurozone can still rather safely be forecast.

3. THE REFORM OF THE STABILITY AND GROWTH PACT

While budgetary policies remain a national responsibility in the European Monetary Union, since its start there have been rules and procedures that are supposed to prevent irresponsible budgetary policies and should ensure sound economic policies.

The European rules for fiscal policy coordination are about to be modified for the third time since the Maastricht Treaty (Schwarzer 2007). Firstly, in 1997, the Stability and Growth Pact added details and hardened the rules of the Maastricht Treaty and spelled out the terms for a more speedy procedure leading to sanctions. At the time, the Pact was widely seen as being one key guarantor of stability for the single currency. The designers of the Pact, notably the German government, did not expect the sanction mechanism ever to be applied. Its deterrent character was expected to be sufficient to ensure sound fiscal policies which would underpin monetary stability.

In 2005, the Pact was reformed in order to enable more political discretion in its application, in particular with the objective of allowing governments to take into account cyclical conditions in single member states as the stabilizing role of fiscal policy had become a concern. Prior to the reform, countries like Germany, France, Portugal and Italy had breached the deficit rules in the years of low economic growth (2002–2004) and were about to face sanctions. In particular the German and French government pressured their fellow ministers in the ECOFIN (Economic and Financial Affairs Council) to temporarily postpone the application of the sanctioning procedures, pointing to the need to grant national fiscal policies a sufficient stabilizing role. A subsequent ruling of the European Court of Justice declared part of the ECOFIN decision to be illegal. This reinforced the political dynamics towards a reform of the Pact.

In 2010, under the impression of the sovereign debt crisis, a new reform of the Stability and Growth Pact has been launched. This time, it is part of a broader reform package to reinforce surveillance and coordination of national policies. A new surveillance cycle, the 'European Semester', shall better link the coordination of budgetary and economic policies and interconnect the European and the national policy cycles. In the future, scrutiny on the European level should come timely enough to actually influence national debates and decisions, in particular on the annual budget. To ensure the impact of European surveillance on national policy choices, a high degree of political commitment on the national level needs to be ensured. The first steps taken to implement the European semester in January 2011 have highlighted this specific problem, with the European

Commission, so far behind closed doors, criticising at least some member states that their national reform programmes lack ambition and in some cases even fall behind previous recommendations to the governments. If the European Commission, backed by the ECOFIN, actually hardens its stance on some governments, the question of political legitimacy will arise as national parliaments will observe an interference with their budget authority. As a response to the criticism that the new mechanisms will strengthen bureaucracy and technocratic inference in policy making, the point is made that not only should national parliaments play a strong part in this process, but also the European Parliament should be involved in the debate on budgetary and economic policies in the EMU.

In addition to these innovations, a likely outcome of the reform of the Stability Pact is firstly, that the variables subject to supervision will be expanded, paying particular attention to excessive debt while previously the focus was mostly on deficits. The enforcement of the rules will be strengthened, meaning more efficient procedures and more weight for the European Commission in implementing them, and possibly also harsher sanctions both in financial and reputational terms. Far-reaching proposals, for instance to completely exclude the ECOFIN from implementing the Stability and Growth Pact, but leaving it solely to the European Commission (Verhofstadt 2010) will very probably not be implemented as the governments are clearly reluctant to cut down their own sovereignty.

Secondly, fiscal responsibility is supposed to be encouraged by setting minimum requirements for national fiscal frameworks in order to make sure they are in line with EU Treaty obligations. Experience with the EU's fiscal rules has revealed the problems of a coordination mechanism which requires peers to sanction each other – and as argued above this problem will very probably persist. Hence, the idea to make national fiscal rules obligatory is part of the attempt to improve national adherence to certain objectives, just like the proposal by the European Commission that member states install independent national budget offices, improve budgetary procedures governing all stages of the budget process, introduce medium-term budgetary frameworks and better control fiscal relations across government layers. But the first rounds of negotiations in the Council working groups reveal that, once again, national sensitivities are likely to lead to an only moderately ambitious agreement. While there are convincing arguments (and real-life experience with the current crisis) that in particular the Eurozone member states should care about better co-ordination, reluctance to strongly improve the setting of budgetary rules in the EU comes precisely from some of the Eurozone's members, while some of the non-members, in particular those on a strong convergence path, actually support tougher rules and mechanisms.

3.1 Strengthening Economic Policy Coordination

Furthermore, economic policy coordination will be improved. It is today widely acknowledged that neither the debt crisis in Spain nor the one in Ireland would have been prevented even if the newly emerging control mechanisms discussed above had been in place. Indeed, persistent and large current account imbalances and diverging competitiveness put the Eurozone under consistent tensions. The large current account deficits and losses in competitiveness were associated with a misallocation of capital and labour, unsustainable accumulation of debt and housing bubbles. Conversely, other member states with external surpluses capitalized on their competitive export sector, but domestic demand lagged behind, amplifying the gap between deficit and surplus countries within the euro area.

The mechanism that is foreseen in both the Van Rompuy Report and in the legislative proposals tabled by the European Commission in September 2010 will provide help in identifying and addressing macroeconomic imbalances, including deteriorating competitiveness trends. Reforms will very probably lead to the introduction of an alert mechanism based on a kind of scoreboard which identifies member states with potentially problematic levels of macroeconomic imbalances through a set of indicators in order to identify timely imbalances emerging in different parts of the economy. The Commission has suggested regularly publishing the results of the scoreboard and providing a list of member states which risk running too large account deficits or surpluses. There would then be a debate in the Council and the Euro Group upon which the Commission would provide in-depth country reviews, taking into account the severity of imbalances and possible spillovers to other member states, as well as the assessment of findings from Stability and Convergence Programmes and the National Reform Programmes.

The Commission has furthermore proposed to install the following rather far-reaching procedure: if it considers that there is a risk of macroeconomic imbalances, it issues preventive recommendations to the member states concerned. In case of repeated non-compliance, there could even be sanctions. Depending on the nature of the imbalances, the policy prescriptions could address fiscal, wage and macro-structural as well as macro-prudential policy aspects under the control of government authorities. The member state concerned would have to set up a roadmap of implementing policy measures. The Commission would monitor the implementation of corrective action by the member states concerned, which would issue progress reports on a regular basis.

Introducing this kind of surveillance of member states' economic policies would be a big step forward, in particular if it obliges both deficit and surplus countries to take economic and budgetary policy choices in line with European objectives. However, without a truly binding competence on the EU level, the risk remains that the new rules will turn out to be a 'toothless tiger', just like the fiscal rules have proven to be since the start of the EMU. Despite the deepness of the current crisis, there is currently little political appetite to create a European economic government that could take binding decisions and that would have a relevant budget to spend on European economic policies.

3.2 A Crisis Resolution Mechanism

The third major issue of the reform is the so-called crisis resolution mechanism. In April and May 2010, the EU adopted short-term measures in order to contain the largely market-driven escalation of the sovereign debt crisis. A lot of criticism has been made, for instance with regard to the rescue package for Greece. But, although in the end Greece's debt problem may turn out to require restructuring, the decision to adopt the package in spring 2010 was right.

The Eurozone so far possesses no permanent instruments with which it could intervene in the event of a member state experiencing acute payment difficulties after 2013, nor an orderly procedure for dealing with insolvent states. In case of a sovereign debt crisis, the danger of contagion is hence especially great in the Eurozone, as markets have demonstrated when the interest rates on Spanish, Portuguese, Irish and also Italian debt spiked in 2010–2011. There is a major risk of so-called self-fulfilling debt crises.

Against the background of the theory of self-fulfilling financial crises, several requirements for a sustainable solution can be identified (see also Dullien Schwarzer 2011). Firstly, excessive deficits should be prevented by intensifying monitoring and coordination of budget and economic policy to prevent countries from getting into an untenable perilous deficit and debt situation in the first place. This is currently being worked on in the context of the reform of the Stability and Growth Pact and the reform of economic policy co-ordination. Secondly, the mechanism should avoid a situation where countries are driven into payment difficulties simply through changes in market expectations even though under normal borrowing conditions they would be able to cope with their level of debt. Thirdly, the mechanism should bridge liquidity bottlenecks to ensure that countries that are structurally solvent retain access to capital for funding state expenditure and rolling over debt. Fourthly, it should prevent moral hazard by making the conditions for assistance unattractive enough that governments still have an incentive to reduce their public debt. And finally, it should allow for a restructuring of public debts of insolvent states quickly and constructively so that they can return to a sustainable path of growth as soon as possible.

In December 2010, the European Council decided that a European Stability Mechanism (ESM) should be set up, before the temporary rescue fund expires in 2013. Details will be negotiated in the first half of 2011. What is known so far is that the ESM will be a crisis mechanism set up to safeguard financial stability in the euro area. It will provide assistance to Eurozone member states in a liquidity crisis. Its main features will build on the existing European Financial Stability Facility (EFSF). In case of a solvency crisis, private creditors will be involved – but how will be decided on a case-by-case basis. It has been agreed that Collective Action Clauses will be included in the terms and conditions of all new sovereign bonds issued by Eurozone member states as the legal basis for the negotiation process. Member states undergoing a restructuring of their debt can still obtain liquidity assistance.

In the course of the reform debate, an additional proposal has been tabled, notably by the President of the Euro Group, Jean-Claude Juncker: he has proposed that member states of the Eurozone issue Eurobonds up to a volume of debt amounting to 60 per cent of GDP. From the perspective of self-fulfilling financial crisis this could indeed be a useful complementary component to the two others.

3.3 A Three-Component Model

Combined, a European liquidity fund, a debt restructuring procedure and joint European bonds for a maximum of 60 per cent of GDP meet the five criteria set out above. They could prevent self-fulfilling financial crises, reduce moral hazard and deal with both liquidity and solvency problems of individual states. The European Stability Mechanisms would provide speedy relief for Eurozone countries with liquidity problems and bridge periods of liquidity shortage. In order to prevent self-fulfilling financial crises the interest on this facility should not be the market rate but instead only slightly above the interest rates paid by other euro states without borrowing difficulties. It would also be important for the credit to be granted under clear and transparent rules. The approach of tying payments to a restructuring programme supervised by the IMF fulfils this criterion. Presenting a realistic plan for restructuring – which by definition can only apply to states that are basically solvent – must be a precondition.

The existence of such a fund would probably stabilize market expectations to such an extent as to prevent speculative attacks on states that are solvent in the medium to long term but insolvent in the short term. In order for the fund to unfold its stabilizing effect the maximum necessary volume must actually be available. Credit facilities amounting to 10 per cent of the Eurozone GDP (or currently about €920bn) would be a sensible order of magnitude. This would be large enough to cover all current problem cases but small enough not to endanger the solvency of the credit-providing states. Under such a rule the volume would grow automatically with the economic output of the Eurozone, ensuring that the guarantees remain adequate in future.

It must be ensured that soft loans from the fund go only to states that are illiquid but not structurally insolvent. They should be granted only if the affected state can present a plausible programme showing how it intends to reduce its debt to a manageable level within a defined period.

In order to address moral hazard, countries must be prevented from making use of the facility without real need. A country wishing to call on the funds must accept largely relinquishing its control over national budget policy. For a period this influence on national politics would be greater than under programmes run by the IMF alone, because the fund would have to have the means to very quickly verify and approve the budget and its implementation together with the European Commission, the Euro Group and possibly the IMF (European Central Bank 2010).

Such an intervention in national budgetary sovereignty can of course produce political tensions and reduce the EU's standing in the affected country, at least for a time. It must therefore be made absolutely clear that governments ask the fund for soft loans voluntarily and are not coerced into doing so by the EU. Intervention in the budget would be the last resort at the end of a coordinating process lasting many years within the Eurozone and EU – a process that is supposed to prevent the worst case ever occurring. So by this stage the member state concerned would have had plenty of time to try out its own ideas for ensuring sustainable state finances and a competitive economy.

As economic policy coordination is strengthened in the Eurozone it will be important to make sure it is properly integrated with the consolidation and reform programme of the highly indebted member state. This must be accomplished in a cooperative manner because the economic policies of the other member states have a decisive influence on the chances of the highly indebted state to reduce its debt. The fund could provide help alone or together with the IMF. At least in the first years of its existence the second method would be advisable (Matthes 2010, Pisani-Ferry and Sapir 2010).

An 'orderly procedure for debt restructuring' is needed when a country's unsound budget policies or unfavourable external economic circumstances leave it unable to service its debt. In this case a solution must be found that balances the interests of creditors with reducing the country's debt burden to a point where it can return to a normal path of growth.

Opponents of state insolvency argue that the political and social costs to the affected government would be unbearable and that the bankruptcy of one Eurozone member would discredit the EU as a whole and undo the convergence achieved thus far in the Eurozone. A state insolvency would indeed come with considerable political costs and it would be better to avoid a default in the first place. But bridging facilities like soft loans or extending the repayment period of loans are useless where a country is truly insolvent. The long-term social and political costs of struggling under a suffocating burden of debt would be considerably greater than those of an orderly insolvency. Virtually unable to achieve economic growth, the country's convergence within the Eurozone would be abruptly reversed. Moreover, the orderly insolvency of a single country would probably do less harm to the reputation of the EU than having member states under permanent de facto external administration and forced to send significant parts of their national income and state revenues abroad.

Critics also warn that the threat of state insolvencies in the Eurozone would harm financial market integration because certain bonds would be too risky for the banks. That, they say, would create new barriers to the internal market and impair its growth potential. Again, the question is whether the alternative – liquidity assistance postponing an inevitable default – would be better. The country would be trapped in a situation of low growth or even lengthy recession that would drive up the insolvency risks for private companies and banks. Debtors from the affected country would be automatically stigmatized.

Finally, it is also suggested that the orderly insolvency of one state would harm the reputation of the other euro states. This effect can be neutralized by providing liquidity assistance for solvent states and adopting clear rules for initiating an insolvency process. In order to minimize the costs and risks of a state bankruptcy, the necessity for debt restructuring should be defined in the clearest possible terms.

An orderly insolvency is preferable to an unorderly default because the latter is usually a drawn-out process where the outcome – for creditors and for the affected country itself – remains uncertain for a long time. In an unorderly default creditors are often treated unequally, with those with the most powerful lobby generally getting better restructuring conditions.

3.4 Eurobonds for a Share of Public Debt

The third component of a mechanism to prevent self-fulfilling financial crises would be to introduce joint Eurozone bonds. This proposal was made in 2009 and in 2010 by Euro Group President Jean-Claude Juncker, and has been discussed in the Euro Group (Strupczewski 2009) and the Van Rompuy Task Force. But some countries, including Germany, have so far vetoed the idea. The idea is to create a European debt title with which member states would be able to fund part of their state debt (Delpla and Weizsäcker 2010). The amounts under discussion range from 40 per cent of national GDP up to 60 per cent.

This security should be inherently secure and liquid. The depth of the market for such Eurobonds would be comparable to that for US Treasury Bills and would guarantee member states similarly low interest rates. The greater market liquidity and security of these bonds – with all Eurozone states assuming joint and several liability – means that interest rates could settle below the Eurozone mean and possibly even below the rate on German Bunds. This would require investors to have confidence in the sustainability of national finances and the efficacy of Eurozone governance mechanisms.

For debt above the cut-off of 60 per cent of GDP the Eurozone states would have to issue national securities for which they alone would be liable. These would only be served after any European bonds obligations had been fulfilled. The national bonds would thus be more risky and consequently raising credit with them would be more expensive than with Eurobonds. That would give member states a clear incentive to avoid borrowing above the 60 per cent limit.

The introduction of these European bonds would not only lower the cost of borrowing for debt below the 60 per cent cut-off, but also create a sensible instrument for encouraging budget discipline. Countries with large debt would reduce their borrowing costs and at the same time submit to greater discipline because the national bonds exceeding 60 per cent of GDP would be associated with risk surcharges. The division into European and national bonds could also help to avoid self-fulfilling financial crises. Growing mistrust in the financial markets would increase returns only on the national bonds exceeding the 60 per cent threshold, making it less likely for a country to be driven into bankruptcy.

While the liquidity fund and insolvency procedure would together be capable of mastering liquidity and solvency problems even without joint bonds, the introduction of European bonds would make it less likely that a country would even have to call on the fund at all. The difficulty in the present situation is that if the risk premium on a country's debt rises, all of its old debt has to be rolled over at the new higher rate of interest. With European bonds up to 60 per cent of GDP, this would apply only to the latter, reducing the danger of a country being driven into bankruptcy in a self-fulfilling financial crisis. In fact, this measure could completely prevent such crises because investors would not fear that exorbitant risk premiums might send a country spiralling into bankruptcy.

3.5 Crucial Issues Ahead

3.5.1 The EU's struggle for economic recovery
The current reform process will lead to a more integrated Economic and Monetary Union. In the best case, policy co-ordination leads to a reduction

of internal divergences while at the same time the member states together implement a useful growth strategy and negotiate the new EU budget in a way that decisively underpins these objectives. Meanwhile, financial markets are calmed down and the sovereign debt crisis is handled well thanks to a new crisis resolution mechanism. The supervision of national budgetary policies and the change of budgetary rules at the national level help member states regain a course of budgetary consolidation and increase the long-term sustainability of public finances. Tensions in the EMU are substantially reduced.

But this is not the only scenario. Economic recovery may not occur as hoped for. In case of a continuous economic slump, budgetary austerity may not lead to the expected consolidation effects if growth is too sluggish. At least some of the EMU's member states would continue to be caught in a negative spiral of budgetary strain, low growth and high unemployment rates which can eventually lead to further debt crises, unstable governments, rising populism and anti-EU sentiments.

3.6 Pressure from the Outside

Reasons for slow recovery may be external to the Eurozone. It cannot be excluded that the US economy runs through another severe economic downturn or that demand from Asia, mainly China, decreases. This effect can be increased if the euro seriously appreciates while other currencies (the US$, the Yuan and/or the Yen) devalue. It is today unlikely that China, for instance, gives up its discretionary exchange rate policy that has led to a persistently undervalued exchange rate of the Yuan. Other emerging countries are under considerable pressure to artificially weaken their own currencies. Against this background, it becomes clear that the European Union and in particular the Eurozone face important challenges that they have to tackle with their international partners, for instance in the G20.

3.6.1 Strategic implications and the Eurozone's external representations
Most probably, European growth rates will be lower than those in other economic areas. In particular, emerging markets grow with high rates, and the Eurozone and the EU lose relative economic weight. One example: in the distribution of regional shares in world GDP, according to IMF (2010) estimates, China will overtake the Eurozone in 2012 and will catch up with the EU-27 around 2015.

The relative loss of economic weight has strategic consequences. The European Union is likely to lose further influence in global discussions on developments in international economics and finance. For instance, with regard to financial market regulation or macroeconomic policy coordination, an economically weakened EU will be less and less able to succeed in convincing its partners of European preferences. This is especially true in a G2 world which some observers see emerging and in which the major policy choices influencing the world economic order are being made between China and the US.

This puts pressure on the European governments to pool their strength and to formally improve the external representation of the EU in matters of international economics and finance. Europe will only be able to secure its place among the major players if it combines a sound economic base (in terms of growth and internal convergence) with an effective representation of its interests on the global scale. If this is not assured and if internal divergences grow further and increase political tensions, the Eurozone – which from a macroeconomic perspective technically is one economy as long as the single currency and the single market exist – will continue not to be perceived and treated as such.

The economic and financial crisis has considerably strengthened the case for an improved external representation of the EU and in particular of the Eurozone in international financial and economic matters. In the course of crisis management, the insufficiencies of the current arrangements became clear. The volatility of financial markets and in particular the spill-over effects between financial market actors, different segments and national markets provide reason for the EU and the Eurozone to act with one voice on the international scene.

Even before the outbreak of the crisis, there were strong arguments for a single European voice on international financial matters. Sharing a single monetary and exchange rate policy makes it logical for the participating member states also to defend a common position in international fora dealing with macroeconomic matters such as the IMF and the G7–G8. This is especially so as the Eurozone has become more exposed to international portfolio shifts due to the substitutability between assets denominated in euros or in US dollars.

Moreover, new approaches to international cooperation in the field of economics and finance have emerged. The agenda (for instance in the G20 format) now comprises various policy questions in which the EU or the Eurozone should make their voice heard. For instance on exchange rate policies or financial market regulation, a consolidated representation of the euro area in international fora would strengthen the euro area's negotiating power and could increase its gains from international policy coordination.

Given the relative decline of the EU in comparison with emerging markets, pooling the external representation in international financial institutions may hence become necessary to maintain influence. In addition, many partners of the EU would prefer dealing with a single interlocutor, rather than with a multitude of different actors. Consolidating the external representation would not only enable the Eurozone to better defend its interest, but could also increase the interest of other players in cooperating with the Eurozone.

Moreover, the EU member states have to face the criticism that the EU is overrepresented in international financial institutions. In October 2010, the G20 decided on a reform of the International Monetary Fund. The package includes a shift of quotas, a change in the Fund's capital stock and a recomposition of the Executive Board. The European countries have to give up two of their current eight seats in favour of large emerging market countries.

The reasons why the external representation of the EU or the Eurozone in economic and financial matters is not improved mostly related to sovereignty concerns. Member states have diverging views and do not want to run the risk of not being able to make their opinion heard internationally. National representation in global institutions and fora offers influence – and political prestige. As a Commission report puts it, 'some euro countries finding themselves in a privileged situation, holding the Chair or the Alternate Executive Director position of their constituencies, may fear a loss of influence from a consolidation of chairs' (European Commission 2008). So there is a rather high probability that countries refrain from giving up their seats, for longer-term gains which are perceived as rather vague.

4. CONCLUSIONS

The economic and financial crisis has revealed the interdependencies and the divergences of the European economies and has highlighted insufficiencies in the governance mechanisms. The sovereign debt crisis has made it particularly clear that those countries which have integrated their currencies share very close ties over the real economies and the financial sectors. They need to strengthen policy coordination and to improve governance instruments.

For the first time since the euro's introduction in 1999, there is a widespread consensus that the EMU needs specific governance mechanisms in the EU and that political integration is needed to bring the member states which share a currency closer together – both economically and politically. The Eurozone will hence form a more closely integrated core of the EU-27. But member states remain extremely prudent to transfer further parts of national sovereignty to the EU level, both with regard to internal governance and external representation.

Even if the European Union agrees encompassing reforms in 2011, it is still possible that the implementation of policy coordination is insufficient.

With regard to binding rules, transfers of decision-making power and sanctions, member states will – despite the effect of the crisis – probably opt for a rather weak compromise in order to protect national sovereignty as far as possible. If the implementation of budgetary and economic policy-making is left to political discretion with a strong role for the ECOFIN, it is possible that the reasons that lead to an insufficient application of the existing coordination mechanisms from 1999 to 2010 will also in the future cause coordination failure. If, meanwhile, European control and inference is increased and the European Commission is strongly upgraded in its capacity to influence member states' policy decisions, problems of democratic legitimacy are likely to arise. In a few years time, the Eurozone might face the next reform debate, circling around questions of democratic legitimacy and, once again, political union (see for instance Collignon 2010).

If, however, the member states do not agree far-reaching reforms which decisively strengthen economic and budgetary policy co-ordination as well as the management and prevention of sovereign debt crises, internal economic and budgetary tensions will persist and may grow. Political destabilization in some member states is a likely side effect. An appreciation of the euro exchange rate or a breakdown of demand from our key trading partners, the US and China, can contribute to aggravating divergence in the Eurozone. An encompassing view on the internal perspectives of the Eurozone and its global challenges should be further developed, drawing conclusions on the struggle over strengthening the euro's external representation.

BIBLIOGRAPHY

Collignon, Stefan (2010), *Democratic Surveillance or Bureaucratic Suppression of National Sovereignty in the European Union?*, Briefing paper for the Committee on Economic and Monetary Affairs, IP/A/ECON/NT/2010-07, September.
Delpla, Jacques and Jakob von Weizsäcker (2010), *The Blue Bond Proposal*, Bruegel Policy Brief, Brussels: May 2010, http://www.bruegel.org/uploads/tx_btbbreugel/1005-PB-Blue_Bonds.pdf, (accessed 2 June 2010).
De Grauwe, Paul (2010), *Why Should We Believe the Market This Time?*, ECMI Commentary, no. 22, Brussels: European Capital Market Institute, 20 February 2009, http://www.eurocapitalmarkets.org/node/416 (accessed 28 May 2010).
De Grauwe, Paul and Wim Moesen (2009), 'Gains for All: A Proposal for a Common Eurobond', *Intereconomics*, **45** (3), 132–35.
Dullien, Sebastian and Ulrich Fritsche (2007), 'Anhaltende Divergenz bei Inflations- und Lohnentwicklung in der Eurozone: Gefahr für die Währungsunion?', *Vierteljahreshefte zur Wirtschaftsforschung*, (4), 56–76.

Dullien, Sebastian and Daniela Schwarzer (2009), *The Euro Zone Needs an External Stability Pact*, SWP Comments 2009/C09, Berlin: Stiftung Wissenschaft und Politik, July.

Dullien, Sebastian and Daniela Schwarzer (2011), *Coping with Sovereign Default in the Eurozone*, SWP Research Paper, February.

European Central Bank (2010), *Reinforcing Economic Governance in the Euro Area (2010)*, 10 June, http://www.ecb.europa.eu/pub/pdf/other/reinforcing economicgovernanceintheeuroareaen.pdf (accessed 12 December 2010).

European Commission (2008), *EMU@10: Successes and Challenges after 10 Years of Economic and Monetary Union*, Directorate General for Economic and Financial Affairs, European, Economy, No. 2.

Henning, C. Randall (2007), 'Organizing Foreign Exchange Intervention in the Euro Area', *Journal of Common Market Studies*, **45** (2), 315–42, 317f.

International Monetary Fund (2010), *World Economic Outlook Update, Restoring Confidence Without Harming Recovery*, 7 July, 7f, http://www.imf.org/external/pubs/ft/weo/2010/update/02/pdf/0710.pdf (download on October 10, 2010).

Matthes, Jürgen (2010), 'The IMF is Better Suited than an EMF to Deal with Potential Sovereign Defaults in the Eurozone', *Intereconomics*, **45** (2), 75–81.

Pisani-Ferry, Jean and André Sapir (2010), 'Crisis Resolution in the Euro Area: An Alternative to the European Monetary Fund', *Intereconomics*, **45** (2), 72–5.

Pisani-Ferry, Jean *et al.* (2008), *Coming of Age: Report on the Euro Area*, Bruegel: Blue Print Series, 89.

Schwarzer, Daniela (2007), *Fiscal Policy Co-ordination in the EMU. A Preference-Based Explanation of Institutional Change*, Baden-Baden: Nomos.

Strupczewski, Jan (2009), 'Euro Zone Bond Idea Taking Shape, May Never Fly', *Reuters*, 20 February.

Verhofstadt, Guy (2010), *How Can We Save the Euro?*, Berlin: Bertelsmann Stiftung.

6. The Fiscal Governance Disorder of the Eurozone: Curing the Symptoms or Curing the Causes?

Carlo Altomonte, Francesco Passarelli and Carlo Secchi

Europe is facing both a short- and a medium-term critical situation. In the short term, the sustainability of public finances of some member states is in question; in the long term, the entire Continent suffers from sluggish growth rates.

The short-term response cannot be undervalued: without convincing responses able to restore the necessary credibility on financial markets in terms of sustainability of public debt, the risk of a breakdown of the Eurozone might become systemic. It is also fairly clear that such a cure requires a two-pronged therapy: one addressing the symptoms of the disease (the crisis of debt in the Eurozone periphery), and one addressing the underlying illness (the unbalanced competitiveness differentials induced by sluggish growth).

Addressing the symptoms boils down to the rescue actions of the member states currently at the heart of the financial turmoil. The recent decisions undertaken by the EU institutions (the set-up of a permanent European Stability Mechanism – ESM, coupled with a Sovereign Debt Restructuring Mechanism – SDRM), represent a first step in coping with the immediate fears of the markets.

Addressing the actual illness requires instead fixing the 'original sin' of the Maastricht Treaty, that is the substantial failure of the 'non-monetary' governance of the euro area. The illness itself can be decomposed in two distinct disorders of governance. First, there is what we can term as a metabolic disequilibrium, in which competitiveness differentials tend to persist in the euro area while fiscal oversight is imperfect: the latter generates pronounced current account imbalances, not easily fixed lacking the medicine of devaluation, as well as potentially significant deviations from budgetary stability. The second disorder is instead related to a general weakness of the organism, with Europe for having experienced sluggish growth rates with respect to the rest of the world economy at least a decade.

Indeed, the European Union has tried since long time to provide an answer to the problem of growth for a by setting up the (in)famous 'Lisbon Strategy' of reforms, an agenda for action which, as it was originally phrased in 2000, aimed at turning Europe into 'the most competitive and dynamic knowledge-based economy in the world' by 2010. By 2005, its dismal start had already generated a thorough review by the new Commission, under the heading of strategy for 'growth and jobs'. By 2008, quite conveniently, the near collapse of the world economy and the ensuing new set of short-term priorities cast the final shadow on the murky performance of the strategy, with the reform agenda and its missed targets gently set aside from the policy debate. Nowadays, however, the issue of EU competitiveness and growth has resurfaced, with proposals for a new, decade-spanning agenda of reforms known as 'Europe 2020' (European Commission 2010a), formally adopted by the European Council in June 2010.

At the same time, the European Commission (EC) has also started to address the issue of economic imbalances. In particular, in June 2010 the EC issued a Communication on enhancing economic policy coordination (European Commission 2010b) in which it suggested a framework for tackling broader macroeconomic imbalances, which should work in a way similar to the Stability and Growth Pact (SGP), equally foreseeing a strengthening of the latter on both its preventive and corrective levels.[1] By and large, the new enhanced policy framework should thus encompass a monitoring of divergences in the current account positions of member states, an analysis of the different competitiveness trends based on a number of indicators, as well as preventive and corrective mechanisms, all parts of a so-called Excessive Imbalance Procedure.[2]

Both initiatives of the European Commission thus aim *ex ante* at trying to fix the two governance disorders we have pointed out. What remains to be seen, however, is whether these two initiatives are able to provide a veritable cure. Should they fail, two outcomes are likely, none of which is pleasant: with persisting imbalances and no adequate institutional framework for assessing them in the long run, the euro area will gradually consume itself in trying to cope with the financial instability ensuing from this, with the European Central Bank (ECB) de facto becoming the 'bad bank' of the Eurozone until confidence in the euro, externally and then internally, vanishes. At the same time, one has to avoid the risk that the design of an appropriate institutional framework able to deal with these imbalances (see 'infra') ends up imposing a straightjacket on growth: if that is the case, over the next decade Europe will possibly become a very stable, but quite a marginal, player in the global arena.

In the rest of this chapter, we will thus try to discuss the extent to which the proposed solutions of fiscal governance are able to cure both aspects (imbalances and growth) of the illness currently characterizing the health of the Eurozone system.

1. ADDRESSING THE IMBALANCES IN THE EURO AREA

The macroeconomic imbalances currently affecting the euro area, and leading to the instability of public debt on financial markets, can be characterized through two different angles, the Hellenic and the Spanish one.

The 'Hellenic' imbalance is quite straightforward: the Economic and Monetary Union (EMU) has experienced a failure in the surveillance of public finances as well as the inability to enforce the existing rules, as witnessed by the notorious problems encountered by the SGP. Just to quote the most striking example, in 2009 the newly elected Government has revised the yearly official public deficit of Greece from 3.5 to around 15 per cent, then leading to the eruption of the country's debt problems.

The latter issue has indeed received a good policy response in the last months: within the previously discussed enhanced macroeconomic surveillance framework, proposals for a reform of the SGP have been tabled, the enforcement powers of Eurostat have been strengthened and the 'European Semester' has been introduced, that is a stricter co-ordination of national budgetary policies, whose general guidelines have to be pre-approved by the June European Council before starting their legislative process in the national Parliaments. Moreover, the new permanent European Stability Mechanism which by 2013 is meant to substitute the European Financial Stability Fund (EFSF), should allow individual member states to overcome the current negative consequences of the bad EU fiscal governance, while imposing stricter enforcement rules to prevent these behaviours from happening again. In the new proposed legal framework it is also envisaged that private creditors should share some of the costs in case of future debt restructurings taking place within the euro area. Hence, no 'reputational' shield from the euro as a whole, with the ensuing moral hazard problem, will exist in the future.

Apart from the 'Hellenic' imbalance, essentially related to problems in the governace of existing fiscal rules, another possibly more serious imbalance, the 'Iberic' one, is also currently affecting the EU. The latter refers to the fact that, within the euro area, the competitiveness differentials (in terms of real exchange rate) of the countries are diverging, leading to the emergence of serious current account imbalances.

With respect to the latter issue, the traditional view has had it that, within a single currency, persistent current account imbalances should not emerge; if they occurred, they would be transitory and of a benign nature, as they would signal the fact that, under capital mobility, savers can lend to international investors in the periphery of Europe to support catching-up processes. Hence, all that was needed to ensure a fair degree of macroeconomic stability was a control on public finances preventing the build-up of excessive public debt and deficit positions.

In reality, it is now clear that the current account imbalances which arose in the early stages of monetary unification are not transitory, but rather, in a context of deep, globalized financial markets, they can grow larger over time; moreover, these imbalances do not have a benign nature, as shown by the unsustainable credit positions developed by certain member states, irrespectively of their absolute public debt levels (for example Spain) (Altomonte and Marzinotto 2010).

Figure 6.1, in particular, describes the evolution of the current account as a proportion of GDP in Germany and in the group of the most indebted countries (Greece, Ireland, Italy, Portugal and Spain). All these countries have experienced, to different extents over time, a trade deficit leading in aggregate to diverging and persistent current account imbalances within the Eurozone; although the crisis has contributed to containing these differences in the last year, the latter effect is likely to be temporary, with the structural imbalances due to persist in the forthcoming periods.[3]

As far as the causes are concerned, the 'Hellenic' imbalances can be dealt with within the original framework of the Maastricht Treaty: it is mostly fiscal in nature, stemming from public accounts out of control (if not plainly manipulated). It involves to a certain extent an inadequate preventive action by the EU institutions, and it has been exacerbated by the lack of a clear-cut institutional roadmap for crisis management. Hence, it is quite straightforward that the Greek crisis has generated, as we have seen, a call for a revision of the fiscal surveillance mechanism and the SGP, as well as the set-up of a crisis management strategy dealing with the possible default, or debt restructuring, of one of the EMU countries (an event completely ruled out under the original Maastricht design).

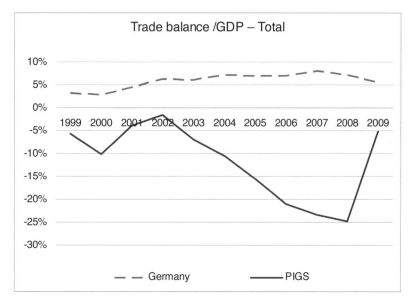

Source: Altomonte and Marzinotto (2010).

Figure 6.1 Trade in balances in EMU, 1999–2009

Quite more worrisome, however, are the 'Iberic' imbalances, as the root of the Spanish crisis cannot be found in the fiscal field: the most perfect implementation of the current or future rules on the SGP would have not prevented troubles from arising in Spain (Marzinotto *et al.* 2010). More generally, the current account deficits (and thus the ensuing imbalances) of Greece and Portugal can be re-conducted to negative public savings (that is public deficits), but the trade deficits of countries such as Spain and, to some extent, Ireland have certainly less to do with public finances and more with other economic distortions. These are related to decreasing real exchange rate competitiveness, coupled with a credit boom and a housing bubble, which has inflated the debt of the private sector, especially of banks. These situations oblige the EU institutions to think out of the box of the Maastricht Treaty, calling for a different governance strategy specifically aimed at tackling these imbalances.

Data show in particular that over the last decade some positive results in terms of nominal convergence (in interest rates and, to some extent, in inflation rates) have been obtained, especially when taking into account the Eurozone as a whole. But the same does not hold true when the emphasis is placed on real convergence: in this case, a grim picture of diverging economic performances (in terms of price–wage trends, not compensated by adequate productivity rates) emerges. Consequently, competitiveness and growth rates have followed different paths inside the Eurozone, as shown in Figure 6.1: the stunning performance of Germany – its current account deficit in 2000 (€ 35.2bn) turned into an impressive surplus in 2008 (€ 165.4bn) – was contrasted with strong deficits and, ultimately, poor growth potentials in other Eurozone countries (for example Greece, Portugal and Spain) (Villafranca 2010).

A framework leading to the governance of these imbalances should thus entail a relatively high degree of flexibility and political judgment, as most of the critical situations at a national level cannot be mechanically associated to the outcome of one or another economic indicator. Specifically, while the preventive arm of the proposed Excessive Imbalance Procedure seems to be properly defined, once the already discussed caveat of avoiding a strict mechanical approach based only on quantitative indicators is taken into account, the implementation of the corrective arm remains problematic. In fact, provided that a clear set of measures can be identified, together with a viable roadmap, it remains to be seen whether the competence of the suggested action falls within the scope of the EU level of governance (for example in the case of a suggested reform of the wage formation mechanism); also, one has to assess whether corrections to the existing imbalances can be effectively implemented by the national governments in a defined time-span (for example in the case of a loss of competitiveness induced by a change in the global pattern of comparative advantages). Moreover, surplus and deficit countries should not be treated symmetrically.

In addition to the general idea that public and private debt have complemented each other and grown indefinitely thanks to systematic imbalances of current accounts, there is another source of instability: the complementarities between private and public debt contributions to systemic risk. Let us consider this issue from a micro perspective, first. When large quantities of high-risk instruments enter the portfolios of private and institutional investors, the demand for low-risk instruments to counterbalance total risk also increases. Typically low-risk instruments that serve counterbalancing purposes are public bonds. In this context one may expect that the demand for safe public debt instruments goes up and, consequently, interest rates on those instruments remain low. At the same time, one would expect that the demand is also quite sensitive to small changes in the relative risk of alternative safe instruments, due to high substitutability. For example, the presence of high-risk instruments in German banks' portfolios has boosted German banks' demand for public bonds (for example Greek bonds), to counterbalance excess risk. As soon as risk on Greek bonds increases even by a small amount, German banks dismiss them massively. This large excess supply of risky bonds generates additional systemic risk which feeds back additional demand for safe bonds. The consequence is a sudden dramatic increase in yield spreads. Projecting this at the macro level, one can say that the presence of high systemic risk makes yields on public debt more sensitive to changes in any country's indicator of financial stability, such as public deficit or perspective growth rates.

All these arguments, thus, should be duly incorporated in the proposals for reforms currently under consideration.

2. GROWTH, POLITICAL ECONOMY AND THE FINANCIAL CRISIS

As pointed out earlier, assessing the 'Iberic' imbalances is possibly more complex than facing the Greek ones, as the former requires actions aimed at fostering growth and productivity convergence in the EU. We argue here that the 'growth side' of the cure entails a rethinking of the policy instruments that ensure stability, and a radical rebalancing of the distribution of powers within the euro area, with possibly a stronger role for central authorities.

In the medium term a likely scenario, not only for the euro area but for most Western governments, is a consistent rise in public debt–income ratios. In this context stability will be ensured by the ability to promote growth, rather than the ability to keep the deficit at very low level. In a sense, the 'G-rowth' aspects of the S-G-P will become of paramount importance in the future.

Looking at the Greek vs. the Iberic imbalances reveals an asymmetry in the working of the SGP. The Greek crisis requires strict enforcement of simple rules. In the short run markets need strong and unequivocal signals of recovered financial stability. First, strict enforcement prevents national governments from cheating and opportunism. Second, simple and unambiguous quantitative rules have an immediate positive impact on the stabilization chances. The market's response is fast and large in this case. However, in the mid run perspective simple and strict limits do not necessarily represent the best strategy. The Iberic case reveals that one-dimensional criteria are not sufficient to shelter national public finances, as stabilization patterns require a positive, and possibly non-negligible, difference between the GDP growth rate and the interest rate. Thus, the three stabilization variables are primary deficit, interest rate and growth rate. There are important relations among these variables, which generate endogeneity in stabilization programmes. For example, reducing the deficit is a positive signal for the markets, which in this case will demand lower yields. The interest rate decreases, and stabilization becomes easier. Fewer resources are used for servicing the debt. Thus in the long run more resources will be available for private investments, with positive effects on growth. Somehow, this example shows that the chain might be unidirectional, and the policy intervention can be uni-dimensional: if deficit is reduced, the other two variables will move in the right direction. This 'virtuous relationship' is the ground for the casual chain assumed by the SGP. The normative aspect of SGP is that in order to stabilize public finances it is sufficient to maintain a low deficit; then growth will complete the remaining part of the job, by consolidating the stabilization pattern. Reality, however, is different. Abstracting away from the recession phase, since the creation of the EMU we have only experienced a long period in which huge efforts to stabilize public debts in several member countries have been accompanied by very low growth rates. Thus the uni-dimensional approach to stabilization and growth is possibly too narrow, if not wrong. In fact, the story might run in a different 'vicious' way: restrictive fiscal policies reduce growth prospects; stabilization becomes more difficult; and the market asks for higher interest rates, which may offset stabilization efforts.

Drastic fiscal measures are useful in the short run to prevent the government budget from collapsing. As in the Greek case, they ensure a rapid and possibly one-shot improvement in the stabilization process, should the situation be extremely serious. After that initial positive shock the market expects that the government implements specific growth polices to consolidate stabilization. Only if growth prospects are good does the process become credible and interest rates may be lowered. In other words, the endogenous 'virtuous' relation between low deficit and low interest rate is non-existent if no significant growth is expected. This is what we call Iberic, and eventually Italian, disease. In this case the alternative approach is multi-dimensional: smart fiscal discipline plus a set of measures to promote growth.

Stability rules must generate incentives for national governments to use the fiscal policy to promote growth, rather than simply staying below quantitative thresholds. Growth policies can be costless, as in the case of market reforms, or in the case of improved public spending. Thus governments should be supported by the European authorities and by the partners in the implementation of those policies. In other cases, growth implies spending, as for investments in research, infrastructures or education. Then growth and deficit may go in the same direction. Only the market can say, in this case, if there is a trade-off or not in the stabilization prospect. The signals are usually clear. The market welcomes fiscal expansions that generate stable growth by lowering the interest rate. Again, a simple textbook analysis can say whether prospects improve or not after fiscal expansions: if the growth rate rises above the real interest rate, and the latter remains stable below, then public debt converges towards a stable level. After a drastic fiscal contraction rate the interest usually decreases. However the chance that it remains low depends on the growth prospects. Thus, the game that a government can play with the market is the following: the government makes a credible growth policy, with possible moderate deficit increase; as a result growth rate increases; then the market reacts by possible interest decrease.

In synthesis, the cure of different diseases must be different. If the disease is irrational public spending, as in the Greek case, then the cure is a drastic deficit reduction. A smooth deficit reduction policy is the cure also when the fiscal expansion is temporarily due to a recession, provided that growth prospects have not been compromised. However, if the disease is lack of growth that is expected for prolonged periods, then fiscal contractions are useless and potentially harmful. In this case the cure must be a credible growth policy.

Growth policies are multidimensional. The deficit–GDP ratio does not give a precise idea of the growth change that is expected in the medium term. It is a too synthetic measure. Fiscal reductions are just an emergency signal to the markets when there is a risk of speculative attacks to public bonds. In emergency cases 'linear' reductions of spending are a strong and effective signal. However, in the medium term the signal should be rather a set, or a package, of fiscal policies with a clear impact on growth. The package is not necessarily unique. A given increase in growth may be determined by alternative package policies. Eventually the choice of alternative packages will have internal distributional consequences. Thus the internal political compromise on growth measures is possibly an issue of bargaining among winners and losers.

Realistically, the Commission may act to facilitate the internal compromise within the euro area. When alternative policy packages are under discussion, it may suggest the ones with better growth prospects. Thus the internal bargaining is restricted to a smaller set of alternatives. Arguably, in these cases the government's role in reaching a compromise is facilitated. The idea here is that the Commission has the ability to interact with governments on the selection of a good growth strategy. This is not the case with the current SGP. In the current situation the governments are rather asked to keep deficit under strict quantitative thresholds. The internal 'political outcome' is clear: everybody must make sacrifices. In these cases likely policies consist of just linear cuts, as many governments have been doing recently. Given the current SGP, this linear-cutting attitude has a political-economy rationale, but it may seriously jeopardize growth prospects. In synthesis, the strict implementation of quantitative fiscal measures may be, and in our opinion is, responsible for the lack of growth in many countries of the euro area. The paradox is that in this situation stabilization becomes a quite difficult task. Moreover, in the absence of growth, stabilization is very sensitive to short-run shocks. The crisis has shown that, after the negative impact of stimulus packages, public finances will improve only in countries that display stable patterns of substantial growth. The others will lag behind and their stabilization processes will be extremely difficult.

A final politico-economic issue concerns the potential contrast between, say, the internal and the external conflict eventually caused by stabilization measures. Consider a member of the euro area. Citizens' needs in that country do not necessarily coincide with the partners' needs. The latter, due to an externality issue, are interested in financial stability. The former are interested in making low sacrifices. In the current case of SGP, stabilization is implemented through strict quantitative measures required to the government. In a sense, the partners' expected needs are preserved, but the citizens' need may not be. In this situation, the conflict may be sharp. The government may have serious difficulties in balancing the internal consensus with the partners' expectations. In other words, strict stability measures may be politically destabilizing and cause huge political cost. If instead stabilization is promoted though growth policies, the conflict is less severe. On the one hand, growth generates resources for compensating the citizens who lose; on the other hand, the stabilization achieved by growth is a common good that benefits the partners. There is less conflict, internally and externally. Eventual political costs are lower, as well as governments' attitudes to bear them.

Summing up, growth is the common good that the EU members should contribute to generate, and it represents the only definitive cure for the current illnesses. Growth-based stability is possibly more difficult to be framed in a normative perspective. But is it may be easier to implement in a political perspective, since growth may smooth conflicts down. Growth packages require a more active involvement and a technical soundness by European institutions. With this respect, a specialized DG or task-force of the Commission that specifically deals with growth issues and interacts with the members' governments might represent a valuable institutional device.

3. HOW TO RECONCILE GROWTH AND STABILITY

Summing up, we have thus seen how growth-based stability is not an obvious feature of a policy framework, as in pursuing the two objectives, more often than not, a trade-off can be generated between short-run goals on stability and long-run ones aiming at growth. There is nevertheless a third area of policy intervention with potentially significant effects on both the short- and the long-term growth rate that could be pursued. The latter stems from the consideration that the cyclical reaction to the crisis of firms and consumers, and the ensuing policy response, might indeed interact with structural features of the economy (essentially the functioning of labour and capital markets) in ways not necessarily conducive to a sustainable growth path (see also Chapter 7). For example, some of the countercyclical responses emerging during the crisis (for example labour hoarding) might actually hamper the recovery if, in some countries, these interact with a peculiar structural rigidity of labour or capital markets.

If that is the case, as we try to argue in this chapter, policymakers should devote attention to the fact that some of these countercyclical responses should be progressively modified if growth is to be revamped. Or, if the policy response is meant to be maintained given the new post-crisis context (for example preserving jobs), other short-term structural changes in the functioning of the product and factor markets might be needed in order to guarantee the consistency of the new policy measure with a scenario conducive to growth.

Of course, to the extent that these interactions are heterogeneous across countries, and we will show this is the case, the same policy responses will have to be tailored to specific country-specific needs, ideally within the new 'National Reform Programmes' to be implemented and reviewed within the broad 'Europe 2020' agenda of reforms.

To start grasping the problem at hands, Figure 6.2 decomposes average growth rates for a number of EU countries, the US and Japan in terms of labour productivity, measured as output per hour worked, and employment (the sum of the coordinates yields the average growth rate of the country in question). We distinguish between the average 2000–2007 growth rates on the one hand and the crisis years of 2008 and 2009 on the other, thus indicating the extent to which productivity and employment have been adjusting in Europe compared to US and Japan throughout the crisis.

As can be seen, the cyclical EU response to the crisis, on average, seems to rely more on a contraction of productivity rather than employment, with firms essentially hoarding jobs, contrary to the US case. The latter path of adjustment is by and large similar for all the major EU economies (Germany, France, UK and Italy), with the only exception being the case of Spain, in which the adjustment to the crisis seems to have operated mainly via the shedding of fixed-term, low productive jobs (especially in construction), with the result that employment has fallen much more than productivity in the short run.

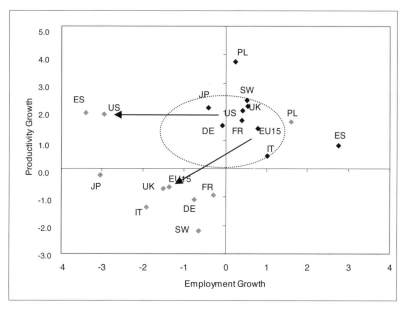

Notes:
◆ 2000–2007
◆ 2008–2009

Source: OECD Productivity Database. Productivity is measured as GDP per hour worked.
Employment is measured as total hours worked.

Figure 6.2 Productivity and employment growth rates in selected countries

The overall picture for 2010 is of course different given the economic
recovery. Data (from the Conference Board) for some EU member states
and the US point to a general pro-cyclical recovery of productivity growth
across all countries, with working hours on average stalling or still growing
negative (Spain). An exception is Germany, where both productivity (1 per
cent) and, most importantly, working hours (2.4 per cent) have accelerated.
Once again, however, productivity growth in the US (2.8 per cent) is at
least twice as fast as the average EU country, with Italy below average
(around 1 per cent) and Sweden above (3.2 per cent).

To provide a confirmation of these macro trends, we capitalize on a
recently available dataset built within the EFIGE (European Firms in a
Global Economy) project, a research project aimed at examining the
pattern of internationalization of European manufacturing firms. The
project mainly operates through a survey collected on representative
samples of firms in the main European countries;[4] in particular, we exploit

here the fact that, in undertaking the survey, firms were asked at the beginning of 2010 about their changes in performance in 2008 and 2009.

The preliminary results of the EFIGE project (Barba Navaretti *et al.*, 2010) show that, on average, some 43 per cent of EU firms have reduced employment during the crisis, and some 39 per cent have done the same in terms of planned investment (overall, the two figures are 0.3 correlated, with around 60 per cent of firms adjusting along both employment and investment across countries). However, while the average reduction of employment has been 16.5 per cent, planned investment has been more than halved (by 55.1 per cent).

The latter micro-based evidence is consistent with the macroeconomic picture: as a response to the crisis, investments have been postponed by firms in Europe while jobs have been relatively better preserved, somewhat contrary to the US experience. Member states have also contributed to such a policy response by supporting a variety of Government-sponsored compensation schemes (for example *kurzarbeit* in Germany, *chomage partiel* in France, *cassa integrazione straordinaria* in Italy, ...) fostering the preservation of employment within firms.

Another interesting facet to explore in this particular crisis is related to the behaviour of credit markets. Always exploiting some of the results of the EFIGE survey, we have analysed the extent to which firms in Europe have suffered from a credit crunch (that is additional credit lines were denied when asked for) and/or have experienced a worsening of the credit condition (that is existing credit lines have become more expensive).

The data shows that, on average, credit crunch phenomena have been certainly present but they have not been pervasive in Europe, with 21.6 per cent of firms having asked for more credit during 2008–2009 and having it denied (51.8 per cent of firms were successful in obtaining extra credit, and 26.6 per cent of them did not ask for more credit). Conversely, however, 45 per cent of firms, on average, have seen an increase in their existing credit cost, notwithstanding the large drop in inter-banking rates resulting from the expansionary monetary policy of the ECB.

More in general, going across the EFIGE results, it is also interesting to point out the substantial heterogeneity existing across member states. For example, a significantly smaller number of German firms have reduced employment and investment during the crisis (31.3 and 27.7 per cent of firms, respectively, vs. 42.8 and 39.2 at the EU average), while the contrary has happened for Spanish firms (consistently with the previously reported macroeconomic evidence); along similar lines, only 2.3 per cent of firms have experienced a credit crunch in the UK market, compared to 30.5 per cent of Italian firms, while credit costs have increased for 68.7 per cent of Hungarian firms and only 30.2 per cent of French ones.

All the latter thus points to the fact that the short-term responses to the crisis might have interacted differently across member states with structural features of the EU labour and capital markets, in ways not necessarily conducive for growth.

4. CYCLICAL VS. STRUCTURAL LABOUR AND CAPITAL MARKETS FUNCTIONING IN EUROPE

Starting from the analysis of labour markets, it is possible to explore some of their structural features across member states through an appropriate micro-based decomposition of aggregate productivity changes.[5]

In particular we report the result of the decomposition for four European countries: France, considered as an example of a country with 'continental' labour market institutions;[6] Italy, as a prototype of a Mediterranean country; the UK for the Anglo-Saxon model and Sweden as an example of the Nordic institutions. The period covered by the data is 2000–2008. For each country the average growth of productivity over the entire period has been decomposed into four components:

- the *within-firm effect* is the change attributable to the productivity within a firm given its initial market share: a positive sign implies that firms, controlling for their size, are growing more productive over time;
- the *between-firms effect* accounts for the switch of market shares between firms, keeping the productivity constant, that is it captures the gains in aggregate productivity coming from the expanding market of high productivity firms, or from low-productivity firms' shrinking shares;
- the *cross term* gives information about the underlying market adjustment in size and productivity: a positive sign would indicate that market shares and productivity are changing in the same direction, that is firms able to increase (decrease) their productivity are also able to grow larger (smaller) in size–employment, with positive effects for overall growth; a negative sign would show that productivity and market shares are moving in different directions, that is firms whose productivity is decreasing are growing larger and vice versa, with negative effects for underlying productivity growth.
- the *net entry effect* indicates the extent to which the market is able to select firms in accordance with their competitiveness, that is whether firms less productive than a given threshold are forced to exit the market, while relatively productive firms are able to enter.

Figure 6.3 presents each element of the firm-level decomposition for the four considered countries, together with the total resulting productivity growth rate resulting from the sample, compared with the official growth rate computed from the Organisation for Economic Co-operation and Development (OECD) data and used here for validation.[7]

Looking at Figure 6.3 for France and Italy, it is indeed possible to appreciate the potentially contrasting effects on total productivity growth driven by the 'within' effect and the reallocation dimension (between and cross terms). While in both countries the 'within-firm' dimension is positive, that is firms are able to internally grow in productivity, the between and the cross dimensions are very small or negative, thus signalling the fact that relatively rigid labour markets in both countries are such that firms more productive than average find it difficult to grow larger over time in terms of employees, with workers not necessarily moving towards the most productive firms.

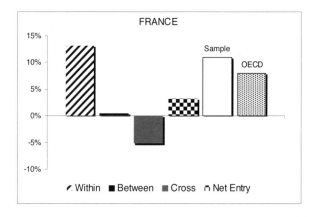

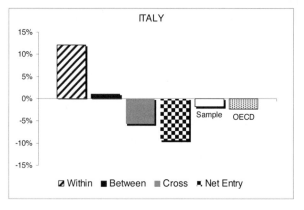

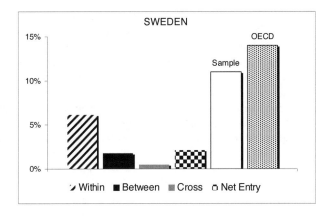

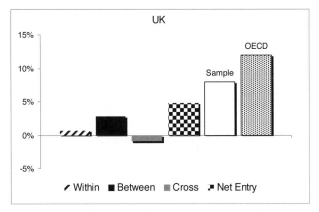

Source: Altomonte (2010). Units on vertical axes are total percentage changes in productivity.

Figure 6.3 Productivity decomposition in different EU countries, 2000–2008

The situation is instead different in the UK and Sweden, where the between- and cross-terms effects combined are positive and larger than in France and Italy, thus indicating that in these two countries' flexible labour markets seems to have allowed incumbent firms to grow in size, with workers allocated along firms' productivity.[8]

In terms of robustness of these results, we have decomposed productivity for firms belonging to the manufacturing vs. services industries (not reported here), obtaining very similar results across our countries. Also, we do not find a significant change in the productivity decomposition for 2008 with respect to previous years, which is not surprising given the 'structural' nature of the exercise. Interestingly, comparing our results with those obtained by Bartelsman *et al.* (2004) for France and the UK (in their analysis they decompose, among other countries, labour productivity for France during 1990–1995 and for the UK during 2000–2001, for the manufacturing sector) the distinctive features of the within, between and cross terms across the two countries they are able to obtain are qualitatively very similar to ours.

Therefore, given on the one hand the structural effects on aggregate productivity of the EU labour markets' functioning and, on the other hand, the cyclical response to the crisis in which jobs have been 'hoarded' within firms, it is clear that a potential short-run obstacle to higher growth rates might derive from a perverse interaction between these two elements. In fact, if part of the workforce remains hoarded in firms which have lost productivity during the crisis, countries with a relatively rigid labour markets (that is where the between and cross terms are smaller) will experience a limited post-crisis restructuring, with low-productive firms behaving as 'zombie' companies with subsidized jobs and high-productive firms constrained in their ability to grow: the consequences on the overall growth rate are obvious.

To prevent this scenario, an ideal set-up would be one in which labour-hoarding policies keep workers active in the 'right' firms, while the functioning of labour markets foster a reallocation of workers towards the firms that have become more productive after the crisis. Such a policy can be summarized in the idea that existing compensation schemes should be reformed in order to allow individual wages to track more closely a firm's productivity. As the latter is a country-specific competence, it is therefore important that, when discussing economic reforms within the 'Europe 2020' framework, an adequate implementation of these labour market policies could be ensured at the national level, where necessary (incidentally, both Italy and France have a relatively centralized wage compensation mechanism).

A second key policy area in which the interaction between cyclical and structural features of the EU economy matters in affecting the EU growth strategy is the functioning of capital markets. We have already discussed micro-economic evidence pointing to the fact that firms have experienced an increase in their cost of credit during the crisis. But has this increase been in line with firms' productivity?

In other words, it is important to assess whether the adjustment of financial markets to the crisis, if anything, will be conducive to productivity growth, that is whether the cost of credit is going to increase relatively less for the more productive firms. If that is the case, the crisis would set in motion a Schumpeterian selection effect, in which the less productive firms would find it increasingly difficult to access capital and therefore exit, with potential benefits for the aggregate productivity. By the same token, a policy seeking to promote corporate access to capital in this context would also result in an efficient (with respect to productivity and growth) allocation of capital across firms.

Conversely, if the functioning of capital markets is such that access to capital is eased for all firms across the board, irrespectively of their productivity levels, or, worse still, if the relatively less productive (but better connected) firms end up having relatively better access to finance during and after the crisis, then the effect of the reallocation of capital induced by the crisis (and/or a specific policy in this context) would harm aggregate productivity, as the most competitive firms would be constrained in their growth.

To provide some micro-based evidence on the issue, we have proceeded in two steps. First, starting from the same firm-level balance sheet data, we have calculated for the four countries considered an average 'index of financial pressure'[9] for the period 2000–2007, relating it to the individual firms' ranking in productivity; moreover, we have decomposed the index for small (less than 20 employees), medium and large firms, in order to control for the effect of size in driving the access to finance.

As for the initial (pre-crisis) levels of financial pressure over the period 2000–2007, the situation is rather homogeneous across countries: less productive firms have the highest financial pressure indexes (between 0.6 and 0.8 in the four countries analysed), with the index then decreasing in a linear fashion as firms become more productive (the index is around 0.3 for the top 80 per cent of the most productive firms). Similar dynamics are present when looking at small vs. large firms, with levels of financial pressure being, not surprisingly, slightly lower for the latter group. All in all, we therefore have 'prima facie' evidence of a positive pre-crisis situation, in which financial pressure and productivity are strongly (inversely) related.

However, the picture radically changes in 2008 (data for 2009 are not yet fully available). In the following Table 6.1 we report the change in the index of financial pressure between the average for 2000–2007 and 2008, once again differentiating it according to the firms' ranking in productivity and by firms' sizes. Not surprisingly, the indexes broadly rise across countries, as in a recession profits typically decline and interest spreads increase. However, of more concern is that in some countries the correlation between financial pressure and productivity is somewhat lost.

France is an example of a 'good' country: the average financial pressure in 2008 in France has clearly increased for the first quintile of the least productive firms (by some 8 per cent for medium to large firms and 5 per cent for small ones). However financial pressure changes get smaller as productivity increases, as it should, with the top 20 per cent of the most productive firms seeing virtually no change (if not a decrease) in their financial pressure in 2008 with respect to the 2000–2007 average.

Table 6.1 Change in financial pressure (2008 vs 2000–2007) according to firm productivity and size (%)

Productivity Rank	France		Italy		Sweden		UK	
	Small	Large	Small	Large	Small	Large	Small	Large
Bottom 20%	5.0	7.6	5.7	0.4	7.0	13.6	4.5	-1.7
20–40%	4.5	6.9	6.3	13.0	4.1	-8.9	4.9	-3.6
40–60%	3.3	1.5	5.5	11.7	1.0	-1.0	2.0	-1.8
60–80%	1.3	0.4	3.8	4.8	-0.6	-1.5	4.5	-1.4
Top 80%	-0.2	-1.9	1.5	2.0	-1.1	-0.4	5.5	-2.3

Source: Altomonte (2010). Small firms are firms with <20 employees. The averages are calculated using the quintiles of the (year-specific) labour productivity distribution.

The situation is instead different in Italy, where we find that the linear relationship between financial pressure and productivity (present before 2007) becomes blurred. In particular, the least efficient medium-to-large Italian firms see virtually no increase in their financial pressure in 2008, mirroring the situation of the most efficient firms. Equally, the least efficient small firms have an increase in financial pressure comparable (6 per cent) to that experienced by firms in higher quintiles of the productivity distribution, with only very productive small firms (from the fourth quintile upwards) being able to benefit from a relatively smaller increase in financing cost.

In Sweden and the UK financial pressure has increased for small firms but decreased for large ones, once again not necessarily in line with their productivity.

We thus have a situation in which the underlying function of credit allocation by financial markets might have changed in some countries during the crisis, in ways not necessarily correlated with the productivity of the firms receiving credit. If the latter situation persists, and is combined with the already discussed figure of 45 per cent of firms experiencing an increase in their cost of credit during the crisis, in some countries we might face a situation in which credit is not allocated along firms' productivity, with detrimental consequences for growth.

More in general, as noted by Rajan and Zingales (1998), in a financial crisis there is a clear link between a firm's performance and its reliance on external finance vs. internal cash flows, with the latter being a better set-up in a crisis context. The EFIGE Survey data also allows us to explore this issue, revealing that on average 44.5 per cent of European firms have resorted to external finances during the crisis, with, however, a very heterogeneous picture, with figures ranging from as low as 20 per cent for German firms to more than 60 per cent in the case of Italian and Spanish firms.

Also for credit markets we thus derive a picture in which the short-term response to the crisis risks altering to a certain extent the proper allocation of credit to firms in ways detrimental for productivity, with the effects being once again very heterogeneous across countries. The latter outcome clearly calls for renewed attention by policymakers, not only at the EU level but also (because of the emerging heterogeneity) at the national level, making sure that the implementation of the new banking regulation is able to ensure an allocation of credit and an access to finance which correlates with the underlying firms' productivity. Incidentally, such a feature of credit markets does not appear among the 'Europe 2020' targets, although it definitely should.

5. CONCLUSIONS

Europe is certainly going through testing times, and as a result much of the current policy debate tends to revolve around the short-term aspects of the recovery, related to the financial stability of the euro area. While the latter is of paramount importance for the future of the EU, much less emphasis is, however, devoted to an equally important discussion on growth-enhancing 'structural' reforms.

The risk of such an approach to the necessary enhanced governance of the euro area is that the resulting policy framework implicitly generates a trade-off between stability and growth-enhancing policies, with the former clearly dominating the latter. While the political dividend of such a setup might be relevant in the short run, over time the resulting institutional framework might impose a straightjacket on growth, with Europe being over the next decade possibly a very stable, but quite a marginal, player in the global arena.

To solve the latter conundrum, it is useful to recall a general rule of economic policy, stating that the number of instruments at hand has to be equal to the number of objectives we want to achieve. It then follows that, if stability and growth have to be jointly pursued, one should identify and use a set of tools able to exert effects on both the short- and the long-term phase of the cycle. Or, *mutatis mutandis*, one should complement policy actions envisaged as a short-term reaction to the crisis with regulatory changes in the structural features of the economy (essentially the functioning of labour and capital markets), in ways conducive to a sustainable growth path. Moreover, policymakers should also bear in mind that the relationship between growth-oriented and stability-oriented policy packages is a trade-off only in the short run, whereas in the medium and long run pursuing both objectives may give raise to potential complementarities: public debt stabilization, currently giving rise to political conflicts amongst countries, ultimately requires a sufficiently high growth rate. Growth represents a common good that benefits all, and thus effective growth policies contribute to smooth conflicts down.

We therefore recommend an integrated approach to the governance of the euro area, able to combine adequate attention to the macroeconomic imbalances with the fundamental quest for higher growth, along the possible lines of action suggested in this chapter. Of course, as long as these interactions among policy tools are heterogeneous across countries, and we have shown that this is the case, the same policy responses will have to be tailored to country-specific needs.

The European Commission has indeed already been working along those lines: in January 2011, on the occasion of the start of the first European Semester of *ex ante* policy co-ordination, the EC has put forward an Annual Growth Survey, identifying 10 priority initiatives aimed at bringing together the different actions which are essential to strengthen the recovery in the short term while preparing the EU to move towards its 'Europe 2020' objectives.[10] In line with the policy suggestions described in this chapter, the EC has identified three main areas for action: the need for rigorous fiscal consolidation for enhancing macroeconomic stability; labour market reforms; and growth-enhancing measures.

These actions, which put on parallel tracks the issue of stability and the issue of economic growth, should then be examined each year by the European Council, in order to provide the reference framework for reforms to which member states should abide by fine-tuning their individual 'National Reform Programmes' foreseen within the 'Europe 2020' agenda.

In principle, therefore, the fiscal governance of the post-crisis Eurozone has been put in place with a convincing approach, identifying the causes of the illnesses affecting the EU, and proposing adequate remedies for both types of 'disorders', that is macroeconomic imbalance and growth. Now, it is up to the sick men, the member states, to start the therapy while taking adequate care of their contingent conditions.

NOTES

1. See 'Proposal for a Council Regulation amending Regulation (EC) No. 1467/97 on speeding up and clarifying the implementation of the excessive deficit procedure', European Commission, COM(2010) 522, 29 September 2010.

2. See 'Proposal for a Regulation of the European Parliament and of the Council on the prevention and correction of macroeconomic imbalances', European Commission, COM (2010) 527, 29 September 2010.
3. As clarified by the European Commission (2010c), the recent convergence may be cyclical (due to the collapse in global demand in surplus countries and the substitution of imports in some deficit countries), with the pre-crisis divergence trend likely to resume once the recovery gains strength.
4. The EFIGE project is led by Bruegel, working together with seven other partners, and has received the support of the Directorate General Research of the European Commission through its Seventh Framework Programme (FP7). It is running from 2008 to 2012. The main tool of analysis of the project is the EU-Bruegel-Unicredit EFIGE survey, a dataset collecting detailed information on more than 150 firm-specific items for a representative sample of 15,000 firms in seven European countries. More information is available at www.efige.org.
5. To be consistent with the macroeconomic analysis generally employed in the policy debates and previously reported, in what follows we will consider individual firms' productivity as proxied by labour productivity (output per hour worked) rather than total factor productivity (the Solow's residual of the production function). At the aggregate level the two measures tend, however, to be quite correlated. A similar decomposition of aggregate productivity has been performed in 2004 on a relatively large sample of countries across the world by Bartelsman, Haltiwanger and Scarpetta (2004). More references, as well as a description of the methodology and a validation of the data, are provided in Altomonte (2010).
6. The representativeness of the available German sample was lower than the French one, and thus we have used the latter country as a model of 'continental Europe'.
7. Official figures are the growth rate between 2000 and 2008 of labour productivity per person employed (for the whole economy) as retrieved from the OECD Productivity database.
8. Results on the net entry effect should be viewed with some caution due to the imperfect measurement of entry and exit from balance sheet data, as at times the observed (that is in the data) entry–exit of firms does not coincide with the actual economic one. For these reasons they are not discussed here.
9. The index of financial pressure is calculated for every firm year following Nickel and Nicolitsas (1999) as Interest Payments – (Profit before Tax + Depreciation + Interest Payments). The ratio is bounded between 0 and 1, with higher values indicating a higher financial pressure. The ratio is set to 1 if profits are negative.
10. See *Annual Growth Survey: Advancing the EU's comprehensive response to the crisis*, European Commission, COM (2011) 11, 12 January 2011.

BIBLIOGRAPHY

Altomonte, Carlo (2010), 'Micro-founding Europe 2020: Firm-level evidence in four European economies', XXII Villa Mondragone International Economic Seminar, Roma, June.

Altomonte, Carlo and Benedicta Marzinotto (2010), *Monitoring Macroeconomic Imbalances in Europe: Proposal for a Refined Analytical Framework*, Note for the Directorate General for Internal Policies, European Parliament, 8 September.

Barba Navaretti, Giorgio, Matteo Bugamelli, Gianmarco Ottaviano and Fabiano Schivardi (2010), *The Global Operations of European Firms*, Second EFIGE Policy Report, www.efige.org.

Bartelsman, Eric J., John Haltiwanger and Stefano Scarpetta (2004), *Microeconomic Evidence of Creative Destruction in Industrial and Developing Countries*, Tinbergen Institute Discussion Papers No. 04-114/3.

European Commission (2010a), 'EUROPE 2020: A Strategy for Smart, Sustainable and Inclusive Growth', COM(2010) 2020, Brussels.

European Commission (2010b), 'Enhancing Economic Policy Coordination for Stability, Growth and Jobs – Tools for Stronger EU Economic Governance', COM (2010) 367/2, Brussels.

European Commission (2010c), 'Surveillance of Intra-Euro-Area Competitiveness and Imbalances', EU Economy No. 1/2010, Brussels.

Marzinotto, Benedicta, Jean Pisani-Ferry and André Sapir (2010), *Two Crises, Two Responses*, Bruegel Policy Brief, March.

Nickell, Stephen and Daphne Nicolitsas (1999), 'How does financial pressure affect firms?', *European Economic Review*, **43**(8), 1435–56.

Rajan, Raghuram and Luigi Zingales (1998), 'Financial dependence and growth', *American Economic Review*, **88**(3), 559–86.

Villafranca, Antonio (2010), *Piggybacking Pigs. The Future of Euroland After the Greek Crisis*, ISPI Policy Brief No. 179, March.

7. Overcoming Europe's Long Term Growth Crisis

Fabian Zuleeg

Europe's economies have gone through a period of unprecedented crisis: a financial crisis which quickly turned into an economic one, followed by a public finance and Eurozone crisis. And Europe is not clear of crisis yet with continuing unease in the financial markets about European sovereign debt in the weakest performing economies.

Much has been done at the European level to counteract the crisis, from the European Economic Recovery Plan (European Commission 2008) to the rescue plan for the Greek economy and the subsequent umbrella fund which was called upon to support Ireland towards the end of 2010. Alongside short term crisis measures, the strategic direction of policies was reoriented to combat the impacts of the crises, including most notably the 'Europe 2020' strategy and the EU Budget Review which make exiting the crisis a primary priority.

Most of Europe is now on the tentative road to recovery, but in addition to short term impacts it looks increasingly likely that the crisis will result in long term impacts. Europe is thus facing a far greater crisis in the coming years: the prospect of continuously low growth, in part caused by the structural changes which resulted from the crisis in part caused by the long term challenges Europe faces, including increasing resource prices, ageing of its population, global competition and the need to finance climate change adaptation and mitigation. This growth crisis will have far reaching impacts – on Europe's position in the world, its economic and social models, on public debt and the future of the Eurozone.

This contribution analyses the growth challenge the EU faces and how European policy has put increasing emphasis on growth (and jobs) in recent years. It then examines what Europe can do to overcome the growth crisis, focusing in particular on how to generate the investments which are needed to put Europe on a path to higher growth potential.

1. AIMING FOR GROWTH

The European Union has always been concerned with the economic development of its member states with a particular emphasis on the poorer regions and countries. In this, Europe has always emphasised the need to pursue sustainable development, that is growth which does not hurt social and environmental objectives. This focus is enshrined in the objectives noted in the Treaty on European Union, which states that the EU aims to achieve 'the sustainable development of Europe based on balanced economic growth and price stability, a highly competitive social market economy, aiming at full employment and social progress, and a high level of protection and improvement of the quality of the environment'.

A strong focus on growth at the European level has been especially prominent in the last decade. The Lisbon Strategy set out the goal for the first decade of the millennium, for the EU 'to become the most competitive and dynamic knowledge-based economy in the world, capable of sustainable economic growth with more and better jobs and greater social cohesion'.[1] In the revised Lisbon Agenda, the focus is even clearer with the main aims summarised as 'growth and jobs': 'The Commission proposes a new start for the Lisbon Strategy, focusing our efforts around two principal tasks – delivering stronger, lasting growth and creating more and better jobs'. It also emphasises that growth is central to achieving wider objectives: 'renewed growth is vital to prosperity, can bring back full employment and is the foundation of social justice and opportunity for all. It is also vital to Europe's position in the world and Europe's ability to mobilise the resources that tackle many global different challenges' (European Commission 2005).

The emphasis on growth (in the context of sustainable development) has continued into the current decade, reinforced by the economic crisis. In his political vision for the Barroso II Commission, the Commission President identifies growth, jobs and the transformation to a sustainable economy as three of the five fundamental challenges the EU faces. His objective is 'Restarting economic growth today and ensuring long-term sustainability and competitiveness for the future' (Barroso 2009).

Europe's new growth strategy, 'Europe 2020', which was completed in 2010 makes 'smart, sustainable and inclusive growth' its overarching objectives. It stipulates that Europe needs 'a strategy to help us come out stronger from the crisis and turn the EU into a smart, sustainable and inclusive economy delivering high levels of employment, productivity and social cohesion'. 'Europe 2020' notes that growth is under threat: 'the crisis has wiped out years of economic and social progress and exposed structural weaknesses in Europe's economy. In the meantime, the world is moving fast and long-term challenges – globalisation, pressure on resources, ageing – intensify' (European Commission 2010c).

The same focus on economic growth and the crisis is noticeable in the EU Budget Review (European Commission 2010e). It clearly focuses the EU budget on achieving the aims of the 'Europe 2020' strategy: 'above all, it should be designed as one of the most important instruments to help deliver the 'Europe 2020' strategy for smart, sustainable and inclusive growth'. It notes that 'growth for jobs is our overarching priority, concentrating on getting more people in jobs, boosting our companies' competitiveness and building an open and modern single market'.

2. THE LONG TERM GROWTH CRISIS

But despite the sustained focus on growth, the European position is far from enviable. Even before the crisis, growth rates in many parts of Europe were already relatively low. In part, low growth rates reflect the maturity of many European economies where high growth is unlikely as there is less of a catching up effect. But the EU also contains many economies at a lower level of development where the expectation must be for a faster growth rate. When separating out the performance of the 'catching-up' economies, the low growth problem is even more apparent: 'since the mid-1990s the growth performance of the euro area as a whole, despite some good individual country performances, has failed to keep pace with developments elsewhere in the EU (including the UK) and also in the US. This is especially the case for a number of the larger euro area economies' (McMorrow and Röger 2007).

In part this is due to cyclical factors and one-off events, such as for example the post-unification boom, followed by a slump in Germany. But long term structural factors are also at work. As recognised by the Commission in the 'Europe 2020' strategy, the current difficult economic position of the EU is not due to the crisis alone. The EU faces a number of long term challenges which are impacting on its economic performance, in particular globalisation, resource scarcity, climate change and population ageing.

2.1 Globalisation

Globalisation was the driving force behind the Lisbon Agenda, with a particular fear that Europe was falling behind its main competitors in terms of productivity and competitiveness, focusing especially on Europe's position in relation to the US. Concerns regarding global competition were coupled with the relatively slow transformation of the European economy towards emerging new economic models, in particular the knowledge economy. As the Lisbon Agenda put it, Europe needed to adapt to the 'quantum shift resulting from globalisation and the challenges of a new knowledge-driven economy'.

Since the Lisbon Agenda was put in place, there have been many new developments, not least the stunning rise of the emerging economies as global economic powers, spearheaded by China. This rise has culminated in the seismic shift of economic power which became apparent during the economic crisis with the emerging economies recovering faster and becoming the motors of the global recovery. At the same time, the shift to the knowledge economy has accelerated with large global firms emerging from the internet economy. Technological progress is now inextricably linked with globalisation, fuelling the pace of development, further integrating the global economy and creating new challenges and opportunities.

These developments have made a European response to globalisation even more important. For highly developed economies, creating value in an environment of global competition must involve focusing on economic activities with a high value added, in particular knowledge-based activities. At the same time, many more basic jobs can be outsourced to emerging economies, resulting in a difficult transformation process. The implications of globalisation are profound for Europe's economies: not all are ready to take full part in a global knowledge economy.

2.2 Resource Scarcity

The global challenge for the EU is also clearly apparent in the area of resource scarcity, be it in energy, commodities or food. As global demand increases, prices are also increasing, most notably spiking in 2008 and starting to rise again in 2010–2011 after the economic crisis had dampened down demand. 'Commodities are partying like it is 2008. The oil price stands at its highest since October of that year, just shy of $100 per barrel. World food prices – as measured by The Economist's index – are back at their peak of July 2008' (*The Economist* 2011).

As input prices rise and scarcity of certain materials becomes apparent, there is a clear impact on economic growth, employment creation and inflation, with extreme examples provided by the oil crises in the 1970s which resulted in stagflation – low growth and high inflation simultaneously. The negative impacts are felt directly by the population, making everyday shopping, heating and driving less affordable.

Scarcity of resources is also becoming increasingly apparent in a new area: the global war for talent. Individuals who have a high potential to add significantly to a country's GDP such as top-level scientists, entrepreneurs or those possessing scarce skills can choose location on a global labour market. This hunt for soft, scarce and super skills (Collett and Zuleeg 2008) is going to increase in future. In addition, the availability of skilled and motivated human resources is one of the key drivers for innovation. Given the importance of innovation for the knowledge economy, being able to attract and retain talent is becoming a major factor in global competitiveness.

2.3 Climate Change

Another global development which is impacting strongly on the EU is the issue of climate change. There is a – in Europe, relatively small – direct impact of climate change on economic growth with a much larger impact coming from the policies which are being designed to address climate change mitigation (for a deeper analysis, see Chapter 8).

The direct impact of climate change on Europe is far less than it is in many other areas of the world, where the impact is often strongest where the least capability exists to adapt. Nevertheless extreme climate events and changing climate patterns are already having implications for Europe. In addition to potentially severe impacts on human health, extreme heat waves or extreme winters can also result in energy shortages and a dampening of economic activity as well as impacting on economic infrastructure such as roads and rail and reducing the viability of parts of industries, for example in tourism or agriculture. In many cases, there is the possibility to take adaptive measures to reduce the costs[2] but these impacts and the costs of adaptive measures will dampen growth.

Mitigating for climate change will have a similar effect but it is likely to be even more significant if the transformation to a virtually carbon free economy is the ultimate aim. Given the costs required to reduce CO_2 emissions of households, industry and transport, this will have a growth dampening effect. While in the long term the transformation is likely to also increase economic opportunities (for example through the creation of 'green' jobs and trade of green goods and services), in the short to medium term there will be significant transition costs.

2.4 Population Ageing

While the factors listed above are global factors, with EU member states only having limited ability to influence these processes, population ageing is an issue which is very much anchored in European societies. The combination of increased life expectancy with lower fertility, only partially mitigated by migration, is leading to a significant ageing of Europe's populations. The proportion of the elderly population as a percentage of total population within EU-27 (European Commission 2009b) is set to rise from 17.4 per cent in 2010 to 20.1 per cent in 2020. By 2035 more than one quarter of the population is set to be over 65, reaching 30 per cent in 2060. In Germany, it will already be over 30 per cent in 2035, with Italy reaching this level in 2040. But despite differences in population trends, the overall ageing of the population is affecting all of Europe.

The ageing population will impose significant costs on Europe, as shown in the following table which shows estimated age-related government expenditure from 2007–2060 (increases shown in percentage points of GDP):

Table 7.1 Age-related government expenditure (2007–2060)

	Level 2007	Change 2007–2035	Change 2007–2060
Belgium (BE)	26.5	5.6	6.9
Bulgaria (BG)	16.6	0.8	3.7
Rep. Czech. (CZ)	17.9	0.9	5.5
Denmark (DK)	24.8	3.6	2.6
Germany (DE)	23.6	2.6	4.8
Estonia (EE)	14.3	0.1	0.4
Ireland (EI)	17.2	3.7	8.9
Greece (EL)	22.1	9.1	15.9
Spain (ES)	19.3	4.3	9.0
France (FR)	28.4	2.7	2.7
Italy (IT)	26.0	2.0	1.6
Cyprus (CY)	15.4	4.5	10.8
Latvia (LV)	13.2	0.6	0.4
Lithuania (LT)	15.8	1.8	5.4
Luxembourg (LU)	20.0	9.1	18.0
Hungary (HU)	21.6	0.7	4.1
Malta (MT)	18.2	4.4	10.2
Netherlands (NL)	20.5	6.9	9.4
Austria (AT)	26.0	2.3	3.1
Poland (PL)	20.5	-2.7	-2.4
Portugal (PT)	24.5	1.1	3.4
Romania (RO)	13.1	5.0	10.1
Slovenia (SL)	22.9	6.9	12.8
Slovakia (SK)	15.2	1.6	5.2
Finland (FI)	24.2	6.1	6.3
Sweden (SE)	27.2	1.5	2.6
United Kingdom (UK)	18.9	2.7	5.1
EU-27	23.1	2.7	4.7
EU-15	23.5	3.0	4.8
EU-12	18.3	0.4	3.4

Source: European Commission (2009b).

Table 7.1 shows that in EU-27, age-related costs will rise from currently 23.1 per cent of GDP to 25.8 per cent in 2035 and 27.8 per cent in 2060.

In addition to these direct costs, there will also a wider impact on growth. Population growth is one of the components of economic growth[3] so the impact of low population growth is felt directly. But there is also a potential lack of economic dynamism associated with population ageing, especially if labour market participation of older age groups is low.

Table 7.2 Potential annual GDP rates as a result of demographic change

	Avg	2007	2010	2015	2020	2025	2030	2035	2040	2045	2050	2055	2060
BE	1.8	2.5	2.5	2.3	1.9	1.6	1.6	1.7	1.8	1.7	1.7	1.7	1.7
BG	1.9	6.4	4.0	3.0	2.4	2.0	1.7	1.5	1.4	0.7	0.3	0.7	0.8
CZ	1.8	5.2	4.2	3.0	2.5	1.6	1.4	1.1	0.9	0.9	0.7	0.9	1.1
DK	1.7	2.3	1.7	1.7	1.6	1.8	1.5	1.6	1.7	1.9	1.9	1.7	1.6
DE	1.2	1.4	1.9	1.9	1.5	0.9	1.3	1.1	1.1	1.2	1.0	1.0	1.0
EE	2.1	7.8	5.0	3.2	2.6	2.3	2.2	1.3	1.0	0.7	0.6	0.8	1.2
EI	2.4	5.2	4.1	3.4	2.9	2.6	2.3	2.1	1.8	1.5	1.6	1.8	2.0
EL	1.8	3.8	3.0	2.7	2.9	1.8	1.3	1.1	1.0	1.1	1.2	1.3	1.4
ES	1.9	3.7	2.9	3.1	3.4	2.5	1.8	1.3	0.9	0.8	1.1	1.4	1.6
FR	1.8	2.1	2.0	2.0	1.9	1.8	1.7	1.8	1.8	1.8	1.8	1.8	1.8
IT	1.4	1.5	1.5	2.1	1.9	1.7	1.4	1.1	1.0	1.2	1.3	1.4	1.4
CY	2.8	3.6	3.8	3.8	3.9	3.2	2.9	2.6	2.3	2.0	1.8	1.8	1.8
LV	1.8	8.6	5.0	3.0	2.1	2.0	1.8	1.0	0.7	0.2	-0.1	0.4	1.1
LT	1.8	8.0	5.0	3.6	2.5	1.8	1.5	0.8	0.8	0.5	0.2	0.2	0.4
LU	2.7	4.5	5.0	4.0	2.7	2.3	2.1	2.2	2.2	2.2	2.2	2.0	2.0
HU	1.7	2.9	3.3	2.8	2.4	2.1	2.1	1.5	1.1	1.0	0.8	0.9	1.0
MT	1.7	2.9	2.3	2.7	2.7	1.9	1.7	1.4	1.2	1.0	0.8	0.8	1.0
NL	1.5	2.1	1.9	1.7	1.5	1.3	1.2	1.4	1.5	1.6	1.5	1.4	1.3
AT	1.7	2.2	2.2	1.9	1.9	1.6	1.5	1.6	1.5	1.5	1.5	1.4	1.5
PL	1.7	5.9	4.2	3.1	2.5	2.5	2.0	1.0	0.5	0.3	0.3	0.3	0.5
PT	1.8	1.3	2.0	2.1	2.1	2.1	2.5	2.2	1.8	1.5	1.2	1.3	1.4
RO	2.0	6.4	5.2	3.9	2.9	2.2	1.6	1.8	1.1	0.6	0.3	0.6	0.3
SL	1.6	4.9	3.4	3.2	2.6	1.4	0.8	0.7	0.7	0.7	0.8	1.0	1.1
SK	2.0	6.5	6.2	4.2	3.4	2.3	2.0	0.8	0.5	0.3	0.2	0.3	0.5
FI	1.7	3.4	2.6	1.9	1.7	1.5	1.5	1.6	1.6	1.6	1.5	1.4	1.5
SE	1.9	3.5	2.7	2.2	1.9	1.9	1.7	1.8	1.9	1.8	1.7	1.6	1.7
UK	2.1	2.7	2.7	2.4	2.0	2.0	2.1	2.1	2.1	2.1	1.9	1.8	1.8
EU–27	1.7	2.7	2.5	2.3	2.1	1.8	1.7	1.5	1.4	1.4	1.3	1.4	1.4
EU–15	1.7	2.3	2.2	2.2	2.0	1.7	1.6	1.5	1.5	1.5	1.5	1.5	1.5
EU–12	1.8	5.7	4.4	3.3	2.6	2.2	1.8	1.2	0.8	0.6	0.4	0.6	0.7

Source: European Commission (2009b).

The Table 7.2 shows clearly the long term impact of population ageing, with growth rates declining from around 2.5 per cent currently (pre-crisis) to around 1.5 per cent or below by 2035. In Germany, the motor of the European economy, the long term growth projection is only 1.2 per cent, with Italy at 1.4 per cent. The decline in growth prospects is especially stark in the 'catching up' countries – the EU-12 have relatively healthy growth initially but fall behind the EU-15 by 2035.

2.5 The Role of Policy

The global trends noted above and even population ageing, given its deep-rooted nature, are difficult to change through public policy. Even where options exist, such as, for example, attempting to close off one's economy against globalisation, accelerating in-migration or not reducing CO_2 emissions, they are economically or politically unattractive. But this does not mean that policy is powerless. The key role for public policy is to facilitate the transformation and adaptation to the trends noted above.

This can be done very successfully, which can be demonstrated by the differential performance of European economies in the field of competitiveness. Despite broadly similar starting points (at least among Europe's more developed economies) some are among the global top performers in terms of competitiveness, while others have fallen behind.

Table 7.3 Ranking of EU-27 countries in the World Economic Forum's Global Competitiveness Index (2010–2011)

Sweden	2	Cyprus	40
Germany	5	Spain	42
Finland	7	Slovenia	45
Netherlands	8	Portugal	46
Denmark	9	Lithuania	47
UK	12	Italy	48
France	15	Malta	50
Austria	18	Hungary	52
Belgium	19	Slovak Rep.	60
Luxembourg	20	Romania	67
Ireland	29	Latvia	70
Estonia	33	Bulgaria	71
Czech Rep.	36	Greece	83
Poland	39		

Source: World Economic Forum (2010).

A number of EU member states are among the top ten, with Sweden on rank 2, Germany on 5, Finland on 7, the Netherlands on 8 and Denmark on 9. Understandably, the former Communist new member states rank lower but some have made impressive progress with Estonia on 33. However, of the old member states, the Mediterranean countries struggle with Spain on 42, Portugal on 46, Italy at 48 and Greece on 83. It is not coincidental that these are also the countries where most of the focus of the Euro-crisis has been.[4] This becomes even clearer when considering the long term economic sustainability of Europe's economies, with Portugal, Italy and Greece all in unsustainable positions (Zuleeg 2010).

In part, this can be explained by different starting points, but it is also due to a lack of sustained economic reform in some countries in response to the challenges noted above. This policy failure was at the heart of the Lisbon Agenda, which aimed to encourage structural reform throughout Europe. Many countries accepted that 'the solution to their slow growth problem requires a longer-term policy perspective. A sustainable medium-term recovery process needs to be built on a Lisbon-inspired structural reform agenda aimed at effectively addressing the EU's fundamental growth challenges, presently posed by the accelerating pace of technological change, globalisation (most recently in terms of the growing tradability of large parts of the service economy) and ageing populations' (McMorrow and Röger 2007). The structural reform agenda is now being taken forward through the 'Europe' 2020 strategy, which aims to boost the European growth rate in light of the economic crisis and the long term challenges noted above.

Policy can have a significant impact. For example, for the Lisbon Agenda, one estimate notes that 'the progressive introduction of the five key measures linked to the Lisbon Strategy (that is the services directive; reduction of the administrative burden; improving human capital; 3 per cent R&D target; and increases in the employment rate) could boost the euro area's economic and employment growth rates by more than ½ a percentage point annually for more than a decade' (McMorrow and Röger 2007). But the economic crisis has aggravated an already difficult environment.

3. IMPACT OF THE ECONOMIC CRISIS ON EUROPE'S GROWTH

3.1 Recession

The immediate impact of the economic crisis has been a recession across Europe. EU-27 GDP fell by 4.2 per cent in 2009. While there is a recovery from 2010 onwards, it is relatively weak with the average EU growth rate from 2010–2012 at 2 per cent or below. There is, however, significant variation within the EU, with deep recessions in 2009 in the Baltic States

(Estonia -13.9 per cent, Lithuania -14.7 per cent and Latvia -18.0 per cent) and contractions of around 8 per cent in Finland, Ireland and Slovenia. In 2010, Bulgaria, Latvia, Ireland and Spain continued to contract (albeit at a marginal rate of between -0.1 per cent and -0.4 per cent), whereas Romania's economy is set to shrink by -1.9 per cent and Greece's by -4.2 per cent.[5]

3.2 Reduced Economic Potential

In addition to the decrease in GDP, it looks increasingly likely that there has been a reduction in economic potential unless new growth drivers can be mobilised. This scenario – of a lower potential growth rate as well as the original dip in GDP – is illustrated in the Figure 7.1.

Potential output level

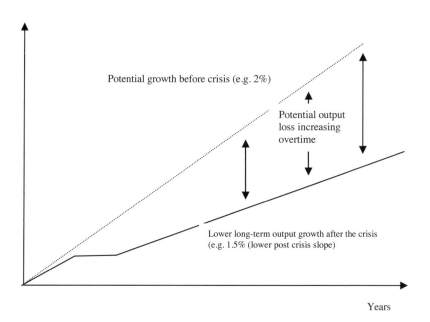

Source: European Commission (2009a).

Figure 7.1 Long-term output growth

The impact on long term growth potential can come directly from, for example, reduced investment in innovation during the crisis, leading to long term output losses, especially when seen in conjunction with strong global competition: the crisis has accelerated global structural changes, with emerging economies attracting a bigger share of global investment and economic activity. In addition, within the EU, sectors which tended to be drivers of economic growth before the crisis, such as construction, real estate or the financial sector, are unlikely to provide such an impact in the near future. A Commission working paper concludes that 'The likelihood of a lasting impact on potential growth appears to be higher in the current crisis than in previous recessions due to the duration of the crisis, its global nature and the changes in attitudes towards risk' (European Commission 2009a).

The outlook is not very positive for the near future: 'medium term potential growth for Europe is projected to remain low and estimated at around 1.5 per cent up to 2020' (European Commission 2011) (see Chapter 3). This is in part due to the long term challenges Europe faces: 'the challenge to be faced up to by policymakers is heightened by the fact that the pre-crisis potential growth rate was already low, mainly due to poor TFP (Total Factor Productivity) growth. In addition, beyond the crisis, population ageing is expected to reduce potential growth in the EU over the medium to long run, owing to the ensuing sharp contraction in the labour supply'. The EU is thus potentially facing 'a permanent loss in wealth, a sluggish growth rate ("sluggish recovery") possibly leading to high levels of unemployment and social distress, and a relative decline on the world scene'. Such a reduction in the growth potential can, however, be mitigated by the right policies as explored later on.

3.3 In Debt

Like any recession, the crisis resulted in a deterioration of public finances, through a reduction in public revenues and an increase in spending through 'automatic stabilisers' such as unemployment benefits and other social support mechanisms. In recognition of the severity of the economic crisis, governments around the world also used – mostly debt-financed – fiscal stimulus programmes to get over the worst of the crisis. But the large deficits (and banking liabilities in some countries such as Ireland) are resulting in mounting public debt burdens. Table 7.4 shows deficits and resulting interest expenditure and debt levels (as a percentage of GDP).[6]

Despite the immediate crisis having passed, deficits are remaining relatively high at over 5 per cent on average in 2011 and over 4 per cent in 2012. The variation remains very large with Ireland still forecast to have a deficit of over 9 per cent by 2012, while Sweden will be running a budget surplus. Overall, there is a clear picture of continuing budgetary deterioration. By 2012, average gross public debt will be over 80 per cent

of GDP in the EU, up from around 60 per cent before the crisis. Four
countries will have debt exceeding 100 per cent of GDP: Belgium with 102
per cent, Ireland with 114 per cent, Italy with 120 per cent and Greece with
a staggering 156 per cent. Portugal, France and the UK will be somewhere
close to or above 90 per cent.[7]

There are many uncertainties over these forecasts, not least the strength
of the recovery in some countries. In addition, interest payments for any
new debt being accumulated are at low levels with monetary policy still
expansionary.[8] However, given the inflationary pressures on the EU
economies, interest rates are set to increase in the short to medium term.
But even without such an increase, the cost to some countries is significant.
While debt financing costs will be around 3 per cent of GDP on average in
the EU, Greece is in a precarious situation at 7.4 per cent of GDP.

Table 7.4 Deficits, interest expenditure and gross debt as a percentage of GDP

	Deficits				Interest expenditure				Gross debt			
	2009	2010	2011	2012	2009	2010	2011	2012	2009	2010	2011	2012
BE	-6.0	-4.8	-4.6	-4.7	3.6	3.5	3.5	3.6	96.2	98.6	100.5	102.1
DE	-3.0	-3.7	-2.7	-1.8	2.6	2.4	2.4	2.4	73.4	75.7	75.9	75.2
EE	-1.7	-1.0	-1.9	-2.7	0.3	0.4	0.4	0.4	7.2	8.0	9.5	11.7
EI	-14.4	-32.3	-10.3	-9.1	2.2	3.0	3.5	4.4	65.5	97.4	107.0	114.7
EL	-15.4	-9.6	-7.4	-7.6	5.3	6.0	6.2	7.4	126.8	140.2	150.2	156.0
ES	-11.1	-9.3	-6.4	-5.5	1.8	2.0	2.4	2.8	53.2	64.4	69.7	73.0
FR	-7.5	-7.7	-6.3	-5.8	2.4	2.6	2.7	2.8	78.1	83.0	86.8	89.8
IT	-5.3	-5.0	-4.3	-3.5	4.7	4.6	4.8	4.9	116.0	118.9	120.2	119.9
CY	-6.0	-5.9	-5.7	-5.7	2.5	2.3	2.4	2.4	58.0	62.2	65.2	68.4
LU	-0.7	-1.8	-1.3	-1.2	0.4	0.4	0.4	0.5	14.5	18.2	19.6	20.9
MT	-3.8	-4.2	-3.0	-3.3	3.2	3.1	3.1	3.1	68.6	70.4	70.8	70.9
NL	-5.4	-5.8	-3.9	-2.8	2.2	2.2	2.3	2.4	60.8	64.8	66.6	67.3
AT	-3.5	-4.3	-3.6	-3.3	2.7	2.8	2.8	2.9	67.5	70.4	72.0	73.3
PT	-9.3	-7.3	-4.9	-5.1	2.8	2.9	3.7	4.0	76.1	82.8	88.8	92.4
SL	-5.8	-5.8	-5.3	-4.7	1.4	1.6	1.7	1.8	35.4	40.7	44.8	47.6
SK	-7.9	-8.2	-5.3	-5.0	1.4	1.4	1.8	2.1	35.4	42.1	45.1	47.4
FI	-2.5	-3.1	-1.6	-1.2	1.2	1.2	1.3	1.6	43.8	49.0	51.1	53.0
Euro area	-6.3	-6.3	-4.6	-3.9	2.8	2.9	3.0	3.2	79.1	84.1	86.5	87.8
BG	-4.7	-3.8	-2.9	-1.8	0.8	0.7	0.8	0.9	14.7	18.2	20.2	20.8
CZ	-5.8	-5.2	-4.6	-4.2	1.3	1.3	1.8	1.9	35.3	40.0	43.1	45.2
DK	-2.7	-5.1	-4.3	-3.5	1.8	1.8	1.9	1.9	41.5	44.9	47.5	49.2
LV	-10.2	-7.7	-7.9	-7.3	1.5	1.8	2.1	2.3	36.7	45.7	51.9	56.6
LT	-9.2	-8.4	-7.0	-6.9	1.2	1.9	2.2	2.6	29.5	37.4	42.8	48.3
HU	-4.4	-3.8	-4.7	-6.2	4.6	4.1	3.8	3.7	78.4	78.5	80.1	81.6
PL	-7.2	-7.9	-6.6	-6.0	2.5	2.8	2.9	3.0	50.9	55.5	57.2	59.6
RO	-8.6	-7.3	-4.9	-3.5	1.6	1.9	1.9	1.8	23.9	30.4	33.4	34.1
SE	-0.9	-0.9	-0.1	1.0	0.9	0.9	0.9	1.0	41.9	39.9	38.9	37.5
UK	-11.4	-10.5	-8.6	-6.4	2.0	2.7	3.0	3.2	68.2	77.8	83.5	86.6
EU	-6.8	-6.8	-5.1	-4.2	2.6	2.7	2.9	3.0	74.0	79.1	81.8	83.3

These levels of debt are unsustainable and necessitate fiscal consolidation. However, in the short term, care will need to be taken to avoid a spiral of lower public spending resulting in lower growth and thus lower revenues, necessitating further fiscal consolidation. Given the scale of the debt mountain, this will require more than a simple cutback in expenditure and a slight increase in taxation – there is a need to reorganise public services fundamentally. The importance of fundamental public sector reform is noted in 'Europe 2020': 'fiscal consolidation and long-term financial sustainability will need to go hand in hand with important structural reforms, in particular of pension, health care, social protection and education systems. Public administration should use the situation as an opportunity to enhance efficiency and the quality of service' (European Commission 2010c).

A lack of public sector reform will impact negatively on Europe's future growth. Minimising the level of inefficient or ineffective spending is essential to free up resources to be used elsewhere in the economy. This is especially true in Europe, where the public sector is proportionally larger than in the rest of the world. As well as potentially tying up crucial resources, the public sector has an important role in the long term development of a country in creating the framework conditions for growth by focusing expenditure on spending that can boost long term economic potential, for example through education and skills, and by providing public infrastructure. The public sector can also boost the competitive advantage for European firms, for example by supporting the development of 'green' goods and services and by fostering innovation. But even if the necessary reform is achieved, it is unlikely that the public sector in most countries will be able to provide sufficient public investments which are needed to increase further growth potential.

3.4 Divergence

In addition to the long term growth crisis there is also increasing divergence within the EU, which is a major driver behind the current Eurozone crisis: 'excessive economic, financial and fiscal imbalances built up in some euro area countries during the upswing, hindering the efficient operation of the monetary union, and led to growing vulnerabilities. These contributed to especially severe economic and fiscal crises in some countries, leading to spillovers mainly through financial markets across the euro area' (OECD 2010). This divergence clearly predates the economic crisis, most notably regarding the balance of payments performance. However, the crisis has made the situation even worse: 'when the financial crisis hit, those countries with large current account deficits were the most exposed and faced the combined pressures of rebuilding of household and corporate balance sheets, impaired financial systems and weak public finances' (OECD 2010).

The immediate impact of the crisis might mean that some of the weakest economies in the Eurozone will be left even further behind. While countries such as Germany are rebounding strongly, recording 3.6 per cent growth in 2010, the largest rate since unification, economies such as Portugal and Greece record low growth and investment rates. Investment in the Eurozone fell by -11.4 per cent on average in 2009, and a further -0.8 per cent in 2010, but it is set to recover to 2.2 per cent and 3.6 per cent in 2011 and 2012, respectively. In contrast, in Portugal and Greece, as well as Cyprus, investment is still falling in 2011 and 2012. A similar picture emerges in relation to labour productivity, where Greece and Portugal see a fall in 2011, with 2012 seeing below Eurozone average growth in labour productivity in these countries.

The key question is whether this is a temporary phenomenon or whether it is a continuation of long term divergence. While the need to rebalance economic policies in the weaker economies is clear, with a consequent short term negative impact on growth, it seems unlikely that those economies with a fundamental structural problem will manage to catch up in the near future. Currently, wage moderation is essentially the main tool for these weakest economies to restore competitiveness and it seems unlikely that this will be sufficient.

4. A NEW GROWTH MODEL?

The crisis has led many to question the global economic model, with its recent overreliance on unsustainable expansion based on consumption financed by private borrowing and public debt, speculation – especially in the financial markets – and an overriding focus on growth. The crisis has shown that the focus of our societies must go beyond growth, focusing instead on the well-being of our citizens,[9] which is also the objective enshrined in the Lisbon Treaty: 'the Union's aim is to promote peace, its values and the well-being of its peoples'. Rather than being an aim in itself, growth must thus be understood as a tool, among other tools, which can be harnessed to achieve greater well-being.

This makes it essential that growth does not have a detrimental effect on other objectives or that it is achieved by unsustainable means. Growth must be sustainable in every sense of the term – economic, financial, environmental and social. A key component in our considerations must be intergenerational equity, which in this context can be understood as not fuelling today's growth by depriving future generations of resources, for example through excessive public debt levels. But while it is clear that any growth should be sustainable, it is still essential to have growth. A low–

zero growth model which is being advocated by some would have significant detrimental impacts as explored below.

5. THE IMPACT OF LOW GROWTH

While very high levels of growth are not desirable for mature economies – as they increase the danger of overheating – low growth rates can have a number of detrimental impacts. Here, we focus on three impacts: the labour market and social cohesion, public debt and the sustainability of Europe's economic and social model, and the role of Europe in the world, economically and politically.

5.1 Labour Market and Social Cohesion

One impact of the crisis which has been felt in most countries is a sharp increase in unemployment. While some countries' labour markets have been performing better, the overall unemployment rate stands at around 10 per cent, as compared to around 7 per cent before the crisis. This should not come as a surprise: there is a close relationship between growth and the change in the unemployment rate (here measured in percentage point change).[10] Figure 7.2 shows this relationship for Germany.

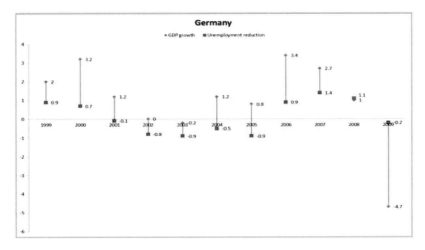

Figure 7.2 Relationship between GDP growth and unemployment reduction (Germany)

The figure shows that over the last decade, low growth rates are not sufficient to improve the unemployment situation but that it usually requires 1.5–2 per cent growth to see an improvement in the labour market.

This relationship only breaks down significantly in the crisis, where the sharp contraction did not result in a corresponding increase in unemployment, potentially indicating the effectiveness of Germany's labour market interventions such as '*Kurzarbeit*'.

A similar picture of the relationship between growth and unemployment can be observed in France and the UK (with a break-even point in the labour market of just above 2 per cent) (Figure 7.3 and 7.4).

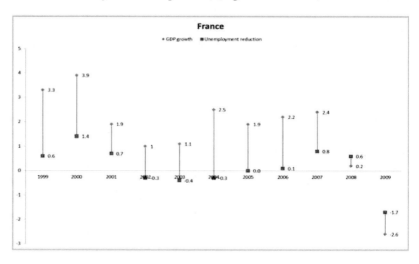

Figure 7.3 Relationship between GDP growth and unemployment reduction (France)

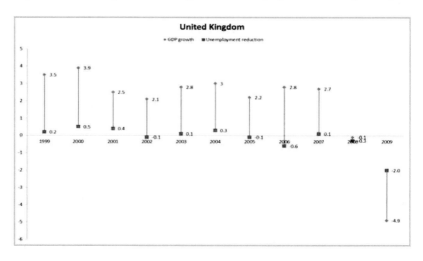

Figure 7.4 Relationship between GDP growth and unemployment reduction (UK)

In countries which are still catching up, the break-even point can be even higher, also depending on the existing tightness in the labour market. For example, in Spain it appears to be around 2.5 per cent, in Poland around 3 per cent and in Ireland around 5 per cent before the crisis, as demonstrated in the Figures 7.5–7.7).

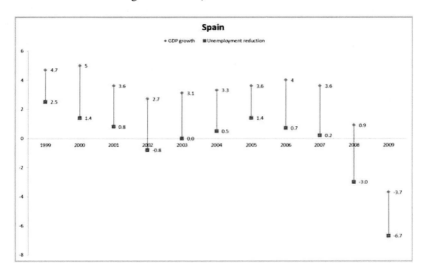

Figure 7.5 Relationship between GDP growth and unemployment reduction (Spain)

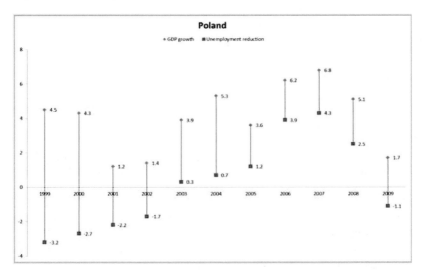

Figure 7.6 Relationship between GDP growth and unemployment reduction (Poland)

While the relationship does not always hold, it clearly shows that in general a positive level of growth is needed to achieve a reduction in unemployment. This positive level of growth seems to depend on the level of maturity of the economy and the level of unused capacity in the labour market, with catching up economies and those with tighter labour markets requiring more growth to achieve a further reduction in unemployment. While policy also seems to matter, at least in the short run, achieving high employment rates and low unemployment will require a significant positive level of growth. This is also entirely consistent with the aforementioned focus on well-being: exclusion from the labour market is a critical factor in the well-being of citizens and is directly linked to the incidence of poverty and social exclusion.

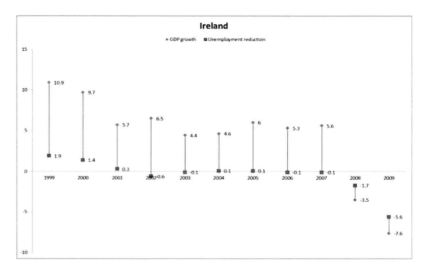

Figure 7.7 Relationship between GDP growth and unemployment reduction (Ireland)

5.2 Growth and Debt

In addition to the social impact of low growth, such a loss of growth potential would also make it increasingly difficult to deal with the sovereign debt crisis. The level of debt depends rather obviously on growth being measured as a percentage of GDP, so any reduction in growth also slows down the rate of fiscal consolidation. This is aggravated if the deficit exceeds the growth rate of the economy, increasing the debt to GDP ratio. And low growth makes deficits more likely, resulting in an increased use of automatic stabilisers and reduced revenues.

The combination of low growth and an increasing debt burden will also put a severe burden on the acceptability of structural reform and fiscal consolidation for the population. If the large amount of economic pain inflicted does not have a visible 'pay-off' it seems unlikely that reforms can be sustained indefinitely. Increasing debt burdens will, in the most severe cases, test the sustainability of Europe's economic and social model, especially when the long run challenge of demographic change also starts to impact. Rising interest payments, severe expenditure cutbacks and reduced revenues, coupled with increased need for support, could well make the provision of even basic public services unaffordable and could bankrupt public insurance systems.

5.3 Europe's Role in the World

Europe's external influence would also be reduced with low growth figures. Politically, a greater growth differential between the emerging economies and the EU would mean that in international negotiations, in standard setting and in international institutions the disproportionate role of European countries would increasingly be questioned, especially since it coincides with a relatively small and stagnating population. This would make it increasingly difficult for Europe to promote its values to other parts of the world, which was already apparent in the climate change negotiations in Copenhagen (see Chapter 8). Here lies another significant problem of low growth in Europe: if Europe cannot prove to the rest of the world that more sustainable growth is possible, it is more likely that other countries will continue with the current unsustainable high growth model.

Europe's influence and attractiveness would also decrease in the global economy. With increasing doubts over the fundamentals (especially when coupled with increased divergence) the euro will continue to be under pressure. A low growth environment also makes Europe unattractive for investments and puts Europe at a disadvantage in the global competition for talent. These are especially concerning in an environment where both investment and human capital formation are under pressure from long term challenges and the crisis.

6. DRIVING GROWTH

To prevent these negative impacts, a significant focus of EU policy must be on driving forward sustainable economic growth, with a particular focus on growth in Europe's weakest economies. As a starting point, the EU has agreed on a successor to the Lisbon Strategy: the 'Europe 2020' strategy, which aims to stimulate 'smart, sustainable and inclusive' growth.

6.1 Strengths and Weaknesses of 'Europe 2020'

The 'Europe 2020' strategy is, in many ways, an improvement on its predecessor. It has a clearer focus with only five headline objectives – on innovation, labour market participation, education, combating poverty and climate change mitigation – as well as specifying seven flagship initiatives with – more or less concrete – areas of action for the EU. 'Europe 2020' also recognises that the main problem with the Lisbon Strategy was not its ambition but the implementation, especially in the weaker parts of the European economy. 'Europe 2020' aims to create more buy-in at the highest level, giving the European Council a much greater role, to drive forward implementation.

But there are also shortcomings which will make it difficult to achieve the ambitions of 'Europe 2020'. There is insufficient attention on the public sector and the aim to drive forward structural reform is not matched with sufficient specific implementation mechanisms. There is also insufficient integration with the current debate on economic governance where current proposals aim for a much higher degree of economic integration, especially in the Eurozone, with an increasing focus on structural reform. For example, the Annual Growth Survey notes that 'To avoid stagnation, unsustainable debt trends, accumulated imbalances and ensure its competitiveness, Europe needs to accelerate the consolidation of public finances, the reform of its financial sector and to frontload structural reforms now' (European Commission 2011). In the end, the question about implementation is still open: are the proposed mechanisms strong enough to overcome significant resistance in many member states, especially in the context of a very difficult economic environment?

To ensure that 'Europe 2020' objectives can be delivered, that is to manage to put Europe on path towards 'smart, inclusive and sustainable growth', this contribution focuses on two specific areas for action that can potentially generate public and private investments into future growth: new-enhanced European-level investment mechanisms and the further development of the Single Market.

6.2 Investing for Growth

To overcome the long term growth crisis will require significant investment, which is a particular challenge in times of public sector austerity where the ability of the public sector to invest is going to be limited. The need for investment is far reaching. It includes invest-to-save schemes, for example to increase efficiency and effectiveness in the public sector through greater use of ICT (information and communication technology) or the transformation to a green economy through facilitating investments in energy efficiency. There are also very significant infrastructure needs across the EU, both in forms of traditional infrastructure such as roads and rail but also in terms of new infrastructure in relation to smart grids and next generation broadband. Policy must also aim to encourage private sector investment, especially in innovation and R&D: 'it is crucial that policies are also geared towards sustaining investments in physical capital, R&D and Innovation during the downturn which will bring considerable long-run gains in potential output level' (European Commission 2009a).

To achieve smart growth, there is also a need to accelerate investment in education and skills formation to, in the long run, increase the value-added of European goods and services and ensure European competitiveness in light of significant ongoing investment efforts by the emerging economies in this area. In addition, Europe's public services and social protection systems can, with the right investment and reform, become drivers of growth by ensuring that all parts of the population can engage in the future economy.

However, as noted before, the public means to achieve these objectives are limited. This means more focus needs to be on how to encourage investment by companies and also by households, for example in the area of education and lifelong learning.

6.3 Addressing Divergence

Generating such investment will be particularly difficult in the economically weaker European economies which need to boost competitiveness and productivity. But the benefits from such investments are potentially significant – both for the countries concerned and the economically stronger countries in the EU from where the investment must come or at least be underwritten. In the recipient countries, it will help to encourage the catching up process as well as counteracting austerity measures, helping to make public finance reform less painful and more socially acceptable. Helping to develop these countries in the direction of smart, sustainable and inclusive growth will also encourage European companies and individuals to provide additional investment. It also demonstrates, in a productive way, European solidarity. At the same time, it would reduce divergence in the Eurozone.

The investment can have a particularly strong impact in a time of weak economic activity as there is unused potential in the economy. While in a booming economy, public investment can potentially draw scarce resources away from productive private investments (so-called crowding out), in a weak economy these resources are available. This can have the beneficial effect of not only increasing future productivity but also maintaining jobs.

6.4 Generating Investments

More needs to be done at the European level to generate this investment. The EU budget for the post 2013 period, especially structural funds and cohesion funding, can help to provide some of the framework conditions necessary for private investment. But this will require significant reforms; for example, much more emphasis needs to be given to building human capital.

These funds also have the potential to leverage private investment. This has, however, proven to be difficult in the past, given the level of administration involved and the uncertainties at the interface between competition–procurement policy and European funding. In future, there is a need to build much closer public-private partnerships which can 'help bring public and private financing together for priority investments, notably in energy, transport and ICT' (European Commission 2011). Activities of the European Investment Bank should also be greatly expanded to provide more low-cost investments, especially where private capital availability is limited in the aftermath of the economic crisis. The idea of EU project bonds,[11] proposed in the Budget Review (European Commission 2010e) also needs to be implemented, to provide crucial investment in pan-European infrastructure projects.

To fully benefit from these new financial instruments, they should ideally fulfil the following criteria:

- Recycled loan funding – where interest and capital repayments are reinvested;
- Low financing costs – where the investment benefits from the low cost of financing at the pan-European level;
- Creating European added value – enabling investments which could not be done effectively at the national level;
- Leveraging private investment, including company investments and financial sector capital;
- Addressing European divergence – being focused on regions which are in danger of being left behind; and
- Avoiding crowding out – by being focused on areas where economic activity is low and excess capacity exists.

If the new instruments being created can fulfil these criteria, they can contribute significantly to meet Europe's investment needs. But in itself, creating new financial instruments is not sufficient: at the same time, the framework conditions for private investments need to be improved.

6.5 A Broader and Deeper Single Market

The most important framework for private investments the EU can create is to develop the Single Market further. The Single Market is already the most significant result of European economic integration but it is far from complete. Companies have the ability to generate the amounts of investment necessary to drive future growth but require an integrated market which makes it worthwhile. Specifically, to drive future investment in areas such as telecommunication and especially energy, more needs to be done to create a true Single Market in these sectors.

Many of the problems encountered by firms and consumers within today's Single Market are not due to the overall framework of rules but to its incomplete or indecisive implementation. In future, rules must be applied uniformly and consistently across the EU with a particular focus on ensuring that legislation is evaluated *ex post* to ensure that it has delivered the desired market integration.

This is particularly important for the services directive. While much has been achieved in the free movement of goods, the services directive has only been in force for just over a year and it still has many shortcomings. In addition the free movement of capital remains elusive from a consumer perspective where cross-border access to capital remains limited. The free movement of people remains one of Europe's proudest achievements but it, too, needs to be updated to reap the full benefits: Europe needs a Single European Labour Market with measures which encourage mobility and open European labour markets to the rest of the world.

Not only is more work required in realising the original four freedoms, but the Single Market also needs to be made ready for the future knowledge economy. To generate additional growth and enable the transformation to the knowledge economy, the creation of the Digital Single Market is critical, which is recognised in 'Europe 2020': 'the aim is to deliver sustainable economic and social benefits from a Digital Single Market' (European Commission 2010c). This requires making progress on a number of thorny issues including, for example, harmonisation of consumer and data protection, common standards for e-invoicing and e-signatures, a pan European patent, IPR (Intellectual Property Rights) and licensing framework and significant investment in hard (broadband) and soft (skills) infrastructure.[12]

If progress can be made the potential benefits for the EU economy are large: it could add at least 4 per cent to EU GDP, help create European digital companies of scale, as well as helping to integrate EU labour markets, combating climate change and countering the effects of population ageing.[13] It would bring many benefits to consumers, not least to a new ICT-savvy generation which expects a free online market where they can, for example, download music anywhere in Europe.

At the EU level, there has been much progress: the Digital Agenda (European Commission 2010a), the Citizenship Report (European Commission 2010b) and the consultation on the Single Market Act (European Commission 2010f). The latter two followed on directly from the Monti Report (Monti 2010) which provided a comprehensive blueprint for the development of the Single Market. However, it remains to be seen exactly how ambitious, integrated and visionary the concrete proposals will be and what, in the end, will be translated from ambition to reality, given the difficult economic and political environment as well as protracted European decision-making mechanisms.

7. INVESTMENTS FOR FUTURE GROWTH

The challenge Europe is facing is enormous: without decisive action, Europe is not only facing a long term growth crisis but also increasing divergence, leading to further pressure on the Eurozone. The long term growth crisis has to be addressed, as low growth translates into weak labour markets, an increasing debt crisis and a diminishing of Europe's role in the world.

If new loan-based instruments, with a particular view towards generating the investment needed to underpin 'Europe 2020', are developed at the same time as developing the Single Market further, in particular the Digital Single Market, much could be achieved in generating the investments which are needed to drive future growth. Europe does not have many opportunities to generate future growth: it is critical to use these available tools to address Europe's long term growth crisis to ensure the well-being of all Europeans in the long term.

NOTES

*   Elements of this chapter are also discussed in an article for the Think Global Act European project, contributed by Maria Joao Rodrigues and Fabian Zuleeg.
**   With thanks to Benedetta Guerzoni, Programme Assistant, EPC, for research support and in particular the graphs on the relationship between unemployment and growth.
1.   http://www.europarl.europa.eu/summits/lis1_en.htm.
2.   The evidence suggests that adapting to/mitigating climate change is a cost-effective solution (see HM Treasury 2006). Never the less there are significant costs involved.
3.   In the neoclassical growth model or Solow growth model, growth depends in the long run primarily on technological change and population growth.

4. In addition to Ireland, where the magnitude of the crisis has been aggravated by significant problems in the Irish banking system.
5. Economic data taken from the Autumn 2010 forecast, European Commission (2010d).
6. Ibid.
7. For some of these countries, such as Belgium and Italy, the high debt levels precede the crisis, while others such as the UK and Ireland have seen a very marked deterioration in direct response to the crisis. For Greece, the situation is particularly precarious, having a high debt level before the crisis and seeing a marked further deterioration during the crisis.
8. However, for those countries affected by the sovereign debt crisis, the risk premium charged by the markets means that they are already paying significantly more than they have in recent years.
9. For a detailed exploration of the concept of well-being and its applicability to European policy making, please visit the website of the Well-being 2030 projects, a joint research project between EPC and the European Commission (http://www.epc.eu/prog_forum. php?forum_id=8&prog_id=2).
10. Given the still fragmented nature of European labour markets and the differences in economic cycle between different states, the analysis of unemployment reduction and growth rates is on a country-by-country basis. Data is taken from Eurostat, National Accounts and own elaboration with Eurostat, The Labour Force Survey.
11. These are different from the proposal of Eurobonds which are intended to provide low cost refinancing of public debt.
12. For details see http://www.epc.eu/dsm/6/Policy_recommendations.pdf.
13. For further details see http://www.epc.eu/dsm/.

BIBLIOGRAPHY

Barroso, José Manuel (2009), *Political Guidelines for the Next Commission*, Brussels, 3 September.

Collett, Elizabeth and Fabian Zuleeg (2008), *Soft, Scarce, and Super Skills: Sourcing the Next Generation of Migrant Workers in Europe*, Washington, DC: Migration Policy Institute.

European Commission (2005), 'Working Together for Growth and Jobs – A New Start for the Lisbon Strategy', Communication to the Spring European Council, COM(2005) 24 final.

European Commission (2008), 'A European Recovery Plan', Communication from the Commission to the European Council, COM(2008) 800 final.

European Commission (2009a), *Impact of the Current Economic and Financial Crisis on Potential Output*, Directorate-General for Economic and Financial Affairs, Occasional Papers 49, June.

European Commission (2009b), 'Economic and budgetary projections for the EU-27 member states (2008–2060)', *The 2009 Ageing Report*.

European Commission (2010a), 'A Digital Agenda for Europe', COM(2010) 245 final/2.

European Commission (2010b), 'EU Citizenship Report 2010: Dismantling the Obstacles to EU Citizens' Rights', COM(2010) 603 final.

European Commission (2010c), 'Europe 2020 – A Strategy for Smart, Sustainable, Inclusive Growth', Communication from the European Commission, COM(2010) 2020.

European Commission (2010d), *European Economic Forecast*, Autumn 2010.

European Commission (2010e), 'The EU Budget Review', Communication from the European Commission to the European Parliament, the Council, the European Economic and Social Committee, the Committee of the Regions and the National Parliaments, COM(2010) 700 final.

European Commission (2010f), 'Towards a Single Market Act', COM(2010) 608 final/2.

European Commission (2011), 'Annual Growth Survey: Advancing the EU's Comprehensive Response to the Crisis', Communication from the Commission to the European Parliament, the Council, the European Economic and Social Committee and the Committee of the Regions, COM(2011) 11 final.

HM Treasury (2006), *Stern Review Report on the Economics of Climate Change*, *The Economist* (2011), 'Back with a vengeance', 20 January.

McMorrow, Kieran and Werner Röger (2007), 'An analysis of EU growth trends, with a particular focus on Germany, France, Italy and the UK', *National Institute Economic Review*, **199** (1), January.

Monti, Mario (2010), 'A New Strategy for the Single Market: At the Service of Europe's Economy and Society', Report to the President of the European Commission, José Manuel Barroso, 9 May.

Organisation for Economic Co-operation and Development (OECD) (2010), *OECD Economic Surveys: Euro Area*, December 2010.

World Economic Forum (2010), *The Global Competitiveness Report 2010/2011*.

Zuleeg, Fabian (2010), *European Economic Sustainability Index*, Brussels: European Policy Centre.

8. 'Europe 2020': the Shift to a Revised Climate Strategy

Antonio Villafranca

1. INTRODUCTION

In the past two decades global warming has been attracting more and more attention not only from international civil society but also from political leaders across the world. The international scientific community has already warned of the risk that world temperature will increase by 1.7° to 2.4°C by 2050, should carbon dioxide (CO_2) emissions not be successfully curbed over the coming decades. Such an increase may reach the dangerous threshold of 4°–6°C – compared to pre-industrial levels – by the turn of the century, with unprecedented and unknown effects on our planet.[1]

The European Union has decided to be a frontrunner in fighting climate change and is currently the only region in the world that has already set binding targets for the post-Kyoto period (that is from 2013 to 2020). Building on the concept of sustainable growth, various measures (CO_2 emission reductions, higher energy efficiency and use of renewables) will be adopted as part of a new growth strategy ('Europe 2020'). But the unilateralism of the EU intervention may prompt internal requests for economic protection, especially in view of possible non-equivalent measures taken by other large world emitters, including the US and China. As a result, trade conflicts at the international level and further requests for a revised strategy at the EU level may emerge over the coming years.

In a nutshell, this chapter intends to assess the European initiatives in the environmental field under the 'Europe 2020' strategy, by taking into account the ongoing changes in the international context (also leading to a revised governance model of fighting climate change) and the ensuing trade-related issues.

Section 2 will highlight the urgent need for common action to reduce CO_2 emissions in order to mitigate global warming over the next decade, while section 3 will show the limits of the current governance model in putting such a reduction into motion. As demonstrated by the failure of the Copenhagen Summit and the modest results of the Cancún Summit, the crucial issue of burden-sharing is far from being effectively addressed by the current governance model; this is inevitably leading to a new governance architecture whose potential impact on the EU policies needs to be carefully assessed. Section 4, in particular, will describe the European unilateral initiatives in the environmental fields (including their costs) and will also put the spotlight on possible requests for protection by European industrial lobbies (and some EU member states), should other leading economic powers not be willing or able to put through equivalent measures. Section 5 will therefore attempt to assess whether, and to what extent, the European Union will face the threat of carbon leakage and unfair competition over the next decade. In this regard, section 6 will show that there is a likelihood of future trade conflicts stemming from possible countermeasures (including Border Tax Adjustments) which the EU may adopt in an attempt to re-level the international playing field.

Building on this analysis, the final section will provide policy recommendations for the EU – both in terms of internal changes and a strengthening of its external dimension – not from the point of view of changing its targets under the 'Europe 2020' strategy but rather to make them more consistent with the changing international context.

2. CUTTING EMISSIONS: THE NEED FOR COMMON INTERVENTION

Climate change is a serious threat for the entire human race and requires a common response if it is to be tackled effectively. The environment may be considered an unparalleled constraint to demand-driven capitalism if new energy resources, technology and coherent political decisions are not able to match economic requirements with environmental sustainability. The scientific community has repeatedly warned that the situation may dangerously worsen over the coming decades as carbon dioxide (CO_2) emissions are expected to grow both in OECD (Organisation for Economic Co-operation and Development) and non-OECD countries, thus aggravating global warming and requiring wide-ranging and expensive mitigation and adaptation policies. As shown in Figure 8.1, by 2035 total world emissions are projected to grow from 29 to 42 billion metric tons (bmt) – a more than 40 per cent increase from the 2007 levels.

But it is noteworthy that the contribution of countries around the world to such an impressive increase can vary widely, depending above all on economic potentials and catch-up processes.

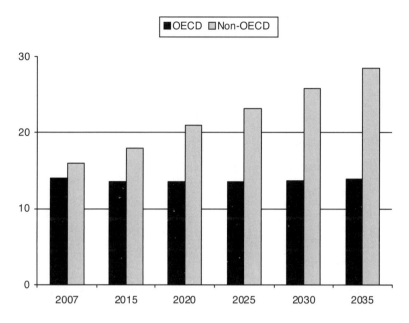

Source: EIA, International Energy Statistics database (as November 2009), www.eia.gov/emeu/international. Projections: EIA, *World Energy Projection System Plus* (2010).

Figure 8.1 World energy-related carbon dioxide emissions, 2007–2035 (billion metric tons)

The OECD countries are by far the most responsible for the stock of CO_2 already emitted in the atmosphere, but their future contribution to global emissions will decrease. In particular, their emissions will grow by 4 per cent (from 13.68 to 14.20 bmt) over the next 25 years, but responsibilities for this cannot be evenly distributed among these countries. Figure 8.2 shows that Australia, Canada and above all the US (currently the largest world emitter) will keep on increasing their emissions, while on the contrary the OECD European states and Japan will successfully curb them. As discussed below (see section 6), this may prompt trade-related conflicts not only between emerging and mature economies but also between OECD countries

Conversely, the emerging countries cannot be blamed for today's stock of CO_2 in the atmosphere, as their contribution has been modest in the past decades. But the same does not hold true when it comes to future emissions. Provided that non-OECD countries are expected to grow at a much faster pace, it comes as no surprise that their emissions will skyrocket from 16.02 bmt in 2007 to a shocking 28.19 bmt in 2035 – a significant 80 per cent increase. China, other Asian countries and Brazil will score high in the ranking of the annual growth of CO_2 emissions, while India, Africa, Central-Latin America and Eastern Europe will follow suit (Figure 8.3).

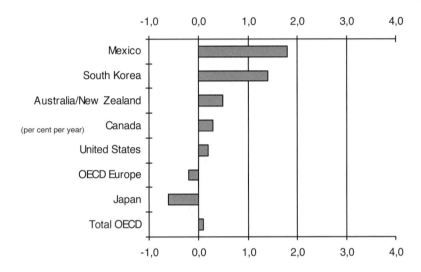

Figure 8.2 Average annual growth in energy-related carbon dioxide emissions in OECD economies, 1990–2035

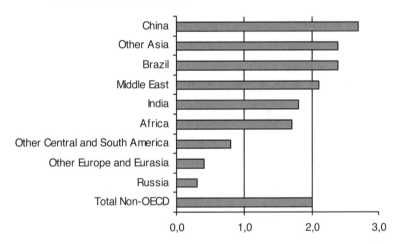

Source: EIA, World Energy Projection System Plus (2010).

Figure 8.3 Average annual growth in energy-related carbon dioxide emissions in non-OECD economies, 2007–2035

To make things worse, the competitive advantage of the emerging countries will continue to be mainly rooted in low production costs for the foreseeable future. As a result, these countries will need cheap (but very polluting) energy resources to support double-digit growth rates and follow a catch-up path towards the mature economies.

More generally, despite recent efforts to increase the use of renewables in both mature and emerging countries, fossil fuels are inevitably expected to play a major role in national energy mixes over the next decades, with coal and oil ranking first and second respectively in terms of projected CO_2 emissions by 2035 (Figure 8.4).

billion metric tons

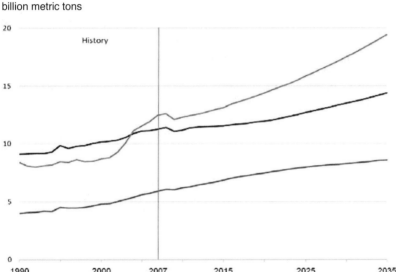

Key: gas (first line from the bottom) coal (second line), liquids (third line).

Source: EIA, International Energy Statistics database (as November 2009), www.eia.gov/emeu/international. Projections: EIA, *World Energy Projection System Plus* (2010).

Figure 8.4 World energy-related carbon dioxide emissions by fuel type, 1990–2035

To sum up, an effective fight against climate change requires a common effort by OECD and non-OECD countries. However, future burden-sharing has to take into account not only projected industrial production levels and energy demand (for both fossil fuels and renewables) but also the negative contribution each country has already made to the stock of CO_2 in the atmosphere. In other words, the resulting governance model must be able to properly balance the effectiveness and efficiency of actions with solidarity and 'fair' distribution of costs. This is an extremely difficult task because global warming is an unprecedented and truly global challenge. It is global in its causes as CO_2 emissions enter the atmosphere irrespective of their country of origin, but it is also global in its effects as they impact on plants, animals and human beings around the world, even if the type or size of the effect – from devastating hurricanes to desertification – and the ensuing adaptation costs can vary widely depending on geography. As a consequence, such a global challenge requires an equally global response in order for it to be successfully managed. Some regions (that is the European Union) are attempting to be frontrunners in the fight, partly in view of the competitiveness advantages stemming from the development of new green technologies, but their efforts will have a minor (or negligible) impact on mitigation if they are not coherently included in a governance model shared by all the other industrialized economies and the major emerging markets.

To make things worse, it should be noted that what is more worrying about global warming is not the intensity of the phenomenon but rather its speed, with some effects (especially in terms of extreme meteorological events) being already felt today, and other major – and potentially dramatic – effects expected in the coming decades. Speed is a severe constraint, as historical evidence shows that political change (if there is any) requires much time to occur. In other words, there is a risk that time will run out well before the complex international political system spontaneously builds up a shared and effective governance model. The following section address this problem by analysing the current 'vertical' governance model, its shortcomings and modest achievements and, as a result, the need for a new strategy as part of a more shared and 'horizontal' model.

3.   TOWARDS A NEW GOVERNANCE MODEL

The 2009 Copenhagen Summit intended to set the stage for a post-Kyoto agreement defining clear burden-sharing across countries. In particular, it aimed to solve two shortcomings of the Kyoto Protocol: the involvement of key countries (both industrialized and emerging countries) in lower world emissions, and the setting of binding targets for the medium–long-term. These two objectives were strictly intertwined: an effective fight against climate change requires emission reductions by the end of the century, but these reductions will be significant only if they are put forward by all the largest emitters, thus also including the US and the BRIC (Brasil, Russia India and China). As a result, solving the burden-sharing problem (in line with the principle of common but differentiated responsibility) is key to addressing both the widening of the Annex I countries and the setting of medium–long-term targets.

Despite long negotiations and top political representation, the Copenhagen Summit turned out to be a failure. Modest results were achieved only in terms of long-term targets,[2] but the main problem of burden-sharing (and consequently of the involvement of other key countries) is still far from being solved. In December 2010, much hope was put on the other COP (Conference of the Parties) meeting in Cancún. This time the results were more significant: a mechanism to reduce emissions from deforestation and forest degradation in developing countries (REDD+ – Reducing Emissions from Deforestation and Forest Degradation); targets for global warming by 2050 (under 2°C); a $100bn per year fund for developing countries by 2020; other initiatives on urgent climate actions and on technology transfer. However, no answer was given to the crucial question of burden-sharing.

Therefore, it should be wondered why huge efforts and long negotiations were not able to address this problem effectively. The answer is strictly related to the multilateral governance of fighting climate change that has been developed over the past 20 years. It is based on the United Nations Framework Convention on Climate Change (UNFCCC), whose biggest achievement is the Kyoto Protocol. The last two COP meetings made the drawbacks of this multilateral and multilevel (global, regional, national–sub-national) governance model crystal clear.

Figure 8.5 schematically presents all the major actors involved in the current multilevel governance of climate change. As mentioned above, the cornerstone of this model is the UNFCCC, which can be defined as a Multilateral Environmental Agreement (MEA). At the global level it interacts with other actors, including the World Bank, the International Monetary Fund, the G8–G20, and the OECD. They all contribute to the setting of global targets and other relevant objectives (trade-related issues, UN Millennium Goals, availability of adequate financial resources and so on).

The EU, and potentially other regions are important actors in the middle level, as they can work as 'transmission belts' from the global level to the national–sub-national level. In doing so, they can better address the issue of burden-sharing among member countries by counterbalancing efficiency requirements (that is the best allocation of resources and implementation of actions) with other aspects such as solidarity. In other words, a large burden can be put on the richest countries (even if this turns out to be less efficient) in such a way as not to interfere with intra-region catch-up processes. The EU ETS (Emission Trading Scheme) provides a good example of the attempt to offset efficiency and solidarity. Overall costs would be lowered if actions were implemented in Eastern European countries, but this would hamper their economic potential, so EU policies have striven to find a trade-off between these two contrasting needs (see the section below). It is also noteworthy that European countries have a big incentive to negotiate at the global level through the European Union, as it can increase their bargaining power vis-à-vis other big economic world powers.

But when it comes to implementing policies, states are by far the most important actors. They are placed at the third level, but it should also be noted that this governance model is only partially hierarchical, as those very states contribute to the setting of both regional and global targets (by taking part in negotiations) and provide norms and guidelines for the actions to be taken at the subnational level.

A further two actors should be mentioned: the World Trade Organization (WTO) and NGOs (non-governmental organizations). The former has a big role to play in addressing trade-related issues (see section 6 below), while the latter can make a significant contribution to spreading awareness of the urgency of fighting climate change by involving transnational civil society and putting pressure on institutional actors at any level where decisions are taken.

This governance model is the 'spontaneous' result of competencies and actions which have piled up over the past 20 years. It is not the outcome of a conscious, *a priori* construction. Notwithstanding some positive results (the major one being the Kyoto Protocol), it has many drawbacks at all levels, which are hampering its ability to deliver (as the last COP meetings have clearly demonstrated).[3]

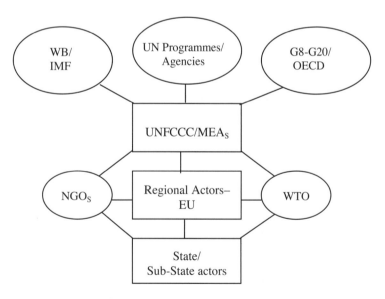

Figure 8.5 Current multilevel governance of climate change

At the global level, there is a problem of efficiency of the intervention due to the growing number of UN agencies and programmes cooperating with the UNFCCC in specific sectors (science, energy, agriculture, fisheries, trade, education, health and so on). This gives rise to inevitable duplication, overlapping and conflicting actions. In other terms, an increasingly confused interaction is emerging among the actors at the global level.

At the middle level, it is key to assess the consistency of some policies implemented by macro regions through international agreements and rules (for instance those set by the WTO). In addition, the actions of regional actors can be contrasted (and their impact lowered) by diverging interests among member countries, especially when they involve change in 'strategic' sectors, as the energy sector is traditionally perceived in Europe.

As far as the subnational level is concerned, the effectiveness, scope and dimension of local interventions are to be questioned. Many initiatives place the emphasis on local polluters and not directly on CO_2 emissions. Besides, the dimension of many interventions – even if focused on CO_2 emission reductions – is often very small and, as a consequence, has a negligible impact on fighting climate change at the global level. New forms of horizontal collaboration (among subnational actors such as regions, cities and provinces) are now emerging[4] and can partially contribute to tone down the dimension of interventions problem, but the other limitations at this level will still remain.

Bearing all this in mind, many scholars have recently strived to present alternative governance models. They attempt to design new frameworks by providing various options: complex formulas to calculate each country's contribution to emission reductions, a portfolio of international treaties, carbon taxes to be levied in all countries (with side-payments for developing countries), linkage of national and regional tradable permit systems, and so on (Aldy and Stavins 2009).

All these proposals are different and evidence many pros and cons, but they all agree on one point: the time seems ripe to move from a vertical and partially hierarchical model to a horizontal and more fragmented (but not necessarily less efficient) model. Under this new framework (see Figure 8.6) the UNFCCC still has an important role to play but it is no longer the key actor. Its former tasks and responsibilities would be shared with other actors to be put on an equal footing. Most importantly, it is no longer the international forum where negotiations on burden-sharing take place. The last two COP meetings made it clear that the UNFCCC decision-making process – based on the seeking of 'consensus' among 193 member countries – cannot deliver on the single most delicate issue (burden-sharing) and therefore needs to be replaced by a new mechanism.

All this would leave room for an emerging international actor, the G20. This could be the ideal forum where top political leaders would take decisions on future burden-sharing. A move from the UNFCCC to the G20 would have many implications:

- The number of countries involved in the negotiations would be dramatically reduced.
- The impact of the potential actions would be roughly the same (as the G20 countries are responsible for over 70 per cent of world emissions).
- The agreement on mitigation (and consequently on burden-sharing) could be traded in the framework of a 'big deal' including other agreements in related fields (that is technology transfers, financial assistance on adaptation policies, lower tariff and non-tariff barriers, creation of an OECD–emerging countries carbon market, and so on).[5]

Decisions taken at the G20 level could provide the overall scheme, but they should be complemented and integrated by other bilateral and multilateral agreements.[6]

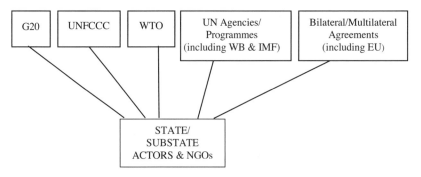

Figure 8.6 Fragmented–horizontal governance of climate change

Under this new framework, the experience and know-how accumulated by the UNFCCC should not be wasted but would be focused on other delicate issues, such as capacity-building for least developed countries, emission monitoring and, possibly, negotiation of an environmental refugee protocol. The latter, in particular, is a problem which will increasingly be at the top of the agenda of many political leaders over the coming decades, thus requiring rules for possible collective action to be defined as soon as possible.

The UN agencies and programmes (including the IMF and the WB, especially when it comes to financial aspects) also have an important role to play, as they may work as agencies implementing the agreements negotiated by the G20 and the UNFCCC. Under this scheme, the WTO's role in all trade-related issues is extremely important (see section 6).

The current vertical governance model has always inspired EU action on fighting climate change. The move toward a horizontal and more fragmented model does not necessarily require a complete rethinking of the EU objectives for 2020, but it would render necessary the re-definition of some EU internal and external policies which cannot be limited to the energy and environmental fields.

4. THE EUROPEAN BET

The fact that the European Commission has invested much time and effort into courageous and ambitious initiatives in the energy and environmental fields over the past years may be surprising. The very credibility of the Commission as the only agenda-setter in the complex inter-institutional balance of power of the EU has been put at stake. Many member countries have raised concerns about these initiatives and repeatedly tried to block them, or at least tone them down. In this respect, the European Treaties have always lent a helping hand to member states, as no competence on energy and environment has ever been handed over to the EU institutions (at least until the Lisbon Treaty). This situation may seem paradoxical as the European integration process was started in the 1950s by acknowledging the need for a common and cooperative management of energy issues (as demonstrated by the setting-up of the European Coal and Steel Community–ECSC and the European Atomic Energy Community–EURATOM). Historically, energy has always been one of the biggest sources of conflict in Europe, especially between France and Germany (for example conflicts over the Ruhr). But notwithstanding such acknowledgement, any attempt to include these competencies in the treaties has repeatedly failed for various reasons: growing strategic national interests in the energy field in the post-war reconstruction period (which also led to the creation of 'national champions' across Europe); the decreasing importance of coal in the energy mix due to the increased use of oil and gas; and uncoordinated national policies on nuclear energy.

Despite this 'hole' in the treaties, the actions taken by the European Union in these fields have been anything but negligible since the 1960s. In particular, the powers and competences given to the EU for the creation of the single market helped identify a 'residual competence',[7] thus leaving room for European intervention. To put it simply, the EU was also enabled to take decisions in fields not explicitly included in the treaties, as long as this was deemed necessary for the creation and completion of the single market.

In the 1990s, European intervention in these fields gained new impetus from some directives[8] aiming to gradually open up energy markets to European competitiveness (through preliminary forms of unbundling in the gas and electricity markets, more transparency in transmission prices, the monitoring of independent national regulators and so on).

But a quantum leap has been taken only in recent years, due to increasing oil and gas prices (especially in the pre-crisis period), spreading acknowledgement of the risks related to climate change and the challenging attempt to be frontrunners in developing new green technologies. After heavy negotiations and mounting conflicts and discontent among member countries, the energy and environmental packages were finally approved in December 2008.[9]

In particular, the environmental package sets unilateral targets for the post-Kyoto period: a 20 per cent reduction in CO_2 emissions, 20 per cent of renewables in the European energy mix and a 20 per cent increase in energy efficiency by 2020. As far as the mitigation target is concerned, the new package increases the number of sectors which are requested to gain allowances under the current Emission Trading Scheme (EU ETS).[10] In addition, from 2013 firms will be increasingly requested to buy allowances in auctions, while today around 90 per cent of allowances are given for free through the so-called 'grandfathering' mechanism under the current EU ETS (which has been designed to meet the Kyoto targets by 2012).

Obviously, all this will come at a price for member states. The Commission chose to calculate the total cost of the package and the ensuing burden-sharing among member states by taking total compliance costs (TCC) into account.[11] The latter include all costs directly or indirectly related to energy production as compared with the business-as-usual hypothesis. In practical terms, this enables calculation of the additional effort requested from each member state to meet its own targets under the new environmental package. Indeed, other methods might be used to calculate the cost of the package. Another option could be the cost-efficiency scenario, which does not place the emphasis on the contribution of each member state but rather on the European Union as a whole. In other words, actions related to the environmental package would be implemented where they are more convenient (in terms of cost-efficiency) in the entire European territory (no matter whether this implies the concentration of interventions in few countries with low emission reduction costs and higher returns on investments). In this case, the total cost of the package would be 0.58 per cent of European GDP by 2020, while the TCC – chosen by the Commission – raises the cost to 0.71 per cent. The rationale behind the choice of the TCC is the unbalanced and, above all, unjust burden-sharing of the cost-efficiency scenario: many actions (and their related costs) would take place in Eastern European countries. Evidently, this would be at odds with one of the founding principles of the EU ETS: the solidarity principle. For instance, the cost borne by Poland under the TCC is 0.06 per cent, while the cost-efficiency scenario would lead to 1.24 per cent of GDP.

However, these costs were calculated by the European Commission by taking 2007 as the reference year. Since then the international economic scenario has changed considerably. First and foremost, the world has experienced the worst economic crisis since the Great Depression and, as a consequence, a dramatic fall in production and CO_2 emissions has emerged.

In this regard, it is noteworthy that emissions are expected to be below the cap over the entire 2008–2012 period, so firms are currently banking allowances and international credits (up to 2.3 Gt CO_2 eq. by 2013), which will contribute to meeting the new European targets by 2020.

Second, assumptions on oil and gas prices need to be profoundly revised due to their increase since 2007. Third, additional targets have been added though the energy and environment packages (including non-ETS targets and renewable energy targets) and other energy efficiency measures introduced as of spring 2009.[12] All this will inevitably have a significant impact on expected CO_2 emissions and on the costs of European targets by 2020. They will probably be about €48bn in 2020, that is 0.3 per cent of GDP, thus resulting in an expected reduction of costs per GDP of between 30 per cent and 50 per cent compared to the same calculation made in 2008.

This is why the Commission has recently proposed to further increase the emission reduction targets from 20 to 30 per cent, if some conditions (in terms of equivalent and proportional targets by other mature economies and emerging countries) are respected. This would imply an additional cost of about €33bn (around 0.2 per cent of GDP in 2020), thus roughly offsetting the cost reduction prompted by the crisis and other intervening factors in the last three years (additional targets, increased oil and gas prices). But this proposal has been repeatedly rejected by various member countries, which underlines the lack of a multilateral agreement in the UNFCCC framework and the fact that, so far, measures announced by other countries have been both non-binding and unequal.

As Table 8.1 shows (presented by the European Commission[13]), the pledges made by Annex I countries under the Copenhagen Accord would enable emissions to be curbed by 12–18 per cent (compared to 1990 levels), thus clearly diverging from the 2°C trajectory (the only significant achievement of the Copenhagen Summit) which would require a much greater reduction (25–40 per cent below the 1990 levels by 2020). In particular when it comes to the US, its pledge to curb emissions (17 per cent vs. 2005 or 4–7 per cent vs. 1990) is strikingly less stringent than the EU legislation.

Table 8.1 Targets pledged by selected developed countries under the Copenhagen Accord

	Emissions (Mt CO$_2$-eq) 1990	Emissions (Mt CO$_2$-eq) 2005	Target % (low pledge)		Target % (high pledge)	
			from 1990	from 2005	from 1990	from 2005
Australia	416 214	524 635	12.9	-10.4	-10.8	-29.3
Canada	591 793	730 967	2.5	-17.0	2.5	-17.0
EU-27	5 572 506	5 119 476	-20.0	-12.9	-30.0	-23.8
Japan	1 269 657	1 357 844	-25.0	-29.9	-25.0	-29.9
Russian Federation	3 319 327	2 117 821	-15.0	33.2	-25.0	17.5
United States	6 084 490	7 082 213	-3.4	-17.0	-3.4	-17.0
Annex 1 total (including US)	18 379 050	17 569 153	-12.0	-8.0	-18.0	-14.0

Note: Emissions from international aviation not included (thus reducing the EU targets compared to 2005).

Source: UNFCCC, submissions provided by Parties in the context of the Copenhagen Accord and of the AWG-KP (all data are excluding LULUCF).

To make things worse, it should be borne in mind that the Copenhagen Accord pledges have not led to national legislations (with the significant exception of the EU member states). Despite the modest results of the Cancún meeting, things have not changed as no agreement has been reached on burden-sharing and no other major world emitter has been willing or able to set binding targets for the post-Kyoto period. As a result, the expected CO$_2$ emission reductions by Annex I countries will likely be even lower than the abovementioned 12–18 per cent. The same holds true when taking into account the pledges of the emerging countries. China has pledged to lower the carbon intensity of its GDP by 40–45 per cent with respect to 2005 by 2020. Besides, it wishes to increase the use of renewable energy in its energy mix and its forest coverage. Notwithstanding the difficult assessment of the stringency of this pledge due to many uncertainties (the GDP accounting method, for instance), once again it seems clear that the pledge is unequal when compared to the EU efforts, and insufficient when considering the 2°C trajectory of the Copenhagen Accord.

Despite this unequal international burden-sharing and the modest effects of pledges in fighting climate change, many economists and specialists agree that the EU engagement is a far-sighted bet. In this case, the spotlight is put on the possibility of escaping heavy European oil and gas dependence (thus improving security of supply), and triggering new economic growth by developing green technology know-how, skills and patents. Building on these assumptions, the environmental package targets have been included in the 'Europe 2020' strategy among the 'flagship initiatives'. This signals the EU's determination to root long-term economic growth in a competitive green economy (see Chapter 7 on the 'Europe 2020' strategy).

But when comparing the costs and benefits of the EU decisions to be engaged in the environmental challenge, it should be borne in mind that the initial costs need to be sustained immediately, while the potential benefits will show up only in the future (and not necessarily the 'near' future). So industrial lobbyists across Europe (especially in the largest manufacturing countries and Eastern Europe) worry that the European efforts are far from enhancing economic growth and rather could hamper economic potential, especially in the light of the austerity plans many member countries have had to put in place due to the European sovereign debt crisis. On top of that, the lack of a multilateral agreement on equivalent efforts by other mature economies or emerging countries is raising fears of carbon leakage and unfair competition. As explained below, this may prompt further requests for countermeasures to rebalance the international level playing field.

5. CARBON LEAKAGE AND COMPETITIVENESS: A REAL THREAT?

Building on the economic literature (Samuelson 1954; Olson 1965; Stigler 1974; Cornes and Sandler 1996), climate can be considered a 'public good', and as a consequence the fight against climate change is likely to prompt 'free-riding' behavior. Nobody is willing to bear the cost of the fight if they can reap the benefits of actions taken (and costs borne) by others.

The Kyoto Protocol has attempted to address this issue indirectly by placing the emphasis on the principle of 'common but differentiated responsibilities'. By recognizing that the fight against climate change is a common responsibility, the Protocol underlines the need for a 'global' response which evidently cannot rely on actions put through by a few countries but rather on efforts made by all countries. By emphasizing 'differentiated' responsibility, it acknowledges that the so-called industrialized (or mature) economies are largely responsible for today's stock of CO_2 in the atmosphere. In addition, unbalanced burden-sharing between mature and emerging countries may unfairly hamper economic growth in the latter.

Nonetheless, this does not imply that emerging countries should not be asked to contribute to the fight, if anything because they will produce the bulk of CO_2 over the coming decades (see Figure 8.1). In addition, given the large trade surpluses piled up by emerging countries over the past decade, the EU, the US and Japan are currently net importers of embodied CO_2 emissions, while China and India are net exporters. As a result, the contribution of emerging countries to the fight is key but it needs to be defined in such a way as to minimize its impact on economic potential and catch-up processes on a global scale. Conversely, their scarce contribution to the fight would give them an unfair advantage which could further increase trade imbalances.

In other words, the fight against climate change and the ensuing burden-sharing problem can have a potentially strong impact on global economic competition.

To make things worse, the problem of unfair competition can also stem from unbalanced efforts by mature economies. In this case, one clear example is the current – and potentially increasing – unequal distribution of costs between the US (which has failed to pass federal bills on CO_2 reductions so far) and the EU (which has already set unilateral binding targets for the post-Kyoto period). In his famous and provocative article 'A New Agenda for Global Warming', Joseph Stiglitz stated that by failing to address the climate change problem, the United States is implicitly subsidizing energy use and engaging in unfair trade practices (Stiglitz 2006).

More generally, attention should be devoted to the issues of unfair competition and carbon leakage. When assessing the impact on competition of the unbalanced fight against climate change, the most precise definition of the former is probably that provided by Reinaud (2005), of the 'firm's ability to maintain and/or expand market position based on its costs structure'.

So differences in cost structures due to unbalanced efforts can prompt changes in terms of trade, trade flows and carbon leakage, not to mention impacts on domestic indicators such as GDP and employment.

As for carbon leakage, the IPCC (Intergovernmental Panel on Climate Change) defines it as an 'increase in emissions outside the country – decrease in emissions inside the country' (Metz *et al.* 2007).[14] In other words, countries worry that carbon leakage will significantly reduce or cancel out efforts made to curb CO_2 emissions and result in domestic production being relocated to foreign countries with no binding targets, thus also triggering a loss of profits and jobs. This is the so-called 'competitiveness-driven leakage' which is an argument often used by industrial lobbyists in the EU and the US. But there are also other forms of leakage, which can be listed as follows (Reinaud 2008):

a)   reduction in world energy prices due to reduced energy demand in countries with binding targets, which, all other things being equal, increases energy demand (and CO_2 emissions) in other countries;

b)   increases in prices of low emitting feedstocks (for example scrap metal for recycling), lowering their consumption in countries with no binding targets;

c)   reduced unitary emissions in plants abroad, as new green technologies and process innovations of countries with binding targets spill over to other countries.

Points a) and b) tend to increase emissions in countries with no binding targets, while point c) goes in the opposite direction and lowers emissions in these countries.

Building on a review of many studies, the OECD has come to the conclusion that a span of 0.5–2 per cent of mature economies' GDP is currently challenged by rising production costs due to the imposition of a carbon cost (Wooders, Cosbey and Stephenson 2009a).

This does not appear to be an unbearable burden for industrialized countries but it involves a relatively small number of large plants which are connected not only to other large plants but also to a variety of small and medium-sized enterprises, and as a consequence accounts for a large number of jobs in their country. Political sensitiveness to such issues skyrocketed after the explosion of the economic crisis, particularly in industrialized countries where the recession or sluggish economic growth may jeopardize standards of living and traditionally generous welfare states (in continental Europe especially). In this regard, specific attention should be focused on the impact on European competition, not only because the EU has been severely hit by the crisis but also because it is the largest economic region with ongoing CO_2 emission reductions under the Kyoto Protocol (that is the EU ETS) and has already planned to achieve other significant results by 2020 (see section 4).

However, as stated by the OECD, there is little empirical evidence of the impact of differences in fighting climate change on competitiveness and carbon leakage. In particular, as far as relocation of plants abroad is concerned, it is noteworthy that climate change policies and measures may play a role in such decisions but are far from being the only factor, as other inputs are included in the decision (wage costs and average education of the local workforce, cost of capital, energy prices, national and local taxes, exchange rate risks, political stability, transport infrastructures and so on).

Nonethless, as Stiglitz (2006) put it, not pricing the global costs of emission (as the US and the emerging countries are currently doing) is *de facto* a domestic subsidy that should allow for countervailing duties, especially in view of the growing differences in implementing measures to fight climate change (as will be the case should a new agreement or an enlarged post-Kyoto agreement not be reached in a couple of years).

6. BORDER ADJUSTMENTS AND WTO RULES

The links between fighting climate change and the international trade rules are clearly perceived by the parties to both the UNFCCC and the Kyoto Protocol. Art. 3.5 of the UNFCCC and Art. 2.3 of the Kyoto Protocol state that by taking actions against climate change, states cannot adopt measures which may represent a means of arbitrary, unjustifiable discrimination or a disguised restriction on international trade. They are also requested to cooperate to promote a supportive and open international economic system leading to sustainable world economic growth and development. In other words, the very objectives of the Convention and the Kyoto Protocol are intended to be consistent with those of the WTO.

However, in the light of potential negative impacts on competitiveness, countries with binding targets (for example the EU member states) and countries which are planning to introduce binding targets (for example the US) are increasingly tempted to use Border Carbon Adjustments (BCAs).

Cap and trade mechanisms with distribution of free allowances are currently in place (the largest carbon market being the EU ETS) and BCAs have been widely discussed both in the EU and the US. Nonetheless, this does not necessarily imply that both measures will turn out to be efficient or effective. Distribution of free allowances (the option chosen by the EU) may not enable states to address issues related to international trade and agreements on climate change (or may simply postpone them), while the use of BCAs, notwithstanding their immediate attractiveness, may raise many practical and legal concerns. Besides, the impacts of BCAs on the national economy (for instance by leading to a reallocation of public and private resources in domestic sectors) should be carefully evaluated.

In this regard, the European Commission has acknowledged that border measures may trigger impacts 'related to increased costs of imported inputs for EU manufacturers, outside the ETS'. In addition the 'higher cost of inputs that would emerge may cause problems for European producers further downstream in the production chain in sectors which are in the ETS but which are not covered by the border measures'.[15]

More generally, all the options available at the border to a country can be listed as follows (Wooders, Reinaud and Cosbey 2009b):

- Border tax adjustments (BTAs) – such as tariffs on imports and/or rebates on exports.
- Mandatory allowance purchase by importers.
- Embedded carbon product standards.

Countries with binding targets can also protect their domestic industries by providing aid (for example subsidies for green technologies) and distributing free allowances (the EU's preferred option).

The effectiveness of the various options on reducing carbon leakage and negative impacts on competitiveness depends on:[16]

- GHG (greenhouse gas) emission of like products from different sources.
- Abatement costs and, more generally, the options producers have to reduce these emissions.
- The ability to pass or the possibility of passing costs on to consumers.

Moreover, the decisions on options and their design depend on other factors, including the ability to gather information about the carbon content of products, the accountability not only of countries as a whole but also of sectors and single plants for their emissions and, last but not least, the cost-effectiveness of an objective calculation of carbon content.

Indeed, none of the abovementioned options is able to fully bridge the gap in competitiveness between domestic and foreign producers and re-level the international playing field. However, design specifics do matter when choosing the most appropriate option. Economically speaking, some options may turn out to be quite costly, while their ability to prevent leakage and loss of competitiveness may be nearly negligible. Moreover, in practical terms a trade-off between the administrative costs (due to difficulties in measuring the CO_2 content of products) and the effectiveness of the various options needs to be made.

As Fischer and Fox (2009) put it,

> border adjustments for climate policy... may not even be very effective at improving overall emissions reductions net of foreign leakage. A border tax on imports only affects the relative price of domestic and foreign goods in the home country. Policies that provide export relief, on the other hand, affect the relative price of the home good in the rest of the world and discourage substitution toward foreign goods at home and abroad, but they also discourage conservation at home. All the policies, however, avoid some of the losses in production associated with a carbon tax.

Notwithstanding the limited impact on national GDP of unequal engagements in fighting climate change and the limits to the use of countervailing measures, it is likely that the demand for carbon equalization schemes will increase in the near future. In the light of the possible failure of negotiations on the post-Kyoto regime, and within the framework of the abovementioned move toward a new governance model of fighting climate change (see section 3), it is likely that disproportionate impacts on GDP will be higher over the next decade (especially in the European Union manufacturing countries) and that demand for countervailing measures will increase.

This problem is being explicitly tackled by the European environmental package which sets binding targets up to 2020. As mentioned above, the EU has decided that free allowances will be provided to industries facing the risk of carbon leakage. In this regard, the European Commission has been asked to prepare a list of sectors at risk, which can be revised every five years. The next revision is expected at the end of 2014, but member states – or the Commission itself – can add to the list on a yearly basis.

Problems do not arise only in relation to the use and effectiveness of BCAs, as there are also growing worries about their compatibility with the WTO rules. As mentioned above, BCAs cannot be designed in such a way as not to be consistent with the international trade rules. However, the possibility of trade conflicts – involving the Dispute Settlement Body of the WTO – seems anything but theoretical, especially in view of the new unilateral measures to be put through after 2013 (for example the EU ETS with auctioned allowances). When assessing the compatibility of BCAs with the WTO rules, GATT (General Agreement on Tariffs and Tarde) Art. II.2 (a) and the Agreement on Subsidies and Countervailing Measures (SCM Agreement) may be a good starting point.[17]

As far as border taxes on imports are concerned, the abovementioned GATT article clearly states that nothing can prevent a country 'from imposing at any time on the importation of any product a charge equivalent to internal tax imposed consistently with the provisions of section 2 of Article III in respect of the like domestic product or in respect of an article from which the imported product has been manufactured or produced in whole or in part'.

Therefore, carbon taxes can be imposed on products (or on the related production process) at the border, as long as they can be considered indirect taxes (while, on the contrary, it is well established that compensations on direct taxes are not viable options). From this viewpoint it should be assumed that carbon taxes are fully legal under WTO rules. However, GATT Art. II.2 (a) leaves room for confusion and possible conflicts, as it remains unclear whether and to what extent fossil fuels used in the production process of goods can be adjusted at the border through carbon taxes, not to mention the difficulty of gathering the required information on the CO_2 content of finished products.

In addition, border taxes must be designed in such a way as to be consistent with one of the most important principles of both GATT and the WTO: the principle of national treatment.[18] GATT Article III.4 better defines this principle by stating that 'all laws, regulations and requirements affecting... internal sale, purchase, transportation, distribution or use' of imported goods cannot be made in such a way as to favour domestic products (or, conversely, discriminate against imported products). In concrete terms, one should draw the conclusion that a Bilateral Trade Agreement (BTA) is in line with the WTO rules as long as an equivalent tax is already levied on a like domestic product.

It is therefore key to decide whether two products are 'like', as the principle of national treatment can be applied only under this condition. Once again, the abovementioned problem arises: two products may be the same in terms of appearance and potential use, and they may also share the same classification under the WTO rules, but nonetheless their production process may differ widely in terms of CO_2 content. Is it sufficient to consider these two otherwise identical products 'alike'? According to the prevailing interpretation of the WTO rules, the CO_2 content of two like products and the type of energy used in their production (for example renewables vs oil) cannot make them 'alike'. The very Appellate Body of the WTO has clearly stated that the 'likeness' of two products must be assessed by taking into account their physical characteristics, end-use, consumer tastes and preferences, and tariff classification.[19] Production methods and the type of energy used for their production do not seem to change the 'likeness' of two products. But these rules also need to be read within the framework of GATT Article XX(b) which allows for exceptional measures when they are 'necessary to protect human, animal or plant life or health'.

To make things worse, it is still unclear whether or not the obligation for importers to buy allowances under the importing country's cap and trade mechanism can be fully considered as a domestic tax.

Other problems arise when it comes to rebates on exports (which are less common than BTAs). In this case, one should take into account footnote 1 of the SCM Agreement which states that 'the exemption of an exported product from duties or taxes borne by the like product when destined for domestic consumption, or the remission of such duties or taxes in amounts not in excess of those which have accrued, shall not be deemed to be a subsidy'. However, this footnote also needs to be interpreted in the light of Annex I of the SCM Agreements, which provides a list of export subsidies prohibited under the Agreement and clearly states, among other things, that states are allowed to provide 'exemption, or remission, in respect of the production and distribution of exported products, of indirect taxes in excess of those levied in respect of the production and distribution of like products when sold for domestic consumption'. In other words, taxes which are levied on products (indirect taxes) could be adjusted at the border, while rebates on exports aiming at equalling taxes on producers (direct taxes) should be considered as prohibited subsidies. Again, this seems a likely outcome but a clear picture is far from being drawn.

To sum up, the subject of compatibility of adjustment measures with the WTO rules appears to be anything but settled, and as a consequence trade conflicts and growing demands for decisions to be taken by the Dispute Settlement Body of the WTO will likely result over the coming years. The time is ripe for states (especially those more exposed to the risk of unfair competition and carbon leakage) and macro regions (thus including the European Union) to set their own strategy to better address these issues.

7. CONCLUSIONS: A NEW STRATEGY FOR 'EUROPE 2020'?

This chapter has addressed the issue of fighting climate change over the coming decades by placing the emphasis on the need for a common effort involving not only the mature economies (which are responsible for the bulk of the CO_2 already emitted in the atmosphere) but also the emerging countries (whose contribution to future emissions will increase). A just and equitable compromise between diverging interests and attitudes (including within the group of OECD countries) needs to be found in the short run, but so far all attempts by the UNFCCC have fallen flat. The impact of delayed mitigation policies on the speed of global warming; will increase the probability of extreme meteorological events which, in turn, will require the adoption of expensive adaption policies and the provision of growing international aid to the least-developed countries. In addition, other key problems (for instance management of environmental refugees, trade-related issues and so on) urge the implementation of new policies and actions, both at the international and national levels.

More generally, burden-sharing and the provision of new norms and rules to better address these issues are key tasks of any governance model for fighting climate change. But, as presented in section 3, the current vertical and at least partially hierarchical model has proven itself unable to deliver both in terms of the involvement of key emitters (that is the US and China) and the setting of binding targets in the medium–long run (by 2030, 2050, and the end of the century).

The failure of the Copenhagen Summit and the limited results of Cancún (with no agreement on the crucial problem of burden-sharing) push us toward a horizontal model in which the UNFCCC will no longer be the cornerstone of the entire governance framework. Therefore, a compromise on burden-sharing may be better found in the G20, while the UNFCCC may re-focus its mission on other aspects (capacity-building, emission monitoring, negotiation of an environmental refugees protocol and so on). The UNFCCC may also be charged with the task of defining global standards and norms to calculate the CO_2 content of products in order to prevent trade conflicts (on the identification of two 'like' products, for instance).

This possible shift to a new governance model will inevitably impact on the EU, which is the largest region in the world with unilateral binding targets for the post-Kyoto period. In particular, the EU should not change the targets it intends to meet by 2020; rather, it should adapt its strategy to the shift in the governance model. When doing so, two issues need to be kept in mind: pledges by other states have not led to national legislations so far; the explosion of the crisis has changed the cost of meeting the European targets. In this regard, it is noteworthy that low production and emission levels prompted by the crisis are allowing firms to bank allowances and international credits (up to 2.3 Gt CO_2 by 2013). This will help lower European costs (from 30 to 50 per cent compared to the expected costs calculated before the crisis) including for the post-Kyoto period. Despite such cost reductions, currently it would not be wise to offset them with more ambitious European targets (that is from 20 to 30 per cent CO_2 emission cuts by 2020) due to the lack of equivalent binding targets of other major world emitters. In addition, the lower costs are not evenly distributed across Europe (with an inevitably greater impact on the largest manufacturing countries) and industries; not to mention the risk of unfair competition and carbon leakage. Indeed, the latter do not appear to pose a real threat for mature economies (including OECD Europe) as 0.5–2 per cent of their GDP is challenged by rising production costs resulting from the imposition of a carbon cost. However, requests for protection may arise, especially in post-2013 Europe when growing shares of allowances will be auctioned. The analysis illustrated in section 6 shows that despite their immediate attractiveness, BCAs may have side-effects (in terms of their cost-effectiveness, impact on the production chain and so on) which may seriously hamper their ability to provide the requested 'protection'. To put it simply, they will hardly succeed in leveling the international playing field. However, this acknowledgment may be misleading as the impact of unfair competition and carbon leakage may be deemed excessive, especially by large firms. They may lobby and put pressure on political leaders to adopt BCAs due to possible job losses (a very sensitive issue in the Europe of today).

But there is also the risk that these border adjustments will clash with the WTO rules. In this regard, as presented in section 6, there is a likelihood of possible trade conflicts on technical aspects (that is the identification of two 'like' products when their CO_2 content differs, rules to be applied to the obligation for importers to buy allowances etc.).

Given all these problems, some policy recommendations can be provided to the EU in relation to its targets enshrined in the 'Europe 2020' strategy. Again, the purpose is not to call into question the 2020 targets but rather to pinpoint some changes in the European strategy to render it more consistent with the changing international context.

In line with a more horizontal and 'fragmented' governance model, the EU should take advantage of its 'would-be' leadership in green technologies and its economic strength as the largest world market. The latter has already enabled the EU to make its own trade standards global standards, and it would be wise to do the same for green technologies and services. In this regard, the EU's credibility and ability to deliver would be increased if its budget were changed accordingly. Indeed, it is a very limited tool whose leverage should be significantly increased (policies should not be entirely funded and co-financing should be facilitated), together with other measures including loan guarantees for funds from the EIB and/or the European Bank for Reconstruction and Development, and – as many suggest – bonds to finance large projects of EU-wide interest in the energy and environmental field (Ferrer 2009).

Moreover, by acknowledging its standing in the world economy, the EU should strive to include mitigation policies in bilateral–multilateral trade agreements with extra-EU countries. In other words, the time is ripe for the EU to scale up its external dimension. The EU is currently either an observer (for example in the UN) or a member (but the states have the final word) of many international institutions (including the UNFCCC and the G20). The WTO decision-making process is a best practice that should be replicated; in this case the guidelines are provided by the Council (which also appoints a special Committee to monitor the negotiations) but the European Commission acts as the formal negotiator on behalf of 27 member countries in the Ministerial Conference. The Council pitches in again when agreements need to be signed. Unfortunately this best practice has not been used in the UNFCCC COP meetings, where internal divisions and over-representation of the EU member states have weakened the EU's bargaining power and led to its demise vis à vis the US and the emerging countries.

At the moment, Mr Barroso and Mr Van Rompuy are the highest placed delegates in the G20 (as well as in the G8), but the WTO procedure (with the Commission at the wheel and the Council monitoring the process) could be used in the G20, where the EU could succeed in having mitigation included in the agenda. Such a change would not be a problem in terms of procedures, because the G20 acts upon informal rules and has no secretariat, so a simple agreement among its members would suffice. This decision-making process may be used for the UNFCCC, including by building on a new tool provided by the Treaty of Lisbon[20] which allows the

Council, following the Commission's recommendation, to appoint the EU negotiator or the head of the EU negotiating team.

The same holds true for the over-representation of the EU in the UN system, including the Bretton Woods institutions. The current opposition of various European leaders to such a solution will likely vanish over the coming years in the light of legitimate requests by under-represented emerging countries.

Finally, the EU should support an OECD carbon market at least in the medium to long run. Indeed, various OECD countries (including Norway, Switzerland, some states of the US, Australia, New Zealand, Japan and so on) are considering adopting a carbon market, and it would be wise to link all such carbon markets. However, making this work at full speed by 2020 does not seem possible, as the extra-EU countries need time to develop the expertise that the EU has being accumulating since 2005. Nonetheless, the next decade is the most appropriate period for establishing the first links between the OECD markets.[21]

To conclude, this chapter has demonstrated that the EU targets for 2020 – within the framework of the 'Europe 2020' strategy – are ambitious but realistic. The impact of the economic crisis is considerably reducing their cost; however, the latter will not be negligible and its impact on specific industries and countries may turn out to be significant, especially in the light of non-equal engagements by other major world emitters. More flexibility should therefore be included in the European targets, and a quantum leap should be taken in EU external representation to make the European targets more consistent with the changing international context and ultimately more acceptable for European firms and citizens.

NOTES

1. See OECD (2008).
2. See Art. 1 of the Copenhagen Accord 'we shall, recognising the scientific view that the increase in global temperature should be below 2°C…, enhance our long-term cooperative action to combat climate change'. See also Art. 2 'We agree that deep cuts in global emissions are required according to science… and take action to meet this objective consistent with science and on the basis of equity'.
3. For a full presentation of this model of governance and its drawbacks, see Villafranca (2009).
4. For instance: 'C40 Cities, Cities for Climate Protection Campaign' (CCP), Climate Alliance, 'Energie-Cités', 'Metro Portland' (Oregon), and so on.
5. For a full explanation of this new governance model, see Pavanello and Villafranca (forthcoming).
6. The recent REDD+ Partnership and the MRV Mitigation Partnership are clear examples of this kind of intervention; they can be seen as new forms of voluntary multilateral international initiatives which are parallel to and might converge with the UNFCCC (or the G20 in the proposed horizontal model) at a later stage.

7. See Art. 308 ECT 'If action by the Community should prove necessary to attain, in the course of the operation of the common market, one of the objectives of the Community, and this Treaty has not provided the necessary powers, the Council shall, acting unanimously on a proposal from the Commission and after consulting the European Parliament, take the appropriate measures'.
8. See, among others, Directive 98/30/EC of the European Parliament and of the Council of 22 June 1998, and 96/92/EC of the European Parliament and of the Council of 19 December 1996.
9. For the energy package: Directive 2009/29/ EC; Decision 406/2009/EC. For the environmental package: Directive 2009/28/EC; Directive 2009/30/EC; Directive 2009/31/EC; Regulation (EC) 443/2009.
10. See Annex I of Directive 2008/101/EC for a complete list of sectors.
11. See European Commission (2008).
12. These measures include the Regulation on CO_2 emissions of new passenger cars, the Eco Design and Labelling Directives, Carbon Capture and Storage (CCS) demonstration plants and so on.
13. See European Commission (2008).
14. Contribution of Working Group III to the Fourth Assessment Report of the Intergovernmental Panel on Climate Change.
15. Ibid.
16. Susanne Dröge (2009) http://www.climatestrategies.org.
17. See ICTSD (2009).
18. See GATT Article III.2. Another WTO basic principle ('the most favoured nation') can also play an important role in assessing border measures, especially if they are likely to result in the discrimination of an imported product on the basis of its country of origin.
19. See 'European Communities – Measures affecting asbestos and asbestos-containing products', WT/DS135/R – Report of the Panel. EC-Asbestos (DS 135).
20. See Art. 218 of the Treaty on the Functioning of the European Union.
21. See the conclusions drawn by Tuerk *et al.* (2009).

BIBLIOGRAPHY

Aldy, Joseph E. and Robert N. Stavins (2009), *Post-Kyoto International Climate Policy*, Cambridge: Cambridge University Press.
Alessi, Monica, Anton Georgiev, and Christian Egenhofer (2010), *Assessments of the Accord and Implications for the EU*, ECP Reports, CEPS.
Bierman, Frank *et al.* (2008), *Climate Governance Post-2012, Options for EU Policy-Making*, CEPS.
Biermann, Frank and Ingrid Boas (2008), 'Protecting Climate Refugees: The Case for a Global Protocol', *Environment: Science and Policy for Sustainable Development*, http://www.environmentmagazine.org/Archives/Back%20Issues/November-December%202008/Biermann-Boas-full.htm.
Biermann, Frank and Reiner Brohm (2005), 'Implementing the Kyoto Protocol without the USA: the Strategic Role of Energy Tax Adjustments at the Border', *Climate Policy*, 4, 289–302.
Cornes, Richard and Todd Sandler (1996), *The Theory of Externalities, Public Goods and Club Goods*, Cambridge: Cambridge University Press.
Cosbey, Aaron (2008), *Border Carbon Adjustment*, International Institute for Sustainable Development.

Cosbey, Aaron (2008), *Trade and Climate Change: Issue in Perspective*, International Institute for Sustainable Development.

Cosbey, Aaron and Richard Tarasofsky (2007), *Climate Change, Competitiveness and Trade*, A Chatham House Report, London: The Royal Institute of International Affairs

Corazza, Carlo (2009), *EcoEuropa. Le nuove politiche per l'energia e il clima*, Milano: Egea.

Curtin, Joseph (2010), *The Copenhagen Conference: How Should the EU Respond?*, Dublin: IIEA.

de Cendra de Larragán, Javier (2006), 'Can emission trading schemes be coupled with Border Tax Adjustment? Analysis vis-a-vis WTO law', *Review of European Community and International Environmental Law*, **15** (2), 131–45.

Demailly, Quirion (2008), 'Leakage from Climate Policies and Border Tax Adjustment: Lessons from a Geographic Model of the Cement Industry', in Guesnerie, Roger and Henry Tulkens (eds), *The Design of Climate Policy*, papers from a Summer Institute held in Venice, CESifo Seminar Series, Boston: The MIT Press.

Dröge, Susanne (2010), *Tackling Leakage in a World of Unequal Carbon Prices*, Climate Strategies, 20 may, final, http://www.climatestrategies.org/research/our-reports/category/32/257.html

Dröge, Susanne (2010), *International Climate Policy. Priorities of Key Negotiating Parties*, SWP Research Paper RP2.

Egenhofer, Christian and Daniel Gros, (2010), *Climate Change and Trade: Taxing Carbon at the Border?*, CEPS Paperbacks.

European Commission (2008), *Impact Assessment of the Package of the Implementation Measure for the EU's Objectives on Climate Change and Renewable Energy for 2020*.

European Council (2009), Presidency Conclusions, 15265, 29–30 October.

Ferrer Jorge N. (2009), *For a Future Sustainable, Competitive and Greener EU Budget Integrating the Climate Change Objectives of the EU*, CEPS.

Fischer, Caroline and Alan K. Fox (2009), *Comparing Policies to Combat Emissions Leakage: Border Adjustments versus Rebates*, RFF Discussion Paper.

Frankel, Jeffrey (2009), *Addressing the Leakage/Competitiveness Issue in Climate Change Policy Proposals, Climate Change, Trade and Investment: Is a Collision Inevitable?*, Washington, DC: Brookings Institute Press.

Geden, Kremer (2010), *The European Union: A Challenged Leader in Ambitious International Climate Policy*, SWP Research Paper.

Ghosh, Arunabha (2010a), *Making Climate Look Like Trade? Questions on Incentives, Flexibility and Credibility*, CPR Policy Brief.

Ghosh, Arunabha (2010b), *Climate, Trade and Global Governance in the Midst of an Economic Crisis*, Briefing at a Public Hearing on Global Governance, 25 March.

Godard, Olivier (2007), *Unilateral European Post-Kyoto Climate Policy and Economic Adjustment at EU Borders*, Ecole Polytechnique, Cahierno, DDX-07-15.

Green, Fergus, Warwick Mckibbin, and Greg Picker (2010), *Confronting the Crisis of International Climate Policy: Rethinking the Framework for Cutting Emissions*, Policy Brief, Lowy Institute for International Policy.

Grubb, Michael and Karsten Neuhoff (2006), 'Allocation and competitiveness in the EU emissions trading scheme: Policy overview', *Climate Policy*, **6** (1), 7–30.

Hague, William (2010), *Russell C. Leffingwell Lecture: The Diplomacy of Climate Change*, Council on Foreign Relations.

Held, David and Angus F. Hervey (2009), *Democracy, Climate Change and Global Governance*, Policy Network Paper, November.

International Centre for Trade and Sustainable Development (ICTSD) (2009), *Competitiveness and Climate Policies: Is There a Case for Restrictive Unilateral Trade Measure?*, Information Note no.16.

Intergovernmental Panel on Climate Change IPCC (2007), *Climate Change 2007: Synthesis Report*.

Ismer, Roland and Karstel Neuhoff (2007), 'Border Tax Adjustments: a feasible way to support stringent emission trading', *European Journal of Law and Economics*, **24** (2), 137–64.

Kurtzman, Joel (2009), 'The low-carbon diet: how the market can curb climate change', *Foreign Affairs*, **8** (5).

Levy, Michael (2009), 'Copenhagen's inconvenient truth: how to salvage the climate conference', *Foreign Affairs*, **8** (5).

Metz, Bert, Ogunlade Davidson, Peter Bosch, Rutu Dave and Leo Meyer (eds) (2007), *Climate Change 2007: Mitigation of Climate Change*, Contribution of Working Group III to the Fourth Assessment Report of the Intergovernmental Panel on Climate Change, Cambridge and New York: Cambridge University Press.

Michonsky, Katherine and Michael A. Levy (2010), *Harnessing International Institutions to Address Climate Change*, New York: Council of Foreign Relations, Working Paper, March.

Monjon, Stéphanie and Philippe Quirion (2009), *Addressing Leakage in the EU ETS: Results from the CASE II Model*, CIRED/Climate Stategies, Working Paper.

Monjon, Stéphanie and Philippe Quirion (2009), 'How to design a border adjustment for the European Union Emission Trading System?', *Energy Policy*, **38** (9), 5199–207.

Organisation for Economic Co-operation and Development (OECD) (2008), *Climate Change: Meeting the Challenge to 2050*.

Olson, Mancur L. (1965), *The Logic of Collective Action: Public Goods and the Theory of Groups*, Harvard University Press.

Pavanello, Antonio and Antonio Villafranca (forthcoming), 'The EU role within the changing governance of climate change', in Julia Lieb, Nicolai von Ondarza and Daniela Schwarzer (eds), *The European Union in International Fora: Lessons for the Union's External Representation after Lisbon*, Baden-Baden: Nomos.

Reinaud, Julia (2005), *Industrial Competitiveness under the European Union Emission Trading Scheme*, IEA Information Papers.

Samuelson, Paul A. (1954) 'The pure theory of public expenditure', *Review of Economics and Statistics*, November.

Smith, Gordon and Paul Heinbecker (2010), *The G20 and Climate Change: the Quintessential Global Governance Issue*, Centre of International Governance Innovation, 9 June.

Spencer, Thomas and Anna Korppoo (2010), *Tools for Building EU Climate Consensus*, The Finnish Institute of International Affairs, Briefing Paper no. 61.

Spence, Michael (2009), *Climate Change Mitigation and Developing Countries Growth*, Commission on Growth and Development, Working Paper no. 64.

Stavins, Robert N. and Robert C. Stowe (2010), 'What hath Copenhagen wrought: a preliminary assessment', *Environment*, **52** (3), Science and Policy for Sustainable Development.

Stigler, George J. (1974), *Free Riders and Collective Action: an Appendix to Theories of Economic Regulation*, Aldershot, UK and Brookfield, USA: Edward Elgar Publishing.

Stiglitz, Joseph (2006), 'A New Agenda for Global Warming', *The Economists' Voice*, **3** (7).

Stormy-Annika, Mildner and Jörn Richert (2010a), *Obama's New Climate policy. Opportunities and Challenges of Climate Policy Change in the US*, SWP, Research Paper RP4.

Stormy-Annika, Mildner and Jörn Richert (2010b), *Going Green? The New US Climate Policy under Barack Obama*, SWP, Research Paper.

Tuerk, Andreas *et al.* (2009), *Report Linking Emission Trading Schemes*, Climate Strategies, Final workshop, Paris, 23 June. http://www.climatestrategies.org/component/reports/category/33.html.

van Asselt, Harro and Thomas Brewer (2010), 'Addressing competitiveness and leakage concerns in climate policy: an analysis of border adjustment measures in the US and the EU', *Energy Policy*, **38**, 42–51.

van Schlaik, Louise (2009), 'The Sustainability of the EU's Model for Climate Diplomacy', in Sebastian Obertür and Marc Pallemaert (eds), *The New Climate Policies of the European Union: International Legislation and Climate Policy*, Brussels: VUBPress,.

Villafranca, Antonio (2008), *Europa e Italia. Chi paga per l'ambiente?*, ISPI, Policy Brief no. 101.

Villafranca, Antonio (2009), 'Feeling the heat. Towards a revised governance of climate change', in Carlo Secchi and Antonio Villafranca (eds), *Liberalism in crisis? European Economic Governance in the Age of Turbulence*, Cheltenham, UK and Northampton, MA, USA: Edward Elgar Publishing.

Wacker, Gudrun (2010), 'Caught in the Middle: China's Crucial but Ambivalent Role in the International Climate Negotiations', in Susan Dröge, *International Climate Policy: Priorities of Key Negotiating Partners*, SWP No. 60, Berlin.

Wagner, Christian (2010), 'India: A Difficult Partner in International Climate Policy', in Susan Dröge, *International Climate Policy: Priorities of Key Negotiating Partners*, SWP No. 60, Berlin.

Wijkman, Anders, Jorge Nunez Ferrer, Christian Egenhofer and Arno Behrens (2009), *For a Future Sustainable, Competitive and Greener EU Budget Integrating the Climate Change Objectives of the EU*, Brussels: Centre for European Policy Studies.

Wooders, Peter, Aaron Cosbey and John Stephenson (2009a), *Border Carbon Adjustment and Free Allowances: Responding to Competitiveness and Leakage Concerns*, OECD, SG/SD/RT(2009)8, July

Wooders, Peter, John Reinaud and Aaron Cosbey (2009b), *Options for Policy-makers: Addressing Competitiveness, Leakage and Climate Change*, International Institute for Sustainable Development, Manitoba, Canada.

World Trade Organization (WTO) – United Nations Environment Programme (UNEP) (2009), *Trade and Climate Change*, Report.

Index